How to Get Your
Dream Job
Using the
Internet

How to Get Your Dream Job Using the Internet

Shannon Bounds

Arthur Karl

CORIOLIS GROUP BOOKS

PUBLISHER	**KEITH WEISKAMP**
EDITORIAL DIRECTOR	**RON PRONK**
COVER DESIGN	**BRADLEY O. GRANNIS**
INTERIOR DESIGN	**MICHELLE STROUP**
LAYOUT PRODUCTION	**KIM EOFF**
PROOFREADER	**GWEN HENSON**

The Coriolis Group, Inc.
7339 E. Acoma Drive, Suite 7
Scottsdale, AZ 85260
Phone: (602) 483-0192
Fax: (602) 483-0193
Web address: http://www.coriolis.com

ISBN 1-883577-68-3 : $29.99

Printed in the United States of America

10 9 8 7 6 5 4 3 2 1

How to Get Your Dream Job Using the Internet *is dedicated to everyone who has learned what looking for a job is all about. Don't despair. There is a better way.*

Acknowledgments

So many people contributed to *How to Get Your Dream Job*, both directly and indirectly, we can't possibly thank them all. We've learned that writing a book is more than just *writing* a book. For every word that's written, there must be an editor, a proofreader, someone to lay it out, and so on. It's a team effort, and we had the best team around.

Thanks specifically to:

- Keith Weiskamp and Jeff Duntemann, for giving us the opportunity to make this book a reality, and for having faith that we would be the rare authors who turned their chapters in on time (or close to on time).

- Ron Pronk, for being a constant source of encouragement and direction, and for always being open minded. Your knowledge made this book happen.

- Tony Stock and Brad Grannis for their patience and diligence with the *Dream Job* cover. Thanks for getting rid of "him."

- Anthony Potts for putting together the CD-ROM, and for providing author pep talks whenever necessary.

- Michelle Stroup for designing the book's layout, and for creating the wonderful icons throughout the book.

- Jaclyn Easton for giving us our first 28,800 modem, and for giving us special insight into the information highway.

- Vic Sussman, for helping us see the Internet as more than a means to an end, but as a "vehicle for social change."

- Tricia McArdle and Donna Ford, for their constant help and support throughout the entire project.

- Vince Emery and Dave Farell, for sending tons of Internet job information our way, which we in turn passed along to you, the reader.

- Tom Mayer, for making sure that bookstores everywhere had heard of our book.

- Our families, for being so understanding about not seeing us (or even talking to us really) for the months we spent as computer-loving hermits.

We'd also like to thank Elizabeth MacLaren of Delorme Mapping, Microsoft Corporation, Colleen Lang of CB Technologies, Sheila Marinucci and Tim Franta of Sun Microsystems, Sheila Carney of Booz, Allen & Hamilton, Aaron Privan of ClariNet Communications, Stormy Hamlin of IPC Technologies, Kristine McLaughlin of Symantec Corporation, Caroline Kohout of General Magic, John Jamieson of Blueridge Technologies, Bradley Richardson and Vintage Books, Damir Joseph Stimac, Derek Powazek, and Ward Johnson.

Contents

CHAPTER 7 MARKET YOURSELF ON THE WEB: CREATE YOUR OWN HOME PAGE 155

CHAPTER 8   BULLETIN BOARD SYSTEMS: HIDDEN JOB OPPORTUNITIES   191

CHAPTER 9   BEEN THERE, DONE THAT: STRAIGHT TALK FROM JOB-HUNTING EXPERTS   215

CHAPTER **1**

Why Using the Internet Can Get You the Job You Want

Chapter 1 Topics

Taking Advantage of Online Technology

Making Online Friends and Influencing People

Introducing Yourself to the World

The Enjoyable Way to Find Work

Whoever said "good things come to those who wait" was obviously already employed. The fact is, job hunting in the 90s takes more than just waiting, and as for finding the job of your dreams, well, in most instances waiting will probably just get you a bad case of empty wallet syndrome. So forget about sitting on the beach sipping margaritas, waiting for a Microsoft executive to stumble across your tanning body only to be instantly awed by the obvious brilliance you display in your five-minute conversation with her. If you have a computer and a modem, you have more than 20 million potential employers at your fingertips.

The Internet is an incredible network of computers that spans the world and connects millions of people. But believe it or not, the Internet that we know and love today originally existed as ARPANET (Advanced Research Projects Agency), a computer network created by the Department of Defense to protect military information stored in computers across the country. Four computers located at different universities (three in California, and one in Utah) were strategically networked through ARPANET so that if one link in the network failed (because of nuclear war, for example), the other computers could continue to communicate with each other.

ARPANET was a hit, and soon more and more computers at universities and military research sites began linking up, communicating, and sharing information. Incredible amounts of networks were created over time, and now the overall group of networks is called the Internet.

Now you know where the Internet came from. In this chapter, we'll explore some reasons why taking advantage of the Internet will help you get your dream job.

Take Advantage of Technology

Reason 1: Doing your job search the "old-fashioned way"—competing with thousands of other career hunters by simply reviewing classified ads and writing and mailing your resume—may not get you the results you want. It almost certainly won't get you the job you want as quickly as you want. "Technology is good. Technology is better. Technology is faster." Make that your job-search mantra.

Be Hip to the Information Revolution

How sick are you of scanning the classified ads for major cities all over the country, licking stamps and envelopes until your tongue is pasty, and then filing away the rejection letters in an ever-growing heap? There *is* a better way. The Internet puts you in touch with thousands of employers who are actively seeking the *right* job hunter, and they are probably looking to the Internet for a reason. They may have found that placing ads in the local newspaper hasn't been producing the applicants they want— applicants who are plugged into today's technology and who have what they think it takes to be successful. Just by being on the Internet, you're proving to them that you're skilled. Many companies recruit for positions on the Internet *only*!

We Thought You Should Know...

A Web page is a graphical, electronic presence on the World Wide Web, a network that links the Internet together in a searchable, user friendly way.

"The Internet is here to stay," says Mark Johnson, Recruiting Operations Manager for Perot Systems Corporation (see their profile on page 93), "and more and more organizations will need to tap into that resource if they truly want to pull from all sources of qualified candidates."

I Wouldn't Say "Lazy" Exactly, But...

In most cases, it's easier for employers to screen electronic or online resumes (which can be emailed or posted online) because they can scan them by keyword. Why not start off on the right foot by making their lives easier? For instance, if the recruiter at AAA Advertising Corporation is seeking a candidate with copywriting experience, she may do a search of all available resumes for the word "copywriting." Seems easy enough, doesn't it? But consider how much more difficult it would be if she had to read every paper resume that was mailed to her in response to a classified ad.

Figure 1.1　Perot Systems' Job Opportunities Web page.

These days, even paper resumes are becoming part of the technological revolution. You may not realize it, but a paper resume (you know, the one with the perfectly aligned columns on your favorite colored paper) that you send to a human resources person might be thrown in the trash immediately after someone scans it directly into the company's resume database. A special kind of software known as OCR (optical character recognition) electronically scans your resume directly into a giant conglomeration of thousands of resumes, which can be searched for by keyword. That's one of the reasons that you'll have to change your entire way of thinking when it comes to resumes.

For instance, let's say that you're interested in a marketing position at a large computer firm. Your natural instinct, thanks to your college technical writing courses and almost every job hunting book you've ever read, might lead you to include statements that use a lot of verbs, such as "wrote technical documents using page layout software." But let's say that the recruiter did a search by the keywords or phrase "technical writing" or a specific type of desktop publishing software package like PageMaker. This calls for a different kind of resume, as we'll discuss in Chapter 5, *How to Create a Killer Electronic Resume.*

A Penny Saved

Another reason why employers may be searching for candidates online is that it can be a less costly way to recruit, for several reasons:

- *Job descriptions or advertisements on the Internet can be longer and more detailed than a classified advertisement would allow.* If you've ever placed a classified ad trying to sell your old TV, you know that you pay by the line, and this means you have a limited number of words to describe your wonderful Zenith. So you'll probably stick to the basic facts and abbreviate a lot. Employers use the same approach when they place a classified ad. They'll probably give you the title of the open position, basic job description, qualifications, and where to send your resume. Then you're on your own in trying to find out more about the company and if you're even interested in the job.

  On the Internet, job listings can be cheap or even free, and can allow the employer to ramble on about why you should want to work for the company, what the town that the company is located in has to offer, who your boss will be, how many employees will be working with you, and more.

- *Less time and fewer man hours will be spent looking at paper resumes because electronic resumes are keyword searchable. Time is money.* You've probably already written your resume and feel certain that it's perfect: Heck, it's about you, so it's fascinating reading! But imagine being the person who receives hundreds of resumes from a classified ad and having to read and sort through them.

A couple of years ago, The Coriolis Group advertised an "Associate Editor" position in the newspaper. Qualifications were pretty standard: editing experience, college degree, knowledge of computers. More than 150 resumes rolled in, and maybe only a little more than half were from people who were actually qualified for the job. One person specialized in making salsa, another was a pilot . . . you get the picture. Our point is that someone had to manually read all of the resumes that were sent in, first to find out if the applicants were even qualified, and then to determine how qualified each individual was compared to other applicants. Seems like a waste of time to read the salsa expert's educational experience.

Bottom line: The Internet allows employers to receive electronic resumes and saves someone the time of manually reading every paper resume that's mailed in. Employers can easily sort through the resumes and screen out all of the unqualified candidates.

- *An employer can get a better understanding of a candidate's skills and personality before ever having to fly him or her out to the company site for a face-to-face interview.* Let's take a look at the normal progression of things in the non-Internet job-searching scenario.

  1. Candidate sends resume, follows up with phone call or letter.

  2. Employer is interested or keeps "your resume on file" (the kiss of death).

  3. If employer is interested, he or she sets up an interview.

Stop right there with "employer sets up an interview." Have you ever considered that if you're applying for an out-of-town or out-of-state job, you have less of a fighting chance than a local job seeker? If you were a recruiter and had two very similar one-page resumes for two different people, and one of those people was down the street, and the other would require an $800 plane ticket, who would *you* call in for a preliminary interview?

But that's true only if the employer had a one-page resume and nothing else to go on. Using electronic mail, an employer and job hunter would easily be able to get to know each other before it was time for the face-to-face interview: personality, details of experience that wouldn't fit on a resume, location preferences, and more. You could also email the documentation from projects that you've worked on or have the recruiter scan your Web page for even more. If all goes well via email, then it's worth it to the employer to fly you out for a personal meeting.

Make Friends and Influence (the Right) People

Reason 2: The Internet is huge and growing every day. With 20 million users, it's a great place to make new friends—many who have influence and know people in high places. Think networking.

You Never Know Who You'll Run Into

As we mentioned earlier statistics say there are more than 20 million Internet users today, and expected growth is estimated at 20 percent per year. Sometimes it seems like everybody from corporate higher-ups to first graders is moving to the information highway.

We recently spent some time browsing the endless aisles of CompUSA, the "computer superstore." In a conversation about cool computer-related stuff, the salesperson who was helping us, and who couldn't have been more than 16, told us that his grandmother had recently gone to see the movie *The Net*. "Really?" we asked. "That doesn't seem to be a grandmother-type movie." He quickly replied that she was having problems with her new Pentium and couldn't get any work done anyway, so she thought she'd catch a flick. Just goes to prove that you never know who'll be surfing with you. In fact, retired senior citizens represent one of the largest growth markets for the Internet. And people in this age group have spent many years gaining job experience, meeting people, and working in the corporate world.

Everybody Knows Someone

Diversity of the Internet audience is a great reason to job hunt online. True, not everyone you meet online will be a corporate recruiter. But someone you meet online, in chat areas or through newsgroups (discussed in later chapters) or other online niches, might know someone who knows someone else who is looking for an employee just like you. Yes, it's the ever-popular networking theory.

Figure 1.2 *Senior citizens are heavily represented on the Internet.*

The traditional methods of networking can be tedious, expensive, and frustrating. You call up someone you've never spoken to before and mention that you're a friend of a friend. God forbid, you might even have to fly somewhere just to meet one of your networking targets. Plus, what are the odds that traditional networking methods will put you in touch with the people you really want to know? Pretty slim. But you never know who you'll meet on the Internet, and who they might know.

While some folks say "It's not what you know, it's who you know," the truth is that it's both. And you can definitely use both in your Internet job search.

Join the Club

Not only do companies and educational institutions exist on the Internet, but you'll be able to find, and perhaps join, one or several organizations that are specific to your discipline. You might be interested in a job with a national newspaper or magazine, for instance. Why not check out the National Press Photographers Association on the Internet. Perhaps you're convinced that you're the next multimedia genius of the world? Why not participate in an online chat with members of the National Multimedia Association of America? Nothing like getting solid advice from the pros, who have probably been in exactly the same situation that you're in right now. And if you spend enough online or email time with the pros, you just might find yourself getting some inside information you can really use, or maybe even a letter of recommendation.

In many cases, by wandering around your favorite organization's Web site, you'll be able to find out when local chapters will be meeting in your area and which speakers they might be featuring. How convenient it would be, let's say, if you, as an aspiring photographer and lover of travel, went to the local National Press Photographers Association and met the Director of Photography of National Geographic who just happened to be the featured speaker for the evening.

Get a list of online professional organizations in Chapter 6, *Schmoozing Online*.

Rumor Has It

How many job hunters are pounding the pavement even as you read this? Way too many to count. Why shouldn't you learn from their successes and failures? They may have picked up some helpful job hunting tips along the way that could save you a lot of time and money (and frustration and embarrassment). They also just might have heard about job openings that are right for you, or could have made some great contacts that you haven't discovered yet. Someone you meet online may be the cousin of the friend of someone whose uncle is the Chief Legal Counsel for the biggest grocery chain in the nation. Job hunting is an evolving process. Why not skip a couple of steps when you can?

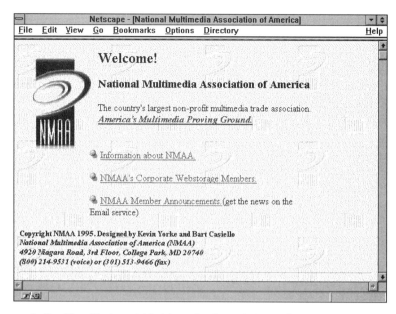

Figure 1.3 The National Multimedia Association of America's home page.

Step Inside

The first person to know that a position is vacant or that hiring will take place is someone who is within the company itself. This doesn't have to be someone in recruiting. It might be a secretary who has heard that the woman down the hall is leaving to have a baby, or the janitor who noticed the vice president packing up his desk and crying. And these folks may be wandering about the Internet, and may belong to the same organizations and newsgroups that you do. It's always helpful to keep your eyes open for inside information, and to subtly make your name known within a company—*before* an official job posting has been made public.

Continental Divide

You've probably already discovered how to meet people in your community. You can join local organizations, attend luncheons, and simply make local phone calls. But what if you're interested in relocating to another state, or even another country? There aren't very many easy and inexpensive ways to research and follow up on employment opportunities far away. The Internet makes it possible for you to discover companies and meet people all over the world, and for the small price that you pay for your Internet connection! You won't even have to pay for a long distance call, and you can communicate with someone as far away as Russia. Depending on where you want to go, we think that using your Internet account for this purpose is well worth the money, and much less expensive than long distance phone calls or than

Figure 1.4 EuroJobs is just one of many sources of international job listings on the Internet.

collecting newspaper classified ads from around the world. (How would you find the classifieds from a Russian newspaper, anyway?)

Many Corporations Are an Open Book—or at Least an Open Page

Reason 3: You don't have to spend hours at the library researching companies anymore. Just look to the Net for "inside information."

Know Your Stuff

Having originated as an educational tool used by scientists and educators, the Internet is much more than just lots of pretty graphics that you may find on the World Wide Web. It's an incredible source for all kinds of information. You can discover everything from the art of stain removal to the precise instructions involved in creating an atom bomb. But most important to you, you'll be able to get important information about potential employers by perusing their Web pages: company profiles, history, descriptions of products and services, positions that are typically recruited for, and the names and email addresses for the relevant human contacts at the company.

This means you won't have to blindly email resumes and applications to the companies on the Web, or even to the companies that advertise in the newspaper. In our research, We've discovered that most recruiters' pet peeve is a prospective candidate's total lack of knowledge of the company. Many companies that are online will be profiled either at their own Web site or in one of the many detailed and valuable online resources. Depending on the type of position you're interested in, you might benefit from the company's current financial statements, stock quotes, future strategy, the life story of the CEO, press releases about new technologies in the works, or the type of food served in the cafeteria.

Introduce Yourself to the World

Reason 4: You can advertise yourself by creating your own World Wide Web page—and it's easier to do than you might think. The key is to design a Web page that fits your target audience—in your case, potential employers.

Getting Employers to Come to You

One fact you should always remember in your job search is that you're advertising yourself. You are a virtual box of Tide in the world of employment. You're telling employers why you're great and why they need you, and maybe even what a bargain you are. One of the best ways to do this is with your own World Wide Web page, which does cost money in most cases, but can be worth the small expense.

Figure 1.5 EDS's home page provides a company description and history.

According to America Online, a commercial online service the company will soon allow its users to create their own Web pages and store them on the America Online Web server. The Microsoft Network is also promising this feature.

A *Web page* is a graphical presentation on the Internet that can offer you links to other places on the Internet and Web. Below is an example of an interactive Web page created by Derek Powazek. This representation of himself and his experience and creativity helped him get his dream job with *HotWired*, a very popular online magazine. It's one of the best personal Web pages we've seen, and is in no way something that is expected of you if you choose to create a Web page. But take a look at what this one offers.

Derek is a photography expert, now a Web design expert, and he chose to include at his Web site pictures of himself, a portfolio of his work, some writing samples, and his resume. Heck, you could even include a picture of Fifi, your overweight Schnauzer, if you think it will help you get a job. (Don't laugh. A lot of employers are also dog lovers.) The possibilities are endless.

We've seen Web sites with people's vacation pictures, sites dedicated to someone's favorite rock star (please, no more Madonna sites!), and yes, lots and lots of pet pictures. If you're looking for a job, consider including anything on your Web page that you feel will help employers get a good "feel" for who you are, but don't go overboard.

This chapter is introductory in nature, so it's not quite the place to teach you how to create a Web page. We do that in Chapter 7.

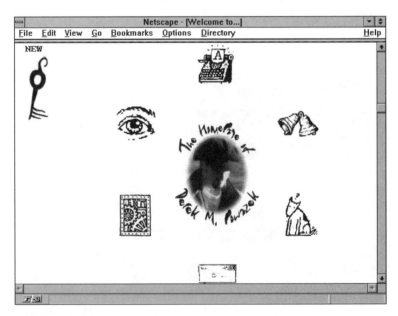

Figure 1.6 Derek's home page.

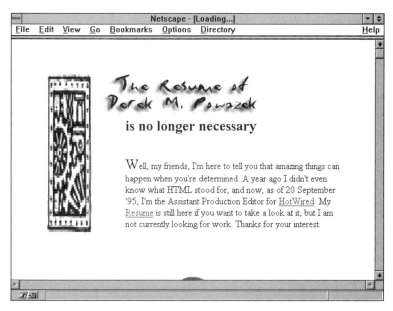

Figure 1.7 Derek's announcement that he found his dream job.

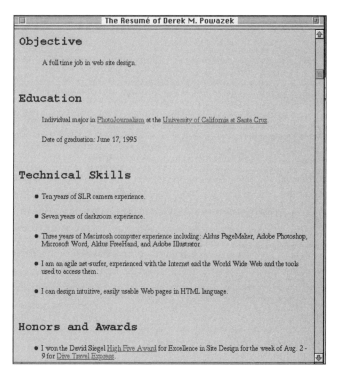

Figure 1.8 A portion of Derek's online resume.

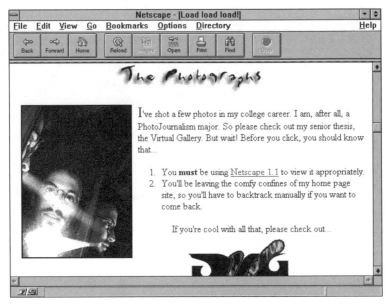

Figure 1.9 Derek's photo portfolio is on this Web page.

Exploit the "World" on the World Wide Web

Reason 5: You'll find international job listings for all kinds of companies, from Mom and Pops to Fortune 500s.

Big Brother

Large, prosperous technology companies were among the first to recognize the benefits of jumping on the information highway. Therefore, they were the first to figure out that they could find really capable job candidates, using the same technology they used to increase company exposure: the Internet. Truth is, you'll find the largest number of opportunities with companies like Intel, Advanced Micro Devices, and IBM.

Companies of this size not only have more employees than smaller organizations, they also may have job opportunities in other states, other countries, other continents. If not for the Internet, just how exactly would you find out that IBM has an open position for a marketing assistant in its South Africa office?

The Corner Store

Don't rule out the possibility of finding job postings on the Web for small and medium-sized companies. A company doesn't necessarily have to spend money on a corporate Web site or page to list jobs with its organization. Any company or group

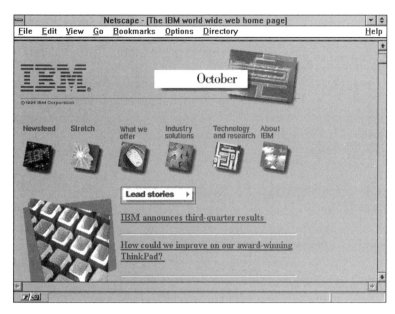

Figure 1.10 IBM's home page.

can pay a small fee to post job openings to many different areas on the Internet, or it can post openings within newsgroups at no charge. This enables small, but growing companies to advertise their need for employees by using a medium that reaches millions of potential candidates. This is great for someone who is interested in working for a company where you don't necessarily have to wear a blue suit and a tie.

Virtual Companies and Contract Positions

Many companies have only an "electronic storefront" and exist solely on the Internet. (In other words, they don't actually have a physical "storefront.") They do all of their business on the Internet. While some of these are only one-person operations, many are growing and are in need of employees: Web page designers, salespeople, marketing experts, data processors, and so on. One of these "virtual companies" could provide the perfect opportunity for you to work out of your home.

If you're interested in temporary or contract work, the Internet has resources and opportunities for you, too. Some companies only advertise for contractors, and some recruiting companies are exclusive to people looking for contract work.

Variety Is the Spice of 'Net Life

Reason 6: You don't have to be a computer expert to get a job using the Internet. Hundreds of "regular" jobs are advertised online.

The Web Is for Every Walk of Life

As we mentioned earlier, technology companies aren't the only ones listing current job openings on the Internet. You'll also find JCPenney, Southwest Airlines, Wal-Mart, and hundreds more. We've found positions for flight attendants, salespeople, artists, writers, teachers—pretty much anything you can think of. The most difficult part is knowing where to find these job openings. That's why, in Chapter 4, we give you some Internet locations where you can find listings. We also give you a basic description of each company and the kinds of positions for which it hires.

Even Microsoft Has Janitors

Don't discount the technology companies, even if you're looking for a non-technical job. Keep in mind that the large, technical companies have a variety of positions within them, and probably list these positions on the Internet as well. This includes secretaries, public relations personnel, marketing personnel, cleaning crew, cafeteria workers, graphic artists, child care workers, human resources personnel, benefits specialists, and more. Most comprehensive sites allow you to search the job listings by keyword, so if you're interested in administrative positions, you can enter "administrative" and click the search button to go straight to the positions you're interested in.

According to John Jamieson, Personnel Manager for Blueridge Technologies, which specializes in document management for Macintosh and Windows, "We've listed both technical and marketing positions on our Web site, and two technical positions at other Internet sites and postings. Interestingly, we have had greater response from the marketing position listings at our Web site than the technical position listings."

Spend a Little, Get a Lot

Reason 7: Using the Internet is the cheap way to find and get a job!

It All Adds Up

Searching for a job is not only frustrating and time consuming, but it can be very expensive. We can't tell you how many stories we've heard from people who paid thousands of dollars to executive headhunters and consultants. And many of these same folks ended up with a position they really didn't want, but accepted so they could pay their headhunter bills. Then there are the costs involved in mailing re-sumes, using professional resume services, making long distance follow-up calls, and more. We're not suggesting that you should cease using all these other avenues, but it's important for you to know that the Internet offers you a lot of resources for a low cost.

Many job hunting resources on the Internet are cheap or even free. This includes posting your resume online. For example, Adams (publisher of the JobBank books)

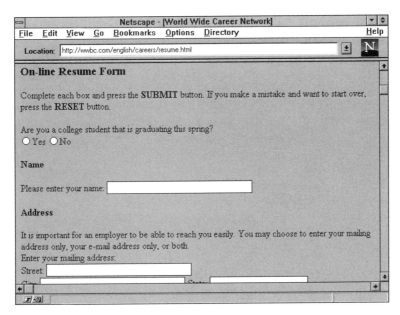

Figure 1.11 *An online resume form.*

has a new job posting area. Corporations pay approximately $1,000 for 60 employment opportunity listings. They're paying, so you don't have to. This is how many job listing areas work. The employer places an advertisement to a service by paying a minimum fee (which could be a cost per ad, or a monthly or yearly fee). Then the company scans the resulting applicants by keyword to find the person it's looking for.

The Internet will save you time, too. Many companies allow you to fill out an online resume form that they provide and then send directly to their recruiter. They ask you a series of questions and you just fill in the blanks with pertinent information, like your name, relevant experience, geographic areas you're willing to move to, and so on.

The Enjoyable Way to Find Work

Reason 8: Searching for a job using the Internet builds character, and it's fun!

Job Hunting That Doesn't Suck

So now you have an idea of all the practical reasons why you need the Internet to get a job. But wait, there's more. The Internet is not only an incredible resource, it's fun to use! With your Internet job search, you'll be tapping into a new culture, meeting new and exciting people, visiting other countries, seeing new art, experiencing amazing technology, and just plain goofing around. What better way to master the information highway and ready yourself for the future of computing? And after you get your dream job using the Internet, you'll be able to call yourself an "Internet expert." You can even use that experience on your electronic resume when it comes time to look for another dream job.

Now it's time to get started. The next chapter gives you an Internet crash course that will get you familiar with basic terminologies and techniques, and explains how to get connected. Good luck, and have fun!

CHAPTER 2

An Internet Crash Course

CHAPTER 2 TOPICS

WHAT'S THE INTERNET, AND HOW DO I GET CONNECTED?

USING EMAIL TO GET A JOB

DISCOVERING MAILING LISTS, NEWSGROUPS, AND FTP'S

NAVIGATING THE WORLD WIDE WEB

In Chapter 1 you found out why you need to use the Internet to get your dream job and how useful the Internet can be. But now you're probably asking yourself "What is the Internet, and what's this Web stuff?" Good questions. Fortunately jumping onto the information highway doesn't have to give you a road rash. In some cases, it can be as easy as inserting a diskette in your floppy drive and making a phone call.

In this book, We're not going to waste your time teaching you every technical term about the Internet and explaining in detail how your computer works. All you *really* need to know is how to achieve your ultimate goal: the dream job. So, we'll just give you the critical information you need to make your online job search successful. In this "Internet Crash Course," you'll learn what the Internet is, find out some basic terms and techniques, and discover what you'll need to know for a successful job search.

What Is the Internet?

You probably often hear about the Internet and information highway on the news or read about it in newspapers and magazines. And maybe you've even seen some of the computer specialty shows like CNN's Computer Connection. The Internet is quickly becoming an important—almost essential—part of our society. But what is the Internet really? We mentioned this briefly in Chapter 1. The concept is almost abstract because it isn't physically located in any single place and isn't run or controlled by any single organization. Basically, it is a "network of computer networks" that allows millions of people throughout the world to communicate with each other, transferring computer files, searching databases, exchanging electronic mail, and even chatting with other Internet users.

The Internet is not any one computer or connection. It's millions of interconnected computers scattered around the globe, all linked by phone lines or other cabling, and all using a common set of communications "protocols," or rules, that allow the computers to "talk" to each other without any misunderstandings or communication errors.

How Do I Connect to the Internet?

Relatively few Internet computers (hundreds, but no more than that) are directly connected to the fastest part of the Internet, called the "backbone." These backbone systems are mostly found in universities, research institutions, and government agencies, or are Baby Bells and long distance services that own their own cables. If you're currently attending a university and your university issues you a free Internet account, chances are that your school is part of the Internet backbone.

But most people and companies have to connect to the Internet through a commercial Internet Service Provider (ISP). An ISP is a subscription service, much like cable

TV. You pay a monthly fee and the ISP provides you with access to the Internet backbone. It works a lot like a toll booth for a bridge or tunnel. You have to pay a fee before you can drive across the bridge or through the tunnel. An ISP, then, is the "toll booth" where you stop and pay before you can access the information superhighway—in other words, the Internet. In fact, an ISP is often called an Internet "gateway" because it's the gate your computer connection has to pass through in order to get onto the Internet backbone.

Why Can't I Connect My Computer Directly to the Internet Backbone?

Actually you can, if you're willing to pay hundreds to thousands of dollars per month to lease high-speed ISDN, T1, or T3 lines. (Don't worry, you don't really need to know what these terms mean.) That's more than the average user is willing to spend. An ISP, on the other hand, spends the money to lease one of these cabling systems, then subleases a small slice of its cable (called bandwidth) to individuals like you. Typical fees for an Internet connection through an ISP are about $20 per month for up to 150 hours of usage per month. In some parts of the country, though, only one or a few ISPs have set up shop; since there's less competition in these regions, you'll often have to pay more for a subscription.

What's the Difference between an ISP and an Online Service?

Good question, and we've discovered that many, many people don't understand the distinction. An ISP provides Internet access, and that's *all* they provide. Once your computer passes through your ISP's gateway, you're on your own, free to explore the chaotic Internet, but also free to get lost on any of a number of information byways.

An online service—like CompuServe, America Online, Prodigy, or The Microsoft Network—provides a much more orderly universe. Online services organize all their features neatly into categories and menus and provide lots of online help to users. Companies that set up shop on an online service pay a fee to do so, or provide a cut of their profits to the online service. The bottom line is that an online service exercises complete control over the vendors and organizations that reside online and controls which areas subscribers can visit and how much subscribers should be charged for browsing the service's different areas.

By contrast, nobody controls the way the Internet is used. Your ISP determines how much to charge you for access to the Internet and how much time you can spend on the Internet. But beyond that, you're on your own—free to explore all of the far reaches of the Net. And as we mentioned earlier, the Internet isn't very organized, because there's no single company or organization to control it, unlike the way online services operate.

Now here's where the line gets blurry. Most of the major online services have come to realize that the only way to compete with the Internet is to provide subscribers with *access* to the Internet. In this sense, an online service is also an ISP. For instance, America Online provides some dialog boxes that allow you to connect to different parts of the Internet, but once you venture out onto the Internet itself, you're beyond the controlled scope of AOL. In other words, AOL provides an interface and a gateway for connecting to the Internet. But once you pass through this gateway, you're technically outside of AOL's control. You now run the potential of getting "lost in cyberspace," a risk that most new Internet travelers have to come to terms with.

Finding Your Way in Cyberspace

Actually, navigating your way around the Internet doesn't have to be all that difficult. It's just a matter of knowing the different categories of Internet access available to you, along with understanding a few of the tools that help you connect to these different "regions" of cyberspace.

There are basically five areas that you, as a job hunter, should know about when it comes to navigating the Internet:

- Email
- Mailing lists
- Newsgroups
- File transfers
- The World Wide Web

We should point out that none of these five "areas" exist in any particular place. They're just ways to organize information stored on the Internet and to organize the way people access and use the Internet.

Email

Email, short for electronic mail, allows you to send and receive messages to and from other computer users who also have email access (Figure 2.2). All of the commercial online services and Internet Service Providers offer their users Internet email. When you subscribe to either an Internet Service Provider or an online service, you will be given an email address. With online services, you basically get a User ID, which then becomes part of your email address. We'll explain this a bit later.

THE BENEFITS

Email opens up a whole new world of communication. You don't need stamps, you don't have to wait for the mailman, and it's much more socially acceptable than

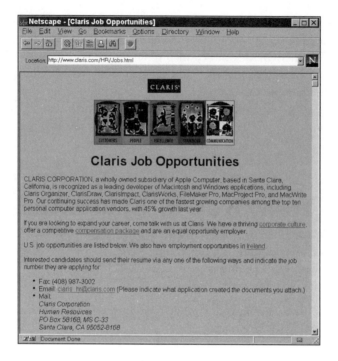

Figure 2.1   Claris gives an email link directly to their human resources department.

calling collect. My brother and I both have email accounts through our businesses. He lives in San Francisco, and I live in Phoenix, and we've found that email is the easiest way for us to keep each other updated on the latest in family news and general gossip. I don't even have to worry about him being able to read my illegible handwriting, or about having to call after 5:00 P.M. or on weekends.

I've especially noticed in my publicity work that even people who are extremely difficult to contact by phone (you know, the kind of person who doesn't want to waste time talking to someone trying to publicize something) check their email . . . and actually read it. According to Vince Emery, author of *How to Grow Your Business on the Internet,* "Email is becoming the dominant way businesses communicate, and is the most-often-used facility of the Internet."

We Thought You Should Know...

Beware of overstepping your bounds with email. Busy, important people may not appreciate unsolicited email. Don't expect the CEO of a company to become your mentor or the brother you never had. Consider the position you're interested in. Then, email to somebody whom you feel has the time or will be willing to talk to you.

When you do contact somebody of importance, be sure to tell him or her that you're trying to advance your career in his or her company's area of expertise, and that you are very interested in what he or she does for a living. Ask for advice. How did they get where they are today? What hints for finding a job can they share with you?

Also, try to detect the person's accessability. If he or she doesn't respond to your email, don't harrass. And whatever you do, don't make it seem as if you're after that person's job. Treat that person as though you are emailing them in order to learn and be enlightened. If you feel that you've established a good rapport over a period of time, ask if the company is hiring. Or ask for a phone number, and make voice-to-voice contact.

Don't be overly ambitious to the point where you earn a reputation as a pest. It's pretty risky to send an email that basically says "Hi! Can I have a job?" There are many more subtle ways of handling this. First, make sure you are targeting the correct person. How do you do this? Start with a company's home page on the World Wide Web. Many corporate Web pages have a general listing of the contact people for the company. If you don't find what you need at the home page, it's time to try alternative methods.

This is a good point to get on the phone, disregarding the Net in favor of person-to-person contact. The Net has helped you learn the starting point for a job search within a company, but from this point on, you're going to be left to your ingenuity. And don't be afraid to start at the bottom. It's amazing what you can find out from an administrative assistant or receptionist, and how helpful he or she can be. Also, try the human resources department, and be honest with the individual you speak to. For instance, you could say, "I'm interested in a position in the marketing department, and I was wondering who I should talk to." It's possible that the H.R. person will say, "Well, you can talk to *me*." Or that individual might direct you to the correct person that you need to talk to.

In any case, inquire about the best way to reach the person in charge of hiring for the job you're interested in. You might even discover that the person you need to talk to hates phone calls and emails, and prefers faxes, which could save you some time and embarrassment.

There are many other ways to get to know someone online, as we'll discuss later in this chapter. Subscribe to newsgroups, participate in online chats, and do your research. Find out who your key contact is at the companies you're interested in and find out as much as you can about him or her. If that individual has done any writing or has recently made the news with an outstanding accomplishment, send a note emphasizing your admiration.

Even the most prestigious member of a company might give you the time of day if you can get his or her email address.

Unfortunately, because email addresses may change often, there is no one place, no one Internet white pages, where you can constantly and accurately find someone's address. But there are several other ways to find an address:

- If you have a phone number for the person, or the person's company, call and ask for the individual's email address. The receptionist who answers the phone may even have it.

- Look at business cards and letters. Many people, including ourselves, list their email address on their cards and every piece of correspondence they send.

- If the person has written books or articles, or has even posted to newsgroups, check to see if he or she has featured a preferred email address for comments or questions.

One of the best things about email is that someone can respond to your message with only the click of a button. He or she can simply write a response to your message and click on "send" instead of filling out the address and subject information that was automatically supplied when you composed your initial correspondence.

THE EMAIL ADDRESS

An email address tells the Internet's network of computers how to route your message, similar to the way postal (snail) mail is routed through a network of post offices. Each part of a person's email address contains specific instructions about where the mail should end up. For instance, my email address is sbounds@coriolis.com. Here's a quick breakdown of my email address and why it appears this way:

- "sbounds" is my user name. It identifies me, is easy for people to remember, and is self-explanatory. Not everyone uses his or her real name for his or her user name. For instance, if a person wishes to remain anonymous, he or she could use something cute as a screen name. My sister-in-law's user name is Funfaktr. Keep in mind, however, that you're trying to find a job—and not just any job, the *perfect* job. Cute is not the way you want to portray yourself to a prospective employer.

Use your real name. (It doesn't matter if you use your first initial and last name, or your first name and last initial.) This will give recruiters yet another opportunity to remember who you are.

If you can't live another day without having a cute screen name, keep in mind that some of the online services, such as America Online, allow you to have more than one screen name at no additional cost. So use your cute name for nonbusiness-related email and chats.

- The @ sign basically means "at" and indicates that the remaining part of the address is the *domain name*, which we'll discuss next.

- "coriolis" is part of the domain name, which every Internet provider must register with an organization called InterNIC. In this case, "coriolis" is not only the name of the company that I work for, it's also part of the domain name that the company registered with InterNIC, and is used by all Coriolis employees who have Internet accounts. When an organization registers a domain name, it has to provide the address of the Internet "server" for the organization. A "server" is just a computer that provides services for other computers (called clients) that directly connect to it. At Coriolis, our server computer is run by our ISP. My computers, both at home and at work, are client machines that link to Coriolis' server system.

  If you obtain an account directly with an ISP, you'll probably be assigned the domain name that the ISP uses. For instance, if I did not have an Internet account through my company, and I used Internet Direct as my ISP, my email address would be sbounds@indirect.com.

- "com" is also part of the domain name, and identifies the type of account that I have: commercial. Other common domain extensions are "edu," which is an educational account, and "org," which encompasses non-profit and other organizations that don't fit into the "com" or "edu" categories. U.S. government agencies, for instance, usually fall under the "org" category. Outside of the U.S., account types are often identified by country code. For instance, yoshi@toshiba.jp identifies an address in Japan, while iand@power.uk identifies an account in the United Kingdom. And by the way, if an Internet address does not include the @ symbol, it's not an email address.

COMPOSING YOUR FIRST MESSAGE

When you choose an Internet Service Provider (see Chapter 3), they will usually give you software that will provide email send and receive capabilities. Easily the most popular email management system currently offered by ISPs (for both the PC and Mac) is called Eudora, seen in Figure 2.2. Eudora is relatively easy to use, and when

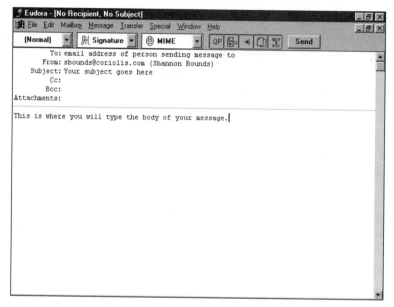

Figure 2.2   The mail composition screen in Eudora.

you sign up with your ISP, instructions should accompany the software. But here are some of the basics to keep in mind.

Email is a lot like an office memo. You need to have an address of the person or organization you want to send a message to, a subject, a return address, and, of course, a message. In an email message, the subject should be treated much like a newspaper headline: Make it short and get your recipient's attention. Some people get hundreds of email messages a day, and the subject line determines which ones they will and won't take the time to read.

While you're probably accustomed to using a variety of fonts—such as Times, Geneva, or maybe more exotic fonts—with your word processor, Internet email is *always* plain text: That means no text formatting allowed, including italics, curved quotes, bolding, and so forth. Get used to this, because when you send your resume electronically, it will also be in text-only format. (An exception is a resume sent or displayed on the World Wide Web in HTML format, an approach that we'll explain in a later chapter.)

Also, as with an office memo, you can copy another person on your message. Let's say, for instance, that I want to send an email to the president of a small but growing company. I want to tell her that I admire her company and believe that I would be a great asset to her organization. I've gone straight to the top, but the top may be just a little too busy to call me up right then and there to set up an interview. So why not copy the company's recruiter or human resources specialist on the note? All I have to do is get the email address for that person as well, and type it into the "cc" box: two birds with one stone.

Although you may have found an email address for someone and know that this person will be the only one who will receive your message, it is still common courtesy to include a salutation (Dear Mr. Watson) at the beginning of the note. You don't want your email to seem like a form letter, do you? Nothing's worse than electronic junk mail!

THE SIGNATURE

A signature, sig for short, is the information that you can add, as a standard feature, to the end of your email message or newsgroup posting (which we'll explain later): a perfect opportunity for you to offer contact information and a little pitch for yourself. It's like a mini advertisement with every email. Once you create and activate your sig, it will automatically tag onto the end of your messages. Theoretically, you don't even have to sign your message if you have a sig file, but do it anyway just in case your signature gets cut off.

Figure 2.3 shows an example of a signature. (Yes, we used one of ours.)

When you create your signature file, always include the basics: your name, email address, physical address, phone number, fax number (if you have one), address of your Web page (if you have one), and anything you think is most important about you. It might be your degree (BS in Finance at Harvard, 1995), your personal slogan ("Hard work is reward in itself"), awards you've won, or even something a little creative, if your field of expertise warrants it.

Let's say you're looking for a job in advertising, a field of employment that's full of creative types who aren't quite as "structured" as, say, bank executives. Your sig might be a good place to let your personality shine through, but think hard before you start writing poetry. Put yourself in the email recipient's place and determine what he or she might find appropriate.

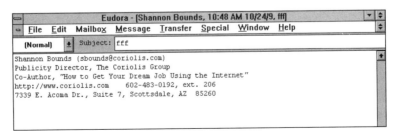

Figure 2.3 An Internet signature, which is added onto the end of each email.

Also keep in mind that most people don't want to spend a lot of time reading someone's signature. A good rule of thumb is to limit your sig to four or five lines, six at the most.

We'll talk about this more in the resume chapter, but an important fact to note is that email or electronic files do not come across the same on every computer screen. When I receive email, my system may allow text on one line to be 90 characters wide, but someone else's email text may only allow lines that are 72 characters wide. Since you don't want your signature to be split up in an awkward-looking mess, play it safe and keep your lines at 70 characters or fewer.

EMAIL THROUGH ONLINE SERVICES

If you use Internet email through an online service, your email address will look different from a person who receives email through an ISP. America Online lets you choose your screen name, but the rest of your Internet email address (the domain name) will always be "@aol.com." So if I had an account with America Online and chose to keep my screen name as sbounds, my Internet address would be sbounds@aol.com. The same is true with Prodigy (sbounds@prodigy.com).

CompuServe is a little different from America Online and Prodigy in that it doesn't give you the opportunity to choose a screen name. When you acquire an account, you'll be assigned a series of numbers that will look something like this: 73711,2318. But if you want to send email to a CompuServe address from another online service through the Internet, you will need to modify the address. First, the Internet doesn't like commas. You must change the comma to a period: 73711.2318. Then you'll have to add the domain name, so the full address will be: 73711.2318@compuserve.com.

We Thought You Should Know...

Always remember to check your email regularly during your job hunt: at least once or twice a day. How long would you go without returning a phone message?

Mailing Lists

Mailing lists are discussion groups consisting of people with a common interest, all of whom receive all the mail sent (posted) to the list. A mailing list is very similar to a newsgroup, discussed later, but doesn't allow users to post messages to individual subscribers, although you can often post information that can be distributed to *all* subscribers. Here's how it works: You subscribe to the mailing list, and the list's sponsor sends (to you and all other subscribers) information on a regular basis. If you have information that you want to distribute to all of the list's subscribers, you can post it to the list's supervisor, who then decides whether to include your information in the next mailing. There are hundreds of mailing lists that exist specifically to provide job and career information, and many of them are extremely focused or specialized; for instance, Job-Net is a mailing list designed to develop and aid the information exchange about job opportunities for Italian people. Mailing lists also allow you to subscribe to electronic newsletters and online magazines.

FINDING A MAILING LIST THAT'S RIGHT FOR YOU

To find a mailing list that's right for you, check out some of the, well, lists of mailing lists. Several people and organizations have created lengthy and detailed compilations that not only describe specific mailing lists' purposes, but identify when the last changes to the lists were made, and how to go about subscribing. Here are a couple of ways to get the lists of lists.

- You can get a long listing of Internet mailing lists from SRI in Los Angeles via email. Be warned: This list is huge. To get it, send an email message to mail-server@nisc.sri.com, and in the message area, type "send netinfo/interest-groups."

- A better way is to use the World Wide Web. Once you've gotten your feet wet in Web surfing (discussed later in this chapter) check out some of these sites:

  Publicly-Accessible Mailing Lists (PAML):
  `http://www.neosoft.com/internet/paml/`

  List of Lists:
  `ftp sri.com/netinfo/`

  Directory of Academic Discussion Lists:
  `http://www.mid.net/KOVACS/"`

  Indiana University Mailing List Archive:
  `http://scwww.ucs.indiana.edu/mlarchive/`

  Directory of Electonic Journals, Newsletters, and Academic Discussion Lists:
  `gopher://arl.cni.org`

  NewJour—The Archive of New Electonic Journal Announcements:
  `gopher//ccat.sas.upenn.edu:70/`

Don't just consider job-related mailing lists. If you're looking for a job in publishing, for instance, why not subscribe to an authors mailing list? You can even subscribe to a religion newsgroup if you think you'll meet potential employers there. The possibilities are endless. For more information about choosing mailing lists and meeting people, see Chapter 6, *Schmoozing Online.*

SUBSCRIBING

When you subscribe to a mailing list, you're basically just sending an email message to list owners asking to receive their electronic mailings. But it's not quite that simple. Some lists are moderated, which means that what is sent to the list gets there via a person who edits the listings. However, most lists are automated by a listserver, which requires no human intervention whatsoever.

Here are some basic guidelines for subscribing to a mailing list:

1. Send an email message to the computer (listserv, listproc, or majordomo) at the site address. An example of this would be the JOBPLACE mailing list, which you would subscribe to by sending email to LISTSERV@UKCC.UKY.EDU. Leave the subject blank unless you're instructed otherwise.

2. In the email message, type the following:

    subscribe name-of-list yourfirstname yourlastname

    for example, *subscribe JOBPLACE Shannon Bounds*

3. After you send this mail, you'll receive a message from the computer telling you that you are confirmed as a subscriber and letting you know how to discontinue your subscription. It's a good idea to keep this message for later, in case you find that you do want to end your subscription. This email will probably also give you the name of the list owner, whom you might want to email if you encounter any problems.

To participate in the list discussion, send email to listname@address.domain (for example, JOBPLACE@UKCC.UKY.EDU).

If you would like more information on using some of the mailing list programs, you can get information written by Jim Milles at the St. Louis Law Library by doing the following:

• Send email to: Listserv@ubvm.cc.buffalo.edu. Leave the subject area blank, and for the message, type in: GET MAILSER CMD NETTRAIN F=MAIL

Newsgroups

Newsgroups are part of an Internet service called Usenet, which provides the largest collection of discussion forums in the world. There are currently more than 10,000 Usenet newsgroups which are very similar to mailing lists, except they provide you with more flexibility in conversing with other newsgroup participants. Specifically, a newsgroup allows you to post messages to a group of people, who can then respond to your message or create messages of their own. It's kind of like posting a message on a bulletin board at the laundromat and having people who are interested in the note post their own responses to your message.

With a mailing list, you receive every posting that the list owner decides to include. Newsgroups, on the other hand, allow you to choose a particular article (topic) that you're interested in. You can then read selected messages and add your own responses if you'd like. Or you can create an article of your own.

In the past, you needed to have a separate newsreader software utility to read and post messages to a newsgroup. However, most Web browsers today include a built-in newsreader, which allows you to view and post messages directly from within your browser.

You don't have to have Internet access to participate in a Usenet newsgroup, although this is the most popular way to access newsgroups. Even if you have Internet access, you might not have access to Usenet (although, as we've already indicated, you get newsgroup access automatically if you have Internet access and Web browsing capabilities).

Newsgroups can be international, regional, local, or organizational. Information is added daily, so constantly monitor your newsgroups for new information and listings.

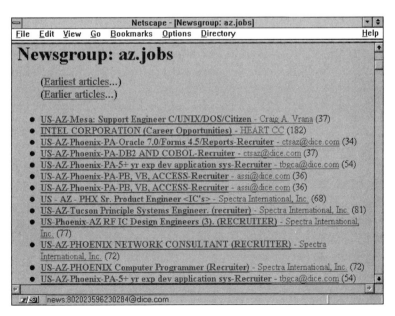

Figure 2.4 This is what the az.jobs newsgroup looks like in Netscape.

NEWSGROUP NAMES

Newsgroup name addresses consist of several parts, separated by dots. The first part of the name describes the general kind of newsgroup, as listed below:

alt   the alternative categories

biz   the business categories

bio   the bio-sciences categories

clari   the premium news categories

comp   the computer-related categories

misc   the miscellaneous categories (kind of like alternative)

rec   the recreational categories

sci   the science categories

An example of a newsgroup would be "misc.job.offered," which you might deduce would be a newsgroup discussing job openings. When several newsgroups are related, their names are also related, as is the case with the newsgroups misc.jobs.misc, misc.jobs.offered, misc.jobs.offered.entry, and misc.jobs.resumes.

SUBSCRIBING TO A NEWSGROUP

When you obtain an Internet account through an ISP, the software that you are given will probably include a newsreader, such as Trumpet News Reader, complete with step-by-step instructions on subscribing and unsubscribing to newsgroups. But you might never need to use the newsreader, since you probably will be able to access newsgroups directly from your Web browser. When you access a newsgroup from your Web browser, you don't actually need to subscribe. You simply type the newsgroup address in this format:

```
news:<name of newsgroup>
```

WORDS TO THE WISE

Don't overdo it by subscribing to tons of mailing lists and newsgroups. Also, make sure to spend some time (days or weeks) reviewing a newsgroup's topics before participating. Most members of a newsgroup have been participating for months, if not years, and they don't appreciate it when a new user tries to "take charge" by asking obvious questions or by adding information that is already common knowledge to the group. Newsgroup etiquette is mostly a matter of common sense and courtesy. Don't offend everyone in the newsgroup by breaking the group's implied rules. Most newsgroups have an FAQ (frequently asked questions) section for new members. Read it!

Just because a newsgroup is job related doesn't mean that you should automatically post your resume. In fact, many employment newsgroups are discussion only, and posting your resume is strictly taboo. You'll find out more about newsgroup etiquette in Chapter 6.

MISCELLANEOUS JOB-RELATED NEWSGROUPS

Here are some job   related newsgroups you might want to check out:

alt.medical.sales.jobs.resumes   medical sales positions
bionet.jobs   biotechnology
bionet.jobs.wanted   biotechnology
comp.jobs.offered   computer related (hardware, software)
biz.jobs.offered   business or non technical
hepnet.jobs   job announcements and discussions
misc.jobs.contract   contract jobs throughout the US
misc.jobs.misc   various jobs throughout the US
misc.jobs.offered   jobs throughout the world
misc.jobs.offered.entry   entry level jobs throughout the US
misc.jobs.resumes   a place to post your resume for US employers to see
pnet.jobs.wanted   people looking for jobs
prg.jobs   programming jobs
vmsnet.employment   jobs sought/offered, workplace, and employment-related issues
za.ads.jobs   jobs sought/offered

EMPLOYMENT NEWSGROUPS FOR SPECIFIC CITIES

Atlanta, GA:	atl.jobs
	atl.resumes
Austin, TX:	austin.jobs
Baltimore, MD:	balt.jobs
Chicago, IL:	chi.jobs
Cleveland, OH:	cle.jobs
Columbus, OH:	cmh.jobs
Dallas-Fort. Worth, TX:	dfw.jobs
Houston, TX:	houston.jobs.offered
	houston.jobs.wanted
Huntsville, AL:	hsv.jobs
Los Angeles, CA:	la.jobs
	la.wanted.jobs

Long Island, NY:	li.jobs
Milwaukee, WI:	milw.jobs
New York, NY:	nyc.jobs.offered
	nyc.jobs.contract
	nyc.jobs.misc
	nyc.jobs.wanted
Pittsburgh, PA:	pgh.jobs.offered
	pgh.jobs.wanted
Philadelphia, PA:	phl.jobs.wanted
Raleigh, NC:	triangle.jobs
St. Louis, OH:	stl.jobs
San Diego, CA:	sdnet.jobs
San Francisco Bay Area, CA:	ba.jobs.contract
	ba.jobs.offered
Seattle, WA:	seattle.jobs.offered
	seattle.jobs.wanted
Washington, DC:	dc.jobs

EMPLOYMENT NEWSGROUPS FOR SPECIFIC STATES OR REGIONS

Arizona:	az.jobs
Colorado:	co.jobs
Connecticut:	conn.jobs.offered
Florida:	fl.jobs
Illinois:	il.jobs.offered
	il.jobs.misc
	il.jobs.resumes
Indiana:	in.jobs
Iowa:	ia.jobs
Michigan:	mi.jobs
Minnesota:	mn.jobs
Nebraska:	nb.jobs
New England:	ne.jobs (Northeast US)
	ne.jobs.contract
New Jersey:	nj.jobs
New Mexico:	nm.jobs
Nevada:	nv.jobs
North Carolina:	triangle.jobs
Ohio:	oh.jobs
Tennessee:	tnn.jobs
Texas:	tx.jobs

Utah:	utah.jobs
Washington, DC:	dc.jobs
United States:	misc.jobs.resumes
	us.jobs.resumes

EMPLOYMENT NEWSGROUPS IN OTHER COUNTRIES

If you'd like to find work in another country, by all means subscribe to newsgroups for the countries you're interested in. But be careful. Spend extra time observing these groups before jumping in to participate. Not only do you have to worry about your general cyberspace netiquette, but you have to take cultural differences into consideration. Also don't be surprised to discover that many of these newsgroups are in languages other than English. It should go without saying, but sometimes Americans need to be reminded of this obvious fact: If you want to work in another country, you'll need to learn that country's language.

Australia:	aus.jobs
Berlin:	bln.jobs
Bermuda:	bermuda.jobs.offered
Canada:	can.jobs
Alberta	ab.jobs
British Columbia	bc.jobs
Ontario	ont.jobs
Ottawa	ott.jobs
Toronto	tor.jobs
Denmark:	dk.jobs
France:	fr.jobs.offres
	fr.jobs.demandes
Germany:	de.markt.jobs
	de.mrkt.jobs.d
United Kingdom:	uk.jobs
	uk.jobs.contract
	uk.jobs.offered
	uk.jobs.wanted
South Africa:	za.ads.jobs
Anywhere in the World:	misc.jobs.resumes

File Transfers (FTP)

File Transfer Protocol, or FTP, is a set of rules that dictates how files can be sent and received on the Internet. When you transfer files via FTP, you're actually sending to or downloading from an FTP server system, which just means that the FTP server is running software that understands and follows the communications and file transfer rules that are universal to all FTP sites. One of the wonderful things about FTP is that it has a standard interface for accessing files, meaning that whether you use a Mac or PC, you should be able to FTP without concern for what platform you are sending to or receiving from.

In most cases, when you FTP, you'll be retrieving electronic files from an FTP server site and downloading them onto your computer. How you FTP depends on what kind of Internet connection you have. Our ISP gave us special FTP software when we signed up. Also, Netscape and Mosaic (and most other Web browsers) allow you to FTP from within the World Wide Web itself. Basically, the advantage of FTP is that it allows you to quickly download large files (which can be text, pictures, sound, multimedia, etc.) onto your computer.

Some FTP sites only allow authorized users to access files. For these sites, you need to enter a user ID and a password to gain access. But many FTP sites support *anonymous FTP* access, which means you can log onto the FTP site by supplying the user name "anonymous," with no password. With many anonymous FTP sites, you don't even need to supply the user ID "anonymous." If you log on without supplying a user ID, the site assumes that you're an anonymous user. Other anonymous FTP sites require you to supply your email address as the user ID, but you don't need to enter a password.

The World Wide Web

The World Wide Web, or Web for short, is a graphical way to view information on the Internet. It allows companies, schools, and casual users like you and us to create pages that can be easily accessed by other Internet users and to view other Web pages—including Web pages for businesses. Web pages are online graphical documents, which can contain text and art, and usually have links to other Web pages.

What's the Difference between the Web and the Internet?

Good question. The World Wide Web is just a *part* of the Internet—but it's by far the most fun part and the most popular part. The Web got its start at a nuclear research facility in France, where a young and enterprising programmer crafted a technology that's now known as *hypertext*. This futuristic-sounding term refers to the ability to click on an underlined or highlighted word in an Internet document and then be immediately transported to a different Internet document, which physically can be stored on a server located anywhere in the world.

A hypertext link is really pretty simple, but to understand how it works, and to understand how the entire Web works, you need to understand another technology called Hyper Text Markup Language (HTML, for short). HTML works in conjunction with a Web viewer (also called a Web browser). Web viewers include Netscape,

Mosaic, and any of the browsers that you can use from online services like America Online or CompuServe.

Here's how it all works: Each Web page is actually composed of HTML commands, which are directions that a Web viewer uses to determine how and where to display text, graphics, video, and other multimedia information. When you use a Web browser, you never actually see the HTML commands. They're all hidden from view. Instead, you see the finished product: pages of nicely arranged graphics and text, plus the hypertext links. Each hypertext link has a Web address associated with it. When we say "associated with it," we just mean that the Web address is contained in an HTML document. So, when you click on a hypertext link, your Web viewer looks in the HTML document, gets the appropriate Web address, and then sends you on your way to a different part of the Internet.

That's the major difference between the Internet and the World Wide Web. To get to many Internet sites—including FTP sites, Usenet groups, Gopher sites, and so on—you just need an Internet account and some simple software. You don't need a Web browser. But if you want to view Web sites—that is, Internet pages that are written in HTML format—you must have a Web browser like Netscape.

The nice thing about most Web browsers, including Netscape, is their flexibility. You're not just limited to viewing Web pages. For instance, you can use Netscape to locate and display information at FTP sites, Gopher sites, Usenet newsgroups, and much more. Netscape is a truly integrated tool; it can take you to just about anyplace on the Internet—not just to Web pages.

URLS AND YOU

To reach a certain page, or place, on the Web, you need to type in a *URL*, which stands for Uniform Resource Locator. Basically a URL tells the computer what kind of link you want to have (Web, FTP, etc.), and gives coordinates (an address) of the Web page you want to reach. For instance, The Coriolis Group (the publisher of this book) has a URL, otherwise known as a Web address, of "http://www.coriolis.com." This is the information that you can enter into the "Location" text box in Netscape, as we'll discuss shortly.

As you spend more time on the World Wide Web, you will be able to easily recognize a Web address. Remember, email addresses always have the "@" symbol, but Web addresses do not. Also, URLs can be case sensitive. If you see a Web address (say in the newspaper, a magazine, or in this book) written as:

```
http://www.GeoTECH.Personal/Html
```

make sure you type it exactly as shown. If you see a capital letter, type a capital letter. If you see a lowercase letter, type a lowercase letter. Some Internet servers are not case sensitive in reading URLs, while others are. It's best not to guess. Always enter a URL exactly as you see it.

EXPLORING THE WEB

The Web can be overwhelming at first because there is so much information out there. It's like exploring a whole new universe. One way to find information on the Web involves the use of a *search engine*. Search engines are programs that allow you to look up information stored in massive databases. To use a search engine, you simply enter the word(s) that describe what you're trying to find. For instance, if you want to find out more about Fortune 500 companies, you could type "Fortune 500" into a search engine. The program will then display a list of Web addresses that will either take you to a Fortune 500 company's Web site or will take you to a site that has additional information about Fortune 500 companies. Using the various search methods that are available, you'll be able to find everything from someone's vacation pictures to the Michael Jackson fan club's home page. Of course, that's not what you bought this book for. You're probably more interested in finding companies that have great job opportunities. But finding the correct Web page for a major company can sometimes be as difficult as locating the correct office in a large building complex.

A major company, like Apple, may have a Web site consisting of several if not hundreds of Web pages that are all linked together. Its *home page*, similar in theory to a cover of a magazine, is usually the first page that a visitor will see. It may just contain the company logo, or may have a table of contents of all the Web pages that relate to the company. The best home pages contain plenty of hypertext links to help you navigate to other, related pages. But for most businesses, it's more important to make sure people know how to find their Web sites. You can't navigate through a site if you can't figure out how to get there in the first place.

Let's say that you've decided you don't want to work for someone else, and have created a new company that sells stationery. You want to put your company up on the Web so that people will become familiar with your company and the products that you offer. You want to include pictures of your products, along with the toll-free number that customers can call to place an order.

After you create your Web presence (of course, you'll have to know a little about HTML to do this—something we'll explore in a later chapter), there are several ways for people to find your business on the Web. You can give them your Web address, in advertisements or on a business card, which they can type into their Web browser to get directly to your home page. Or they can conduct a Web search using one of the various search engines, discussed below. They might find your company by searching for the words "stationery" or "paper" or by searching using your company's name.

Figure 2.5 The Apple Home Page.

Netscape: Navigating the Web

To navigate the Web, you'll need a Web browser such as Netscape, which is currently the most popular and effective browser available (and at this writing, it's still free). You'll probably be given the software for Netscape at the time you sign on with a provider, but if you aren't, call Netscape Communications at 415-528-2555. If you want to know the ins and outs of using Netscape, check out the definitive guide located on the Web at http://mosaic.mcom.com/home/online-manual.html.

We Thought You Should Know...

A Web browser is simply a program that allows you to view documents on the World Wide Web.

Figure 2.6 shows Netscape's opening page. It's what you'll probably see when you log onto the Web with Netscape. At the top of the page is a series of buttons. Directly below, and depending on what version of Netscape you have, you'll see an area called Location or Netsite, which lists the current URL. You can easily change the URL in the Location text box, taking you to another location.

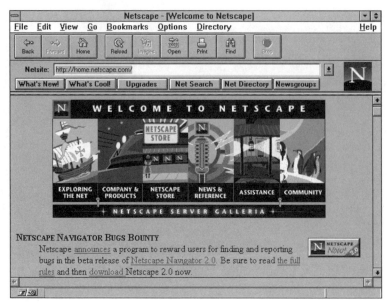

Figure 2.6 Netscape's opening page.

Underneath the Location area is another row of buttons. Here's a quick look at what some of the buttons do:

- **Back** takes you back to the last URL that you visited.

- **Forward** takes you to the URL that you just backed up to.

- **Home** brings up Netscape's home page.

- **Reload** reloads the current Web page in case some of the text or graphics were interrupted during the transfer.

- **Images.** Netscape gives you the option of turning off your graphics so that your Web pages will load faster. If you have chosen this option, instead of auto load, but decide that you want to see the graphics on a specific Web page, you can click on "Images."

- **Open** lets you type in a new URL.

- **Find** allows you to perform a keyword search of the current Web page.

- **Stop** ceases the transfer of information.

- **What's New!** takes you to Yanoff's list, a thorough and frequently updated list of Internet services.

- **What's Cool!** takes you to a list of interesting sites to visit.

- **Upgrades** takes you to a site where you'll be able to get the most recent version of Netsape Navigator.

- **Net Search** takes you to a site featuring search engines like InfoSeek, WebCrawler, and Lycos.

- **Net Directory** takes you to a link to Yanoff's list.

- **Newsgroup** provides you with a quick and easy way to check out and subscribe to newsgroups.

Although you'll probably use Netscape if you have an account through an ISP, if you have Web access through an online service such as America Online, that service may provide its own customized Web browser.

BOOKMARKS

Bookmarks offer a handy way for you to keep from retyping the same URLs of your favorite Web sites every time you log on. This is easy to do in Netscape. When you find a site that you want to bookmark, click on "Bookmarks" in the menu bar. Then when the menu drops down, click on "Add Bookmark." That's it. When you want to go to a bookmarked URL, click on "Bookmarks" in the menu bar, then scroll down to the bookmark for the site you want to view. You're off!

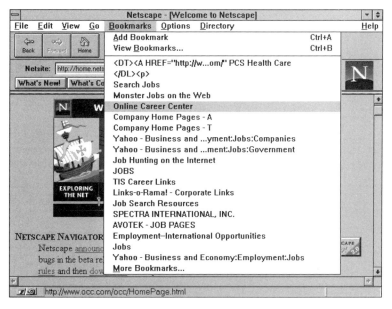

Figure 2.7 Bookmarks in Netscape.

Go Ahead and Explore the Web

After you get connected (see Chapter 3) you'll probably want to do a little aimless wandering to see what's "out there" on the Internet. But how aimless do you really want to be, and where should you start? Let's say that you'd like to do a general search for jobs. This is a broad category, but there are many available search engines that you can use. Here are a few of the best and most popular.

InfoSeek

InfoSeek is a comprehensive Web search engine. Get to InfoSeek by clicking on the "Net Search" button in Netscape or by going to http://www2.infoseek.com. You can conduct a search by entering keywords or phrases. InfoSeek is free for the first 100 results only. If you want more search results, you have to pay. Here are some important tips that InfoSeek offers:

- Enter words or phrases that are likely to appear in the documents you want to find, using the same capitalization you expect to find.

- Identify phrases—for example "music-related jobs"—with quotation marks or by hyphenating the words in the phrases.

- Use a comma to separate proper names (Mozart, Van Halen).

- Use a plus sign in front of a word or phrase that you require in your search (music +jobs).

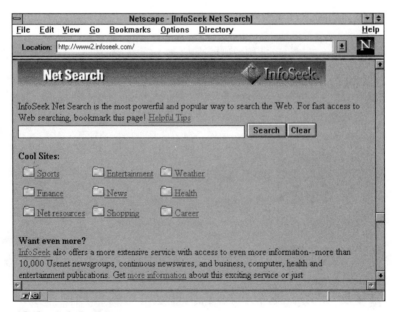

Figure 2.8 InfoSeek.

- Use a minus sign in front of a word or phrase that you don't want to appear anywhere in the resulting document (jobs -accordion).

- Use brackets around terms that should appear in the same area of a document ([music-related job market]).

After you enter your search keywords, click on the Search button or press Enter. After a moment, you will be taken to a page listing the documents that match your search (the "hits"). The title of the document will be underlined and displayed in color, indicating that it is a hypertext link to another Web page. If Netscape identifies that you've already visited some of these sites, they will appear in a different color so that you can easily identify which sites you've already tried and which ones you haven't yet visited.

Lycos

Lycos' search engine lets you efficiently search for document titles and content. You can get to Lycos by clicking on "Net Search" in Netscape or by going to http://lycos.cs.cmu.edu. Lycos contains a database that has millions of link descriptors and documents built by a database program that brings in thousands of documents every day. This engine searches document titles, headings, links, and keywords that it locates in these documents. Lycos catalogs three types of files: HTTP (Web) files, Gopher files, and FTP files.

Searching with Lycos is a little different from InfoSeek. It offers you an area called "Query" for you to enter your search information. Then it allows you to structure

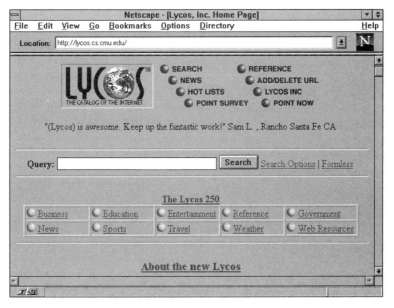

Figure 2.9 Lycos, another popular Netscape search engine.

your search, depending on the type of information you're looking for. Here are some important facts about using Lycos:

- You can enter free-form questions such as "Where can I find a job in music" leaving out capitalization and punctuation.

- You could also just enter the keywords you're interested in, like "music jobs."

- After seaching, you can fine-tune your search by using the Search Options and Display Options.

WEBCRAWLER

WebCrawler allows searches by document title and content. It is operated by America Online, Inc. at their Web Studios in San Francisco and can by found be clicking on "Net Search" in Netscape or by going to http://webcrawler.com. WebCrawler is very straightforward. Just type, in the text box, words describing what you're looking for. Then click on Search, and wait for the results.

When your results are returned, a number will be found next to each document listed (from 000 to 100). This number indicates how relevant each document is to your search, with 100 being the most relevant.

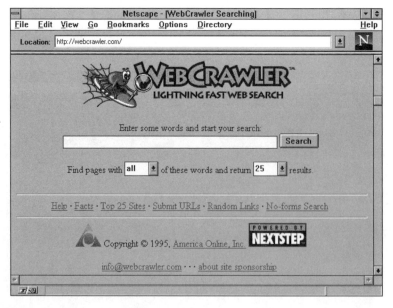

Figure 2.10 WebCrawler.

GENERAL SEARCH TIPS

If you find that you're not getting the results you want, keep the following tips in mind:

- Check your spelling.

- If your search produces too many results, try again, and be more specific.

- If your search doesn't produce any results, don't be quite so specific.

- If a link to something returned on a search doesn't work, keep in mind that Web sites change often and the link might be unavailable for many reasons.

- Try synonyms and variations on words.

YAHOO!

Yahoo! (http://www.yahoo.com) is a subject-oriented guide for the Web and Internet that lists sites and categorizes them into appropriate subject categories. There are numbers that appear in parentheses next to Yahoo! categories, which represent the number of entries in that category. If there is an "@" at the end of a category, it means that that heading is listed in multiple places within Yahoo! If you click on the heading, you'll go to a primary location for that category.

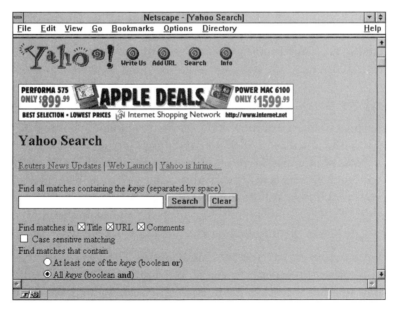

Figure 2.11 *Yahoo!*

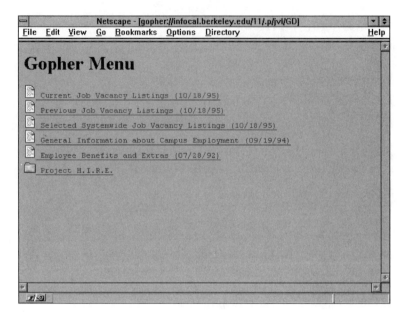

Figure 2.12   A gopher menu.

To conduct a Yahoo! search, go to http://www.yahoo.com/search.html. You can enter your keywords, and Yahoo! will search through its URLs, titles, and comments. You can increase the number of search hits returned by using the pull-down menu that says "Limit number of matches to" and choosing a number. The default number is 100.

Gopher

While gopher is not one of the five things you *must* know about for a successful job search, it is helpful to have a brief understanding. Gophers are basically organizers of high volumes of information into easy-to-use menus. Gopher URLs will begin with the word "gopher." Gopher menus aren't visually appealing like HTML Web pages, but they link you to incredible amounts of information, which can then link you to even more. Gopher menus are infamous for being endless in their link connections. You'll see them very often at university or government Web sites.

You've just completed the "Internet Crash Course." The next chapter, Chapter 3, will get you connected so you can try out all the things you have just read about. You'll learn how to get connected to the Internet and what kind of software and hardware you will need.

CHAPTER **3**

Get Connected

CHAPTER 3 TOPICS

BUYING THE RIGHT COMPUTER

USING A MODEM

ACCESSING THE INTERNET

CHOOSING AN INTERNET SERVICE PROVIDER

After reading Chapter 2, you're probably raring to go on your first Internet job-hunting journey. If you already have online access and don't feel you need a refresher course, go ahead and skip to Chapter 4. If you don't have an online connection or if you just want to learn more about online accounts, you should read this chapter carefully. It will tell you what kind of hardware you need and give you the basics on how to find and use an Internet Service Provider.

The Beginning: A Computer, of Course

If you don't have a computer, and you don't have access to a friend's system or to a computer lab, it may be time to buy a system of your own. Don't feel like you have to have a $3,000 Pentium with 4 zillion megabytes of RAM just because that's what your friend has or because that's what you saw advertised on television last night. You don't have to buy the newest, fastest machine on the market. In fact, you don't even have to buy new. Check out your local Sunday paper's classified ads to determine what kind of equipment is available and for how much. You could probably get by just fine with a 486 machine with 4 megabytes of RAM (Random Access Memory), although 8 megabytes is better. While this book isn't your guide to buying a new computer, we'll just share a few words of wisdom with you.

- If you decide to purchase a new computer, regardless of how much you already know about what RAM and resolution are, buy a couple of magazines that evaluate the performance of the specific models you're interested in. Buyer's guides (like *Computer Shopper*) or special issues of magazines with buyer's guides in them (like *Consumer Reports*) are a great starting point.

- Also, if you decide to buy new, make sure you ask about the specifics of a warranty. Most major computer manufacturers offer a three-year warranty with on-site (at your home or your office) repairs for the first year and off-site repairs for the two years after that. In other words, if anything breaks in the second or third year, you'll be required to take the machine into the store where you bought it or worse, you'll have to send it to the manufacturer for repairs. This can be a little inconvenient to say the least, especially if you're in the middle of a job search. So buy wisely.

- If you decide to use the newspaper or a local computer magazine to shop for a used machine, don't take a stranger's word on anything. Before you buy, test the computer by performing the same kinds of tasks you'll be performing if you do purchase it. The current owner might not have the same software installed that you'll be using, but you should be able to use his or her software to open files and make some changes. This will help you evaluate the speed and performance capabilities of the system—before you commit to making a purchase. If you don't feel comfortable about making such a huge purchasing decision (probably because you feel you lack the computer experience required, take a friend who has some computer experience or who has been through the computer purchasing process.

- Get a decent monitor. The new computer systems at your local computer superstore usually come with a color monitor. Make sure the computer includes a video card that supports *at least* 256 colors. Also try to purchase a monitor that is "non-interlaced" rather than "interlaced." A substandard monitor or video setup can cause headaches and eye fatigue.

- Consider storage. The term *megabytes* refers to the amount of information that a computer can store in memory and on a hard drive. In other words, the term has two basic usages, which often confuses users. The greater the number of megabytes on a hard disk, the more information it can store. You'll often hear megabytes called megs by the technical crowd. A typical hard drive today should be able to store at least 250 megabytes (MB) of programs, files, and other information. Most new computers come with either 8 or 16 MB of RAM (random access memory). You really should have at least 8 MB of RAM if you plan to run Windows 95, despite the fact that Microsoft tells you that 4 MB is "sufficient" (a squirrely word that means "It'll run Windows 95, but the speed might be intolerably slow."). RAM is *upgradeable*, which means you can typically add additional memory chips to increase the total amount of RAM in your system. For instance, if a system is advertised as having 8 MB of RAM, expandable to 128 MB, that means you can add an additional 120 MB before you've "maxed out" the memory capacity of your system. The amount of storage on your hard disk is not upgradeable unless you purchase an entirely new hard disk.

- Consider speed. When we refer to speed here, we're talking about how fast your computer can process information. The speed of computers is usually determined by a number ending in "86" (the big exception is Macintosh computers, which are entirely separate beasts) and then by the number of megahertz (or millions of processing cycles per second) that the system can support. Most new computers today are 486 or 586 (Pentium) main processor chips (called the CPU, which stands for Central Processing Unit). The higher the number of megahertz (Mhz), the faster the computer. For instance, if you were shopping around, you might notice a Pentium/66. That's a Pentium machine that runs at 66 Mhz—a reasonably fast system, even by very recent standards. As of this writing, you can purchase 486/66 machines—both new and used—at very reasonable prices—often well under $1,000. A 486/66 configuration is about as slow as you'll want to go if you plan to run Windows 95. If you just want to run

Windows 3.1, a 486/66 system is plenty fast—and a 486/33 system would do fine, even if you want fast Internet access. Again, make sure you check the amount of memory, or RAM that the system contains. The contents of a Web site can be pretty memory intensive, so even though a 486/33 might be fast enough to support Internet and Web access, it might not be too useful if you have 4 MB of RAM or less. Again, you can easily update the RAM on a system, even an older one.

Reach Out and Modem Someone

First, make sure you have the essentials to get online. Aside from the computer system itself, the most important piece of equipment for using the Internet is a *modem*. A modem is the device that your computer needs to communicate with other computers through a phone line. It converts digital signals, which can be transmitted over a telephone line, and transforms incoming analog signals into their digital equivalents.

Modems can be internal or external. Internal modems are on a card that plugs into your PC's bus, contain their own serial port onboard, and use your PC's power supply. External modems are usually self-contained in their own case, have a separate power supply, and connect to your computer via a serial cable to one of the serial ports on the back of your PC. Whether you choose an internal or external modem will depend on your personal preference. Here are some details to remember when it's time to make a decision.

Internal Modems

- Are usually less expensive because they do not have a case or power supply.

- Are easy to install.

- Don't take up any space on your probably already crowded desk.

- Don't have any external cables (in other words, you don't have to worry about your cat knocking cables loose).

- Don't require a 16550 serial card or cable.

External Modems

- Can be turned on and off independently of your computer (great for when your modem hangs, because you can reset the modem without rebooting your computer).

- Usually have lights—called LEDs and LCDs—that give you information about your current online session.

- Are easily moved.

- May have an external volume control.

So basically, you should consider whether you have room for a modem card inside your CPU case, how much space you really do have on your desk (or floor), what kind of modem is on sale at the time you go shopping, and so on. Beyond that, the kind of modem you'll need depends on which online service you will be using, what you'll be using the modem for, and how patient you are.

Speed

Speed seems to be the most important consideration in modem choice, especially when you pay for an online service by the hour. If you plan to use the World Wide Web, it's important that you realize how long graphics can take to load onto your screen if your modem is slow; it can be almost painful. (That's why a fast modem is far more important than a fast CPU—the extra time is taken up by transferring data to and from computers connected to the Internet, not by the time required to process information inside your computer.) While modem speeds range anywhere from 2400 bits per second (bps) to 28,800 bps, we highly recommend 28,800 for any kind of Internet use. A 28,800 bps modem can send data over a phone line up to twelve times faster than a 2400 bps modem.

If you, like many job hunters these days, don't feel that it's possible to shell out the $150 or so that a 28,800 bps modem will cost you, you can probably scrape by with a 14,400 bps modem if, while surfing the Web, you regularly choose the option to load text without pictures, which means the information will take less time to appear on your screen, since you're just loading text, not graphics. However, this is not something you want to depend on. Not all Web pages offer you an option to avoid graphics. Bottom line: Modems are becoming less expensive every day and will probably be on sale at your local computer superstores. Get the fastest modem you can afford, and consider it an investment.

We Thought You Should Know...

Here's some interesting modem information, courtesy of "Curt's High Speed Modem Page" on the World Wide Web (http://www.teleport.com~curt/modems.html). Feel free to impress your friends with this fascinating "technical stuff and history."

When people talk about modems, you hear the terms baud and bps (bits per second). Here is a little information to help you keep the terms straight. *Baud*, named after the 19th century French inventor Baudot, originally referred to the speed a telegrapher could send Morse code. It later came to mean the number of times per second that a signal changes state.

A *bit* is a single binary digit, which can be represented by a 0 or a 1, so you may think that bits per second and baud are the same thing. However, various data-handling techniques allow more than one bit to be transmitted with each baud in high-speed modemsæthat is, 28,800 bits per second can be transmitted with a substantially lower baud rate. So the proper term to use when talking about high-speed modems is bits per second (bps), not baud.

Access the Internet

If you've read Chapter 2, you already probably realize that you want an Internet account that offers, at a minimum:

- An email address so you'll be able to send and receive electronic mail messages.

- Access to the World Wide Web so you can visit company home pages and experience the incredible amount of resources the Web has to offer.

- The ability to belong to newsgroups and subscribe to mailing lists.

There are a few different ways to gain this kind of access to the Internet:

- Get a direct connection to the Internet itself, which entails spending tons of money and running a cable directly from your house. Let's be serious. Unless you have your own highly profitable business (in which case you probably wouldn't be looking for a job), a direct and permanent connection isn't an option.

- Get an Internet account through an online service, which might be a good alternative for you if some of the features of the online service are extremely important to you, and if you don't plan to spend hours and hours online per week. If you go with this option, find out what kind of access you'll get and what kind of additional job-hunting help the online service might offer. In general, an online service typically gives you a few free hours of access per week, and charges $3.00 an hour or more for additional time spent online. And a few online services charge additionally for time spent on the Internet.

- You could also find an Internet Service Provider (ISP), which allows you to connect to a computer that has a direct Internet connection. Just as with any major purchase, and kind of like choosing a long distance service, you'll need to shop around for prices and features. In most large cities, you can typically open an account that provides up to 150 free hours of access per month (probably more than you'll ever need) at a cost of $20 per month or less.

Choosing an Internet Service Provider

First, you should make sure you don't already have an Internet account. If you are in college you may have Internet access and not even know it. Call the Computer Science Department or your Student Services group to find out. If you work for a large company, you may also be able to get free access for business and personal use. Your company could have a corporate account for which it pays a monthly flat fee, regardless of the number of employees who use it. Find out. You might be pleasantly surprised.

Internet Service Provider Versus Online Service

True, you can send Internet email and access the Internet and even the World Wide Web through most of today's online services, such as America Online, CompuServe, and Prodigy, but as we've already mentioned, these services typically charge by the hour. Even with the resources we list for you in this book, you'll probably want to spend a lot of time on the World Wide Web doing research, looking at job listings, and exploring in general.

This will take more than just a few minutes a day, which means the amount of money you spend can really add up when you are charged by the hour. It will probably be more economical for you to find an Internet Service Provider, if there is one in your community (see the Internet Service Provider list in Appendix A). They may either charge a flat monthly rate, charge a lower dollar amount per hour, or might be able to cut you a smoking deal depending on how much time you'll be spending online. If there is not an ISP in your community and you still choose an ISP over an online service, you will not only have to pay the basic monthly fee for the provider, but long distance charges as well.

Where to Look

There are several ways to find an ISP. First, check out the ISPs listed later in Appendix A of this book. If you don't find what you're looking for, the next most obvious, but not necessarily the most effective, way to find a provider is to check the Yellow Pages under

Internet or Computer. Call a few places and tell them what you're looking for. Compare prices and services, but don't automatically go for the "too good to be true" bargain.

Does your town have any local computer magazines or newsletters? Many ISPs advertise regularly in local publications (sometimes even the newspaper) and may offer specials. You can also check with any of the local computer stores. They will probably be plugged in to the computing community and should be able to tell you some of the best providers around.

Also, keep a sharp eye out for local advertisers who include their Web addresses as part of their print or broadcast ads. Try calling the offices for these companies to find out who their Internet providers are. Chances are, it will be a local provider. If you're congenial enough, a company representative might even be happy to share with you the details about their Internet account (such as number of free hours and charges per month).

Last, but not least, try contacting someone at your town's computer user group. They may even have an Internet SIG (special interest group) whose meetings you could attend to get more inside information. Heck, you might even meet someone who's interested in hiring you!

What to Look For

There are a few things that you'll want to check out in an ISP:

- *Reputation.* Don't instantly hand over your credit card to an ISP just because the name sounds familiar. A lot of customers run into problems, such as an inability to get through to the ISP's lines at key times of the day or evening. They encounter busy signals or are bumped offline in the middle of Internet use. If this is a regular occurrence, word has probably gotten around. This is a good reason to attend a users group meeting or ask your computer-literate or Net-addicted friends which local ISP they recommend and what types of experiences they've had connecting (and staying connected) to their ISP's server.

- *Length of time in business.* Be wary of an ISP that has only existed for a few months and/or is run out of someone's garage. Ask how long the company has been in business, and call your local Chamber of Commerce to determine if the ISP in question is a member or if any problems have been reported.

- *Technical support.* First, find out if technical support with an ISP is free. It would be a pity if you got your communications software package in the mail and had to spend an hour (at $2.95 per minute) on the phone figuring out how to install it.

Second, nothing is more annoying than calling a provider's technical support line in the middle of a crisis and getting a busy signal or, worse yet, a recording saying that tech support hours are between 10 a.m. and 2 p.m. three days a week. The last thing you're going to want to deal with during your job hunt is a lack of help when you really need it.

When you shop for an ISP, ask the provider's sales rep about the hours the technical support staff is available, how many people they have on staff, and what the average time is that a customer can expect to be on hold. Be wary of any provider that tells you they provide "24-hour, online help." What they probably mean is that you can send an email message to their tech support staff any hour of the day or night. But if you can't get online in the first place, 24-hour online tech support is meaningless. And even if you are able to send an "SOS" email message to the tech support staff, that doesn't mean you'll get an immediate response. If you send an email message at 10 p.m. and nobody is monitoring email messages at night, then there's almost no point in sending a critical message during the tech support staff's "off hours."

- *Price.* If you do some research, you should be fine. An Internet account through an ISP should only cost you about $20 to $30 per month, including email capabilities, Web access, and the beginning software. Don't let someone charge you enormous amounts of money for "extras" that you don't need. For instance, our ISP charges a flat monthly fee of $24.95 per month for a SLIP/PPP account, and includes 150 hours of online time at that price. We don't need any of the other bells and whistles (although if you want to create your own home page, you might have to pay extra for this because the files will probably be stored and maintained on your ISP's server).

What Kind of Account You'll Need

We've already established that for a truly successful job search, you'll need email, newsgroup access, and access to the World Wide Web. To be able to do these things, make sure you get a SLIP or PPP account when you sign up with an ISP.

A SLIP account will generally give you the access you need to connect to the Internet and surf the Web. *SLIP* stands for Serial Line Internet Protocol. *PPP* stands for Point-to-Point Protocol and is pretty much equivalent to SLIP, although many consider PPP to be a bit faster and more reliable than a SLIP account. If you choose to get a non-SLIP/PPP account, you'll be able to access the Internet, but not the World Wide Web. A SLIP/PPP account is much more user friendly and is best for the non-techie.

For more infomation on finding an Internet service provider in your area, see Appendix A.

CHAPTER 4

What You Won't Find in the Classifieds: Up-to-the-Minute Job Listings

WHAT THE ICONS MEAN

 FORTUNE 500 COMPANY

 OFFERS INTERNATIONAL JOB OPPORTUNITIES

There are thousands of online job hunting resources on the Internet, but finding them isn't as easy as you might think. If you pay for connection time, and if you consider your time and money precious (as most job seekers do), you probably don't want to spend hours on end just trying to find a good company that might list a couple of jobs.

So we've done some of the work for you. By no means are these listings comprehensive of every Internet company offering jobs because every day the Internet changes. But we spent hours of online time scouring the Internet for a variety of companies that offer all kinds of job openings.

In the following pages, you'll find a list of some of our favorite companies that provide job openings or other important information that can help you achieve employment with that company. For each listing, we give you:

- the name of the company

- the URL that takes you directly to the employment page or job listings

- a brief description of the employment area offered by the company (and typical jobs they hire for)

- a brief description of the company

- the URL of the company's home page

Remember, these are just brief descriptions to help you decide which Web sites are worth your time, to give you an idea of what's out there, and to keep you from spending all your online hours wandering aimlessly. The actual information that you'll find at a company's home page can be very extensive, detailed, and valuable. You might find a sound byte (recorded audio message) from the president of the company, descriptions of all the products offered and their prices, company history, stock information, and more: pictures of the corporate mascot, the company picnic, and even a view of the employee lounge.

As you begin your explorations remember:

- Comprehensive corporate information may not appear on the employment page, but will probably be available at the home page.

- Not all job openings for a technical company are technical.

- Some companies list all of their job openings in one long list, or allow you to search by job categories. Others allow you to search a database by skill keywords, such as "programming" or "marketing."

- Many companies will provide an online resume form for you to fill out. Pay attention! If they only accept resumes created by their form, don't bother emailing your text resume. Follow directions carefully, and use the tips and techniques from Chapter 5.

- In addition to going straight to the companies on this list or searching for companies with a search engine, you can find all kinds of resources on the Web that will lead you directly to a number of companies' employment opportunities. You'll find these resources in Chapter 11.

- This chapter does not include job listings for universities or government agencies. You will find that information in Chapter 11.

Major Companies/Fortune 500s on the Web

3Com

Employment: http://www.3com.com:80/0files/jobs/index.html
3Com offers job opportunities in Administrative, Customer Service, Engineering, Finance, Manufacturing, Marketing, Materials, MIS, and Sales. You can also check the "What's New" section for the most recent job openings.
Company Description: 3Com manufactures networking hardware and has more than 4,500 employees worldwide.
Home Page: http://www.3com.com/index.html

3DO

Employment: http://www.3do.com/company/job_list.html
3DO has tons of job openings in technical *and* non-technical areas: Finance, Marketing, Software, Hardware, Product Engineering, and Developer Support.
Company Description: 3DO was formed to create a new home interactive multimedia technology with closely defined hardware and software specifications.
Home Page: http://www.3DO.com

ADC Telecommunications

Employment: http://www.ps-mpls.com/ADC/CORP_DIR.html employment
This site gives information on ADC's hiring policies and benefits, and lists openings like Senior Product Engineer, Signal Processing Engineer, Software Design Engineer, HRIS Analyst, Account Manager-International Sales, and Applications Engineer.

Company Description: ADC delivers integrated solutions for voice, data, and video networks.
Home Page: http://www.adc.com

AMP Incorporated

Employment: http://www.ampincorporated.com/jobs/jobs.html
This page lists job openings in AMP's facilities in Pennsylvania, North Carolina, South Carolina, California, Virginia, Texas, and Florida. Typical positions are Skilled Trades, Auditor, Development Engineer, Engineering Analyst, Product Engineer, Manufacturing Engineer, Unix Systems Administrator, and more. AMP also has a job section for students.
Company Description: AMP develops and manufactures a wide variety of electronic/electrical interconnection devices.
Home Page: http://www.amp.com

AMR Corporation

Employment: http://www.amrcorp.com/sabr_grp/jobopps.htm
This site lists job openings in the various divisions of the SABRE group: Computer Services, Decision Technologies, Group Finance, Interactive, and Travel Information Network.
Company Description: AMR strives to be the global market leader in air transportation and related information services.
Home Page: http://amrcorp.com/amr/amr_home.htm

AT&T

Employment: http://www.careermosaic.com/cm/att/att6.html
This site gives links to job opportunities with AT&T Bell Laboratories, AT&T Business Multimedia Services, AT&T Customer Service and Part-Time Opportunities, AT&T Global Information Solutions, AT&T Management Employment, and AT&T Microelectronics.
Company Description: AT&T is the world's networking leader, providing communications services and products, as well as network equipment and computer systems, to businesses, government agencies, and consumers.
Home Page: http://www.attgis.com/

Adobe Systems Incorporated

Employment: http://www.adobe.com/JOBS.html
Adobe's employment area lists openings in Engineering (Computer Scientist, Software Engineer); Operations (Inventory Control Analyst, Mail Services Associate);

Information Systems (Business Systems Analyst, Unix Systems Administrator); Sales and Marketing (Product Marketing Manager, Marketing Specialist); and Corporate, Finance, and Administration (Art Director, Administrative Assistant, Financial Analyst).

Company Description: Adobe develops, markets, and supports computer software products and technologies that enable users to create, display, print, and communicate electronic documents.

Home Page: http://www.adobe.com/

Advanced Micro Devices (AMD)

Employment: http://www.careermosaic.com/cm/amd/amd3.html

This site lists exempt positions and college opportunities, including typical entry-level employment opportunities for recent graduates, AMD training programs, cooperative internship and education programs, and contact information. Most positions listed at this site are engineering-related: Applications Engineer, CAD Engineer, Design Engineer, Information Systems, and so on.

Company Description: AMD is the fourth-largest U.S. merchant-supplier of integrated circuits. They produce microprocessors, embedded processors, memories, programmable logic devices, networking applications, and circuits for telecommunications.

Home Page: http://www.amd.com/

Alias/Wavefront

Employment: http://www.aw.sgi.com:80/Corporate/career_opportunities.html

Alias is looking for applicants in the areas of Software Engineering, Information Systems, Marketing, Customer Service, and Sales.

Company Description: Alias/Wavefront focuses on developing "the world's most advanced tools for the creation of digital content."

Home Page: http://www.alias.com

Altera Corporation

Employment: http://www.careermosaic.com:80/cm/altera/altera3.html

This site lists opportunities for recent graduates and describes job openings for Engineers, Layout Designers, Product Engineers, Technical Writers, Software Engineers, and more.

Company Description: Altera creates high-performance, high-density programmable logic devices and associated computer-aided engineering logic development tools.

Home Page: http://www.careermosaic.com/cm/altera

Amdahl Corporation

Employment: http://www.amdahl.com/doc/employment/
This site gives information about internships and college recruiting, and lists openings for the areas of Business Development, Compatible Systems, Customer Services, Electronic Manufacturing, Enterprise Storage Systems, Field Operations, Finance, Human Resources, Information Services, Information Technology Consulting, Marketing, Open Enterprise Systems, and Administration.
Company Description: Amdahl develops and integrates large-scale systems and enterprise-wide solutions that address the business and information needs of leading organizations worldwide.
Home Page: http://www.amdahl.com/

American Management Systems, Inc. (AMS)

Employment: http://www.amsinc.com/greatplc/career/career.htm
This site gives information on the company itself, educational programs, college recruiting, and more. You can also search AMS's job openings database by business area, skills, geographic location, and type of position.
Company Description: AMS is a business and information technology consulting firm that provides a full range of services: business re-engineering, change management, systems integration, and systems development and implementation.
Home Page: http://www.amsinc.com/

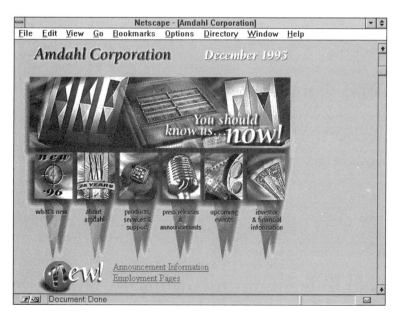

Figure 4.1 Amdahl Corporation's home page with links to employment opportunities.

American Megatrends (AMI)

Employment: http://www.megatrends.com/jobs.Employment.html
This site lists employment opportunities at AMI in Atlanta, Georgia. Typical positions are Engineer, Programmer, Technical Support Representative, RMA Technician, and Test Technician.
Company Description: AMI provides computer BIOS software, motherboards, peripheral cards, and software utilities.
Home Page: http://www.megatrends.com/

 ## Apple Computer

Employment: http://www2.apple.com/employment
Lists current employment opportunities, company information, and more.
Company Description: Apple is the world's number two computer maker (second to IBM).
Home Page: http://www.apple.com

Arris Pharmaceutical

Employment: http://www.arris.com/Career_Opps/Career_Opportunities
Arris' employment area lists current job openings and a U.S. mail address where you can send your resume and cover letter. Typical listings are Scientist, Research Assistant or Associate, and Accountant.
Company Description: Arris is "engaged in the discovery and development of synthetic small molecule therapeutics that modulate the activity of medically important proteins." (Whew!)
Home Page: http://www.arris.com/

Ascend Communications, Inc.

Employment: http://www.ascend.com/aboutascend/jobsindex.html
This site lists job opportunities in the areas of Marketing, Engineering, International, Manufacturing, Customer Support, Finance and Administration, and Sales and System Administration.
Company Description: Ascend Communications produces a broad range of digital wide area network access products that enhance and extend corporate networks for applications such as remote LAN access, Internet access, telecommuting, video conferencing, imaging and integrated voice, data, and video access.
Home Page: http://www.ascend.com/

Aspect Telecommunications

Employment: http://www.aspect.com/hiring.html
Aspect's employment site lists information about the company and its workplace

environment, and employee satisfaction. Job listings are for the areas of Product Development, Sales and Business Applications Consulting, Customer Operations, Channel Marketing and Support, Manufacturing, Information Technology, and Administration.

Company Description: Aspect Telecommunications provides product and service solutions for companies with mission-critical call centers, a primary contact point for their businesses.

Home Page: http://www.aspect.com/

AspenTech

Employment: http://www.aspentech.com/~aspentech/jobs/

The AspenTech employment page lists various job opportunities in technical and non-technical areas. At the time of this writing, the only job categories were "Customer Support, Cambridge, MA" and "Customer Support, Brussels, Belgium, Europe." The positions in these categories included Product Support Engineer and Systems Support Engineer.

Company Description: AspenTech is the largest provider of process modeling technology in the world.

Home Page: http://www.aspentec.com/

Autodesk

Employment: http://www.autodesk.com/job/job.htm

This site lists job openings for Marketing Managers, Telemarketing Supervisors, Technical Writers, Customer Service Representatives, Administrative Assistants, 3D Project Managers, Software Engineers, Programmers, and more.

Company Description: Autodesk is the world's leading supplier of computer-aided design and desktop multimedia software, the world's fifth largest PC-software company, and a leading supplier of Unix-based design tools.

Home Page: http://www.autodesk.com

Automated Concepts Inc. (ACI)

Employment: http://www.careermosaic.com:80/cm/aci/aci4.html

This site gives information on ACI's staff and lists current openings in offices throughout the company. Typical listings are for Marketing Representatives, Programmer/Analysts, LAN Administrators, various management positions, and Practice Manager.

Company Description: Founded in 1966, ACI provides software development, systems integration, and technical services to major corporations and government organizations.

Home Page: http://www.careermosaic.com/cm/aci/

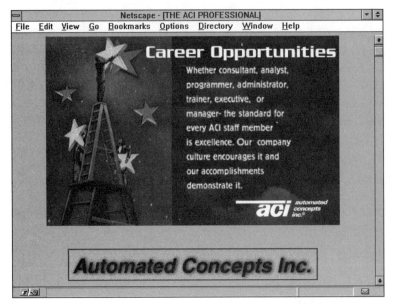

Figure 4.2 ACI's Career Opportunities page.

BBN Planet Corporation

Employment: http://www.helpwanted.com/bbnjobs.html

This career opportunities site lists positions like Customer Technical Support, Micro Networking Specialist, Network Integration Specialist, Router Software Developer, NOC Controller, Senior Network and Computer Security Analyst, and Senior Engineer.

Company Description: BBN provides a new generation of technologies, applications, and value-added services that puts the power of the Internet to work for businesses worldwide.

Home Page: http://www.bbn.com/

BTG Incorporated

Employment: http://www.btg.com/jobs/

This employment area, with more than 11,000 hits at the time of this writing, lists current openings at offices throughout the country. Typical openings include Internet Specialist, Technical Writer, Engineer, Sales, and more.

Company Description: BTG is a technology integration company specializing in open systems development, systems engineering, reusable software, document management, value-added reselling, and the manufacture of customized high-performance computers.

Home Page: http://www.btg.com/jobs/

Bay Networks

Employment: http://www.wellfleet.com/Corporate/Employment/

Bay Networks has job openings in many of its divisions: Hardware Engineering, Software Engineering, Finance and Administration, Information Technology/MIS, International, Manufacturing Operations and Quality, Corporate Marketing, Product Marketing, Materials, Sales, Customer Service, Systems Test Engineering, Technical Operations/Customer Services, Centillion Business Unit, and Xylogics.

Company Description: Bay Networks addresses the needs for switched internetworks supporting next-generation corporate information systems.

Home Page: http://www.wellfleet.com/

Bellcore

Employment: http://www.bellcore.com/HR/

At the time of this writing, this employment area was still under construction, but listed openings for Software Designers and Systems Engineers. The home page has comprehensive information about the company itself and its areas of expertise.

Company Description: With more than 6,200 employees, Bellcore is an architect of telecommunications-network software products and services.

Home Page: http://www.bellcore.com/index.html

Blueridge Technologies

Employment: http://www.blueridge.com/blueridge/positions.html

This site lists Blueridge's East and West Coast opportunities. Typical positions are Sales Manager, Technical Support Specialist, Unix System Administrator, and Software Systems Engineer.

Company Description: Blueridge Technologies specializes in document management for Macintosh and Windows.

Home Page: http://www.blueridge.com/

Booz, Allen & Hamilton (B, A & H)

Employment: http://www.bah.com/shared/careers.html

This site offers information about working as a consultant for B, A & H, career path information, and what it takes to be a successful professional at the company. The home page lists contact information.

Company Description: Booz, Allen & Hamilton is an international management and technology consulting firm committed to helping senior management solve complex problems.

Home Page: http://www.bah.com/

Brooktree Corporation

Employment: http://www.brooktree.com/brooktree/html/job_desc/employ.htm
This site lists technical and non-technical positions in the areas of Communications, Finance, Graphics and Imaging, Information Services, Multimedia, Production, Purchasing, Sales, Software, and Quality Assurance.
Company Description: Brooktree produces high-performance digital and mixed-signal solutions that solve difficult challenges in multimedia, graphics, communications, and imaging applications.
Home Page: http://www.brooktree.com/

CADmazing Solutions, Inc.

Employment: http://www.cadmazing.com/cadmazing/pages/jobs.html
This site listed only a few positions including Design Engineers, Multi Tool Expert, Project Managers for the Services Group.
Company Description: CADmazing Solutions is a technology services company focusing on strategic planning, IC design methodologies, project management, software development, and technology implementation.
Home Page: http://www.cadmazing.com/cadmazing/

CB Technologies, Inc. (CBT)

Employment: http://www.myxa.com/cbtech/employ.html
CBT's site gives a company description and open positions like Software Consultant, Network Consultant, Project Manager, Account Manager, and Account Executive.
Company Description: CB Technologies is a custom software development firm.
Home Page: http://www.myxa.com/cbtech/Welcome.html

CDI Information Services

Employment: http://165.247.64.66/Maps/+bMainToolbar.map?265,18
This is a wonderful employment area that lets you click first on a button to select the CDI office of your choice. You can then click on one of the cities listed in that region and be linked to available jobs locally.
Company Description: CDI Information Services is a division of CDI Corporation (the largest engineering, design, scientific, and technical services company in North America), with more than 25,000 employees worldwide.
Home Page: http://165.247.64.66/index.shtml

Cabletron Systems, Inc.

Employment: http://www.ctron.com/jobs.
This site offers Cabletron employment and sales information, and lists job opportunities in the areas of Engineering, Management Information Systems, Technical Support, Sales, and Manufacturing Engineering.
Company Description: Cabletron Systems is the leading hub manufacturer of the LAN industry, with more than 5,000 employees worldwide.
Home Page: http://www.ctron.com/

Cadence Design Systems

Employment: http://www.cadence.com/employment.html
The Cadence employment site lists current openings for jobs like Engineer, Communications Specialist, Marketing Director, Programmer, Mail Clerk, Human Resources Representative, Business Analyst, Order Fulfillment, Technical Writer, Treasury Specialist, and more.
Company Description: Cadence is the worldwide leader in the development and marketing of design automation software and services that accelerate and advance the process of designing electronic systems.
Home Page: http://www.cadence.com/

Cirrus Logic

Employment: http://www.cirrus.com/career/
This site lists open positions like Engineer, Programmer Analyst, Credit and Collections Analyst, Product Marketing Manager, Document Control Supervisor, and more.
Company Description: Cirrus offers a broad range of innovative chip solutions for personal computing and communications.
Home Page: http://www.cirrus.com/

Cisco Systems

Employment: http://www.cisco.com/public/employment.html
Cisco's employment area gives information about its recruitment information and lists job openings for Business Development, Customer Advocacy/MIS, Engineering, Finance and Administration, Human Resources, International, Kalpana, Lightstream, Manufacturing, Marketing, North America Sales, PC Access Business Unit, and Workgroup.
Company Description: Cisco is the world's largest supplier of computer internetworking systems.
Home Page: http://www.cisco.com/public/www

CLAM Associates

Employment: http://www.clam.com/clamweb/clamjobs.html
CLAM's employment page lists benefits and job openings for Software Development, Quality Assurance, and Professional Services and Systems Integration. CLAM provides a wide range of development, porting, systems integration, education, and support services to aid customers in implementing commercial production systems in Unix.
Home Page: http://www.clam.com/index.html

ClariNet Communications Corp.

Employment: http://www.clarinet.com/jobs.html
This job opportunities page lists job openings like Vice President of Development, Vice President of Marketing, Technical Sales Account Managers, Telemarketing Account Managers, and Assistant Editor.
Company Description: ClariNet publishes the ClariNet e.News, the first and largest electronic news service on the Internet.
Home Page: http://www.clarinet.com/index.html

Cognos

Employment: http://www.cognos.com/about_cognos/1-4.html#job
Cognos' employment site gives basic information about "building your future with Cognos," and gives detailed information on positions for Software Developers, Quality Control Analysts, Technical Writers, Customer Support Specialists, Technical Analysts, Software Specialists, and more.
Home Page: http://www.cognos.com

Computer Associates International, Inc.CA

Employment: http://www.cai.com/career/cajobs.htm
CA's employment page offers general company information and lists Sales and Marketing and Software Development positions, including Marketing Specialists, Technical Consultants, Systems Consultants, and Client Service Representatives. It also lists nationwide openings by city and state.
Company Description: Computer Associates International, Inc. is the world's leading independent software company for multi-platform computing. It has more than 8,000 employees in 30 countries.
Home Page: http://www.cai.com

Cray Research, Inc.

Employment: http://www.cray.com/PUBLIC/COMPANY/EO/
Cray's employment site offers information about the "rewards for working for Cray"

and lists current job openings for Electrical and Mechanical Engineers, Programmer Analysts, Compiler Developer, Sales Analyst, Manufacturing Engineer, Diagnostic Programmer, and more.

Company Description: Cray Research supplies supercomputers designed to improve product quality, lower development costs, and reduce time-to-market.

Home Page: http://www.cray.com/

Creative Labs

Employment: http://www.creaf.com/www/jobs.html

This "fast-growing" company has job listings in the areas of Finance, Marketing, Operations, Sales, MIS, and in its "SHAREVISION" division.

Company Description: Creative Labs specializes in cost-effective hardware and software solutions for the PC multimedia marketplace.

Home Page: http://www.creaf.com/www/jobs.html

Davidson and Associates

Employment: http://www.davd.com/jobs/

This employment opportunities page contains basic contact information and offers job listings for positions like 3D Graphic Artist, Product Marketing Manager, Merchandising Representative, Sales Representative, Programmer, Art Director, Sales Analyst, Technician, and more.

Company Description: Davidson develops, publishes, and distributes multimedia educational and entertainment software for use in both homes and schools.

Home Page: http://www.davd.com:80/home.html

 # Dell Computer Corporation

Employment: http://www.careermosaic.com/cm/dell/dell3.html

This site lists the company profile, global employment opportunities, benefits, and information on the MBA and internship programs.

Company Description: Dell is a leading manufacturer of PCs worldwide.

Home Page: http://www.dell.com/

DeLorme Mapping

Employment: http://www.delorme.com/home.htm

This site lists company information and job opportunities like Windows Programmer, Mac Programmer, Project Manager/Online Services, and Programmer/ Analyst.

Company Description: DeLorme Mapping develops and sells maps, atlases, and multimedia mapping for the consumer, business, and government markets.

Home Page: http://www.delorme.com/home.htm

Delrina

Employment: http://www.delrina.com/about/idxjobs.htm
Delrina's site gives some company history and lists open jobs in Canada and the U.S. Typical positions include Documentation Specialist, Technical Support Representative, Quality Assurance Analyst, and Software Developer.
Company Description: Delrina is a technology company responsible for the creation of products like WinFax PRO, PerForm for Windows, and the screensaver engine used by Berkeley Systems Software.
Home Page: http://www.delrina.com

 ## Digital Equipment Corporation (DEC)

Employment: http://www.digital.com/info/careers/
These are DEC's "Career Home Pages," with a company overview; information on college internships and co-ops; benefits information; contact information; and career opportunities in Engineering, Finance, Legal, Manufacturing, Marketing, Sales, and Systems/Technical Support.
Company Description: DEC is the world's leader in open client/server computing solutions from personal computers to integrated worldwide information systems.
Home Page: http://www.digital.com

Digital PC

Employment: http://www.pc.digital.com/employ/employ.htm
This site contains information about Digital PC products, lists job openings, and allows you to apply for current openings, such as those for Materials Consultants, Software Engineers, Lotus Notes Administrators, and so on.
Company Description: Digital PC is a group of Digital Equipment Corporation.
Home Page: http://www.pc.digital.com/

Digital Systems International, Inc. (DSI)

Employment: http://www.dgtl.com/employment/default.html
This employment page was still under construction at the time of this writing, but it offered job postings like Accounting, Sales, Installation Engineer, Software Engineer, and Technical Support Representative.
Company Description: DSI provides computer telephony systems, software, and services designed to create improved performance and productivity.
Home Page: http://www.dgtl.com/

 ## Dunn & Bradstreet

Employment: http://www.careermosaic.com/cm/dnb/
This is a comprehensive site with locations, information on specific divisions, and

tons of open positions in a variety of areas: Analyst, Consultant, Marketing, Human Resources, Account Manager, Sales, Direct Marketing, Reporter, and more.

Company Profile: The companies of Dun & Bradstreet include Dun & Bradstreet Information Services, Dun & Bradstreet Software, IMS International, Moody's Investors Service, A.C. Nielsen, and Nielsen Media Research.

Home Page: http://www.dnb.com/

EDS (Electronic Data Systems)

Employment: http://www.eds.com/careers/ejc00000.html

EDS's site gives an EDS overview, current job openings, and benefits and campus relations information. Job openings can be searched by keyword or employment category of interest (technical, professional, etc.).

Company Description: EDS is one of the largest information services companies in the United States.

Home Page: http://www.eds.com/home.html

Eli Lilly and Company

Employment: http://www.lilly.com/career/jobline/index.html

This site lists job openings in Information Systems, Scientific, Engineering, Business and Administrative, and positions not requiring a four-year degree. All positions are in Indiana.

Company Description: Eli Lilly is a global research-based pharmaceutical corporation based in Indianapolis, Indiana, that is working to create and deliver superior health care solutions.

Home Page: http://www.lilly.com/

Ericsson

Employment: http://www.ericsson.com/Jobs/

This site lists various job openings in Germany, Sweden, Italy, and Norway. Typical positions include TCM Tester, Systems Test Plant Engineer, DT Engineer, AS Specifier, Area Manager, Sales Manager, Development Engineer-Databases, Radio Systems Manager, and Software Engineers.

Company Description: Ericsson has more than 75,000 employees in more than 100 countries. The company specializes in telecommunications: switching, radio, and networking.

Home Page: http://www.ericsson.com/

Execusoft

Employment: http://www.utw.com/execusoft/reqs.html

This site provides job listings arranged by state (Utah, California, and Colorado). Job postings include Programmer, Engineer, Database Administrators, and so on. They each have codes denoting hourly, salaried, or contract positions.

Company Description: Execusoft is a technology consulting firm providing contract services in areas of computer programming, systems analysis and design, life cycle development, and systems programming.
Home Page: http://www.utw.com/execusoft/homepge.html

 # FMC

Employment: http://fmcweb.ncsa.uiuc.edu/Career/careerHome.html
This site describes career development programs for scientists and engineers. FMC provides career path descriptions with an instant email application so you can easily request more information.
Company Description: FMC is one of the world's leading producers of chemicals and machinery for industry, agriculture, and government.
Home Page: http://fmcweb.ncsa.uiuc.edu/home.html

FTP Software

Employment: http://www.ftp.com/hr/index.html
FTP has job openings for QA Tester, Channel Program Marketer, Staff Engineers, Senior Engineers, Strategic Accounts Support Manager, Technical Support Escalation Manager, Senior Course Developer, Educational Sales Account Manager, Consulting Engineer, and more.
Company Description: FTP pioneered TCP/IP networking over Microsoft Windows as co-authors of the Windows Sockets specification. FTP has the largest independent TCP/IP for the PC development and support staff in the industry.
Home Page: http://www.ftp.com/

First USA

Employment: http://www.careermosaic.com/cm/first-usa/first4.html
The First USA Employment Opportunities page gives a description of what their recruiters are looking for and their corporate values, and allows you to conduct a keyword search for all available positions. You can also search by geographic location, and you'll have access to all First USA locations. Typical positions are in the areas of Production, Marketing, and Customer Service.
Company Description: First USA is a growing credit card institution with more than 900 employees headquartered in Delaware.
Home Page: http://www.careermosaic.com/cm/first-usa/first1.html

First Commerce Corporation

Employment: http://www.neosoft.com/~bcahill/fcom/employ.htm
This employment area lists mostly systems development positions and provides an online resume form.

Figure 4.3   First USA's home page with links to Employment Opportunities.

Company Description: First Commerce Corporation is a $7 billion statewide bank holding company.
Home Page: http://www.neosoft.com/~bcahill/fcom/fcom.htm

 # First Union Corporation

Employment: http://www.firstunion.com/careers/careers.html
At the time of this writing, this employment page was still under construction.
Company Description: A bank holding company made up of eight financial institutions.
Home Page: http://www.firstunion.com

 # Ford

Employment: http://www.ford.com/corporate-info/careercenter
This site gives information on student employment programs: the College Cooperative Education Program and the Summer Internship Program.
Company Description: Ford "strives to become the world's best automotive and financial services company …"
Home Page: http://www.ford.com/

 # Fujitsu

Employment: http://www.fujitsu.com/HR/fossi/employop.htm
This site lists job openings at Fujitsu Open Solutions, Inc. in San Jose, California. Typical positions are for Software Systems Engineer, Test Engineer, Director of Soft-

ware Tools and Processes, Product Manager, Database System Developer, Software Development Engineer, Distributed System Engineer, and more. Fujitsu allows you to fill out their online resume form.

Company Description: Fujitsu is Japan's largest computer manufacturer and the second largest computer manufacturer in the world.

Home Page: http://www.fujitsu.com/

General Instrument Corporation (GIC)

Employment: http://www.gi.com/employ/employ.htm

The employment portion of this Web site lists job openings and qualifications for CAD Application Support Engineer, Supervisors, Engineers, Technicians, Marketing and Sales, Analysts, Business Development Managers, Product Managers, Computer Operator, Customer Service Reps, Trainers, and more.

Company Description: GIC develops technology, systems, and product solutions for the interactive delivery of video, voice, and data.

Home Page: http://www.gi.com/

General Magic

Employment: http://www.genmagic.com/extjob.html

General Magic's site lists current openings in Software Engineering, Customer Engineering, Product Marketing, Marketing, Sales, and Administration.

Figure 4.4 General Instrument's home page with links to job openings.

Company Description: General Magic creates software and hardware for companies like Sony, Motorola, and AT&T.
Home Page: http://www.genmagic.com/

Global Village Communications

Employment: http://www.globalvillag.com/joblist.html
Global Village lists openings for Senior Software Engineer, ISDN Engineer, Engineering Product Enhancement Manager, Engineering Project Leader, Operating Systems Engineer, Windows Engineer, Hardware Technician, QA Engineer, Macintosh Software Engineer, and more.
Company Description: Global Village develops and markets communication products for personal computer users.
Home Page: http://www.globalvillag.com/index.html

the good guys!

Employment: http://www.careermosaic.com:80/cm/goodguys/tgg3.html
This is an extensive career page with information about sales and non-sales positions, benefit descriptions, and application procedures. The open positions are throughout the U.S. and include Sales Counselors, Sales Managers, MIS, Distribution/Operations, Merchandising, Corporate and Administration, Accountant, and Financial Analyst.
Company Description: Based in California, this company consists of retail stores across the country specializing in audio video.
Home Page: http://www.careermosaic.com/cm/goodguys/tgg1.html

HAL Computer Systems

Employment: http://www.hal.com/jobs/
Job opportunities listed at this site are for HAL's corporate headquarters in Campbell, California. Openings include various engineering positions, Utilities and Graphics Manager, Technician, Layout Designer, Buyer, Public Relations Specialist, Account Manager, Operations Manager, Sales Representative, Accountant, Financial Analyst, and more.
Company Description: HAL Computer Systems develops high-performance 64-bit RISC computers for technical, commercial, and business users.
Home Page: http://www-external.hal.com/

Harlequin

Employment: http://www.harlequin.com/full/recruitment.html
Harlequin's site gives general company information and lists job opportunities in the U.S. and Canada in Marketing, Applications, Electronic Publishing, Technical Services, Symbolic Processing, and System Administration.

Figure 4.5 Harlequin's home page with links to employment opportunities.

Company Description: Harlequin creates high-technology software for major clients all over the world.
Home Page: http://www.harlequin.com

Harris Information Systems

Employment: http://www.hisd.harris.com/hr/employment_ops.html
This site lists jobs for Harris Corporation and its subsidiaries, searchable by discipline or by state. Typical opportunities are for Database Engineers, Program Administrators, Quality Assurance Specialists, and Software and System Engineers.
Company Description: Harris is a Fortune 200 worldwide corporation focused on four major businesses: electronic systems, communications, semiconductors, and Lanier Worldwide office equipment.
Home Page: http://www.hisd.harris.com

Hewlett Packard

Employment: http://wwwjobs.external.hp.com:80/
This is a great employment area with information about why you should work for HP. They have facilities around the world, college recruiting, an interactive job search form, interview tips, and an application. Typical opportunities are in Research and Development, Manufacturing, Factory Marketing, Product Assurance, Sales and Service, Finance, Information Technology, Marketing, and more.
Company Description: HP is a large company with a broad mix of technologies and

businesses, including computers, peripherals, components, test and measurement, medical, analytical, and service and support.
Home Page: http://www.hp.com/

Hewlett Packard Europe

Employment: http://www-europe.hp.com/JobPosting/
This service was created by HP's European Personnel Department, listing openings to external candidates in the Barcelona Large-Format and Desktop Inkjet Printers Division, and at the Grenoble Industrial Site. Typical job postings are in the areas of Manufacturing, Marketing, Research and Development, and Information Systems.
Company Description: See above.
Home Page: http://www-europe.hp.com

 IBM

Employment: http://www.empl.ibm.com/
Gives links to employment information for the United States, Canada, Japan, Netherlands, South Africa, and the U.K. For each country, you'll find company information, job opportunities by discipline, instructions on how to submit a resume, and more.
Company Description: IBM is the world's top computer company (hardware and software).
Home Page: http://www.ibm.com/

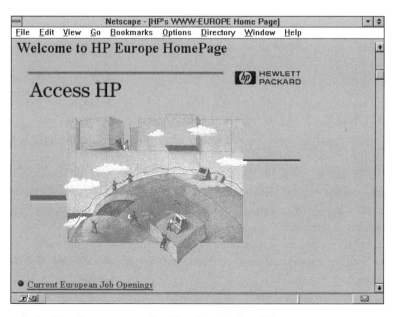

Figure 4.6 The home page for Hewlett Packard Europe.

IPC Technologies, Inc.

Employment: http://www.ipctech.com/jobs/joblist.html
IPC's "JobCache" lists technical positions like Network Connectivity Guru, Sybase/Oracle DBA, Programmer/Analyst, Access/Visual Basic Expert, Mac Expert, and Microsoft Certified Professional.
Company Description: IPC provides a variety of business solutions including Client/Server Consulting, Internet, Web Consulting, and Project Management.
Home Page: http://www.ipctech.com/

Infonet Services Corporation

Employment: http://www.info.net/HR/employment.html
Although you can't send your application or resume via email, check out these opportunities like Financial Analyst, Systems Engineer, Staff Administrator, Telecommunications Analyst, Network Control Specialist, Account Representative, Computer Scientist, and more.
Company Description: Infonet specializes in value-added services and managed networks, which are supported in 54 countries.
Home Page: http://www.info.net

Integrated Computer Solutions, Inc.(ICS)

Employment: http://www.ics.com/Jobs/
This site lists technical and non-technical positions like System Administrator, Technical Trainer, Software Support Engineer, Marketing Director, Marketing Communications Writer, Sales Engineer, Salesperson, and more.
Company Description: ICS designs products that help programmers create applications to meet their standards and develop the environment of their choice.
Home Page: http://www.ics.com

Informix Software, Inc.

Employment: http://www.informix.com/informix/corpinfo/inside/hr/jobs.htm
The employment opportunities page lists a mailing address for resumes and allows you to fill out the provided "Online Resume" for positions in California and Kansas. Typical positions are in Customer Service, Facilities, Finance/Operations, Human Resources, Legal, MIS, Marketing, Strategic Planning, Product Development, and Product Management.
Company Description: With more than 2,200 employees worldwide, Informix is the world's leading supplier of high-performance, parallel-processing database technology for open systems.
Home Page: http://www.informix.com/welcome.htm

International Data Group (IDG)

Employment: http://www.idg.com/welcome/jobs/jobs.html

This site lists tons of job opportunities, including Senior Editor, Sales Representative, Market Research Associate, CFO, Copy Editor, Editorial Assistant, Controller, Webmaster, Accounts Manager, Administrative Assistant, and more.

Company Description: IDG is the world's leading provider of information services for the Information Technology industry.

Home Page: http://www.idg.com

Intel

Employment: http://www.intel.com/intel/oppty/index.html

This site offers information on submitting a resume, college programs, compensation, and benefits. It also provides job listings in the areas of Facilities Design, Engineering, and Maintenance; Finance and Accounting; Hardware Engineering; Human Resources; Information Technology; Legal; Manufacturing; Marketing; Purchasing; and Software Engineering.

Company Description: Intel supplies the personal computing industry with the chips, boards, systems, and software that are the "ingredients" of the most popular computing architecture.

Home Page: http://www.intel.com/

Intermetrics

Employment: http://www.inmet.com/jobs.html

This site has national job openings for both technical and administrative areas in the Systems and Software Services Division, Systems and Software Applications Division, Software Technologies Division, and Microcomputer Division.

Company Description: Intermetrics is a software development and system services company with more than 25 years of experience designing technology-based solutions.

Home Page: http://www.inmet.com/

Intuit, Inc.

Employment: http://www.careermosaic.com/cm/intuit/intuit5.html

Intuit's job opportunities page offers descriptions of open positions like Product Marketing Manager, Software Development Engineer, Software, Quality Assurance Engineer, Technical Writer, and Customer Support Representative. It also lists relevant human resources contacts and addresses (and job hotlines) for four major Intuit locations.

Company Description: Intuit is a leading developer of personal finance, small business accounting, and tax preparation software.

Home Page: http://www.intuit.com

Iomega

Employment: http://www.careermosaic.com/cm/iomega/i5.html
Iomega's job site lists job opportunities, benefits, and corporate information.
Company Description: Iomega "creates information storage solutions that enhance the usefulness of personal computers and work stations in a variety of applications."
Home Page: http://www.iomega.com

JCPenney

Employment: http://www.jcpenney.com/careers/woo/caropps.htm
This site includes employee benefits, store locations, history, and career opportunities in Store Management, Information Systems, JCPenney Business Services, JCPenney Life Insurance Company, Accounting, Auditing, Catalog, and Credit.
Company Description: JCPenney is a large, Texas-based retailer.
Home Page: http://www.jcpenney.com/

J.P. Morgan

Employment: http://www.jpmorgan.com/CorpInfo/Careers/Home_Page.html
Provides answers to employment FAQs (Frequently Asked Questions), profiles recent hires, and discusses career paths for many education and experience levels. Typical positions are in Corporate Finance, Global Markets, Global Technology and Operations, Management Services, Audit, Financial, and Human Resources.

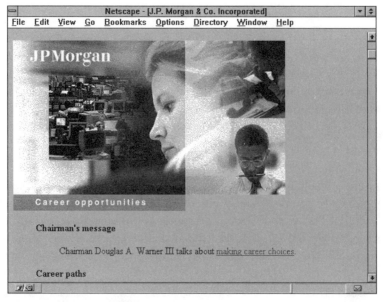

Figure 4.7 J.P. Morgan's Career page.

Company Description: J.P. Morgan is a global financial services firm.
Home Page: http://www.jpmorgan.com/

LEXIS-NEXIS

Employment: http://www.lexis-nexis.com/lncc/about/employment/employment.html
This site lists opportunities in Sales, Customer Service, and the Technical Department.
Company Description: LEXIS-NEXIS provides electronic research services to the legal, commercial, and government markets.
Home Page: http://www.lexis-nexis.com

Lightside

Employment: http://www.lightside.com/~dani/cgi/offers/
This site offers postings for jobs in Australia, Canada, Germany, Holland, Hong Kong, Israel, Italy, Thailand, the United Kingdom, and the United States. Typical positions are 3D Multimedia Programmer, Designers, Artists, Research and Design, Software Engineers, System Administrators, Animators, and 3D Database Artists. You'll also get links to related recruiting services and other Web sites.
Company Description: Lightside provides a variety of Web, Internet, and graphical-design services.
Home Page: http://www.lightside.com

Lockheed Martin

There are several Lockheed Martin companies, so they will be listed separately in this section.

FORMTEK SYSTEMS
Employment: http://www.formtek.com/HR/Jobs.html

LOCKHEED MARTIN ENERGY SYSTEMS
Employment http://www.ornl.gov/employment.html

LOCKHEED MARTIN MISSILES AND SPACE, AND TECHNICAL OPERATIONS
Employment: http://www.careermosaic.com/cm/lockheed/lockheed1.html

SANDERS
Employment: http://www.sanders.com/HR/Sanders_Jobs.html

Company Description: Lockheed Martin is the parent corporation for the previous companies. With more than 170,000 employees worldwide, Lockheed is the world's largest defense and NASA contractor focusing on space, launch vehicles, aeronautics, defense electronics, information systems, and energy/environmental ventures. Typical listings for the Lockheed companies are in Systems Integration, Quality Assurance, Training, Software Engineers, Software System Designers, Artificial Intelligence Scientists, and many others.
Home Page: http://www.lockheed.com/

Lycos, Inc.

Employment: http://www.lycos.com/lycosinc/jobs.html
This site lists technical positions such as Senior System and Network Administrator, Systems Programmer, Computer Operator, Computer Scientist, Software Engineer, Database Administrator, and more.
Company Description: Lycos is a new venture formed to develop and market the Lycos technology, which provides users with an effective way to search the Internet.
Home Page: http://www.lycos.com/lycosinc/index.html

MCI

Employment: http://www.mci.com/about/jobs/positions/home.shtml
At this site you can search job opportunities by state or by job category: Administrative, College Opportunities, Engineering-Hardware, Engineering-Network, Engineering-Software, Engineering-Support, General, Management, Marketing, and Professional Sales.
Company Description: MCI is one of the world's largest and fastest-growing diversified communications companies.
Home Page: http://www.mci.com/

Macromedia

Employment: http://www.macromedia.com/Industry/Job/mm.job.openings.html
This site has tons of job openings updated weekly. Typical positions include Engineering, International Sales, Quality Assurance Manager, Programming, PC Support, Creative Director, Marketing Communications, Multimedia Production, Web Site Administration, and more.
Company Description: Macromedia has created a family of software tools used by more than one million business users worldwide.
Home Page: http://www.macromedia.com

Magnet Interactive Group (MIG)

Employment: http://www.magnet.com/Employment/
This site lists positions for 3D Animator, Accounts Payable Specialist, Customer Service Manager, Game Concept Artist, Game Designer, Game Producer, Illustrator, MIS PC Systems Engineer, Software Engineer, and more.
Company Description: MIG is an interactive multimedia publisher and developer that creates interactive entertainment, edutainment, and online communications for both corporate and consumer markets.
Home Page: http://www.magnet.com

Mass Mutual

Employment: http://www.massmutual.com/viewtop/ifmar1.html
Mass Mutual's employment area gives the company's general philosophy, and allows you to fill out a form and email a request for more employment information.
Company Description: One of the nation's oldest and most respected life insurance companies.
Home Page: http://www.massmutual.com

The MathWorks, Inc.

Employment: http://www.mathworks.com/newjobs.html
The MathWorks job openings page lists both technical and non-technical opportunities in Engineering, Documentation, Computing Resources, Quality Assurance, Operations, Marketing, Sales, and Technical Support.
Company Description: MathWorks develops and markets interactive engineering and scientific software products.
Home Page: http://www.mathworks.com/

Maxis

Employment: http://www.maxis.com/simbusiness/open-jobs/open=jobs.html
This page lists quite a few job openings in the areas of Marketing, Product Development, Customer Support, Sales, Manufacturing, Management Information Systems, and in the Maxis Technology Group.
Company Description: Maxis is an entertainment software company, best known for its innovative simulations that let players learn through explorations, seeing results of decisions without winning or losing.
Home Page: http://maxis.com/index.html

McCaw Wireless Data, Inc. (AirData)

Employment: http://www.airdata.com:80/hiring/
The AirData Employment Center lists position openings like Systems Engineer, Networks Manager, Independent Strategic Relations Manager, Marketing Manager, and Technical Assistance Center Manager.
Company Description: McCaw Cellular pioneered the standard for sending data over today's cellular networks.
Home Page: http://www.airdata.com/index.htm

Megatest

Employment: http://www.rahul.net/megatest/pages/openings.html
Megatest lists their job openings and descriptions in the areas of Development Engineering, Operations, Information Systems, and Finance and Accounting.
Company Description: Megatest Corporation is a leading supplier of automatic test equipment for the semiconductor industry.
Home Page: http://www.rahul.net/megatest/

Microsoft Corporation

Employment: http://www.microsoft.com/Jobs/
Microsoft's employment area lists international job opportunities, information on all of Microsoft's groups (desktop, consumer, etc.), and even lists a calendar of dates, times, and places that Microsoft will be recruiting.
Company Description: Microsoft is the world's number one independent software company.
Home Page: http://www.microsoft.com
Email address for resumes: y-wait@microsoft.com

MicroWorks

Employment: http://www.getnet.com/micro/employ.html
This is a short employment page with contact information and locations to send a resume. MicroWorks typically searches for technicians to provide on-site services for contract accounts around the Phoenix, Arizona area.
Company Description: MicroWorks specializes in providing 24-hour on-site computer support for small to medium corporate clients.
Home Page: http://www.getnet.com/micro/

Miller Brewing Company

Employment: http://www.careermosaic.com/cm/miller/miller11.html
This is a very extensive employment site, with information about the company, products, news, the history of beer, and college recruitment. Typical positions are in

Strategic Planning and Finance, Marketing (Domestic and International), and Human Resources.

Company Description: Miller is one of the most successful beer brewers in the world.

Home Page: (Career Mosaic) http://www.careermosaic.com/cm/miller/

Millipore

Employment: http://www.millipore.com/corporate/hr/index.html

This site describes open positions in Research and Development, Marketing, Sales, Manufacturing, Information Systems, and Finance/Administration.

Company Description: Millipore is a company focusing on applying "purification technology" to critical research and manufacturing problems. Services range from the bacteria testing of water to sterilization of iopharmaceutical proteins.

Home Page: http://www.millipore.com

MITRE Corporation

Employment: http://www.mitre.org:80/jobs/

This site lists job openings in offices in several states. Typical positions are Telecommunications Systems Engineers, Information Technology Support, Software Engineers, Signal Processing, and Business Reengineering.

Company Description: MITRE is a multifaceted engineering company that provides technical and strategic guidance in information, communications, and environmental systems.

Home Page: http://www.mitre.org/

Molex

Employment: http://www.molex.com/jobs.html

This site gives a brief description of Molex and provides job listings for positions like Product Marketing Specialist, Project Engineer, CAD CAM Application Engineer, Quality Assurance Engineer, and Sales Representative.

Company Description: Molex manufactures electronic, electrical, and fiber optic interconnection systems; ribbon cable; switches; and application tooling.

Home Page: http://www.molex.com/

NYNEX CableComms

Employment: http://www.nynex.co.uk/nynex/job1.html

This site lists jobs such as Support Analyst, Database Administrator, and Business Analyst.

Company Description: NYNEX is one of the world's largest telecommunications corporations, providing advanced communications services to over 12 million customers.

Home Page: http://www.nynex.co.uk/nynex/index.html

The National Institutes of Health

Employment: http://helix.nih.gov:8001/jobs/
This site lists job opportunities for health care and science-related senior positions.
Company Description: The National Institutes of Health is one of the world's foremost biomedical research centers.
Home Page: http://www.nih.gov/home.html

 ## National Semiconductor

Employment: http://www.careermosaic.com/cm/ns/ns4.html
This is a good, descriptive job site, with special programs like college co-ops. Typical career paths include various Engineering positions, Financial Analyst, Human Resources Associate, and Marketing Communications.
Company Description: National Semiconductor is a transistor company, currently moving from analog to mixed-signal markets.
Home Page: http://www.careermosaic.com/cm/ns/ns1.html

NetManage

Employment: http://www.netmanage.com/netmanage/jobs.html
NetManage lists all kinds of opportunities, both technical and nontechnical, including Production Assistant-Entry Level, Training Developer, Trainer, Product Manager, Investor Relations Specialist, Accountant, Technical Support Engineer, MIS Manager, Event Manager, Software Development Engineer, Software Engineer, and more.
Company Description: NetManage is the "leading supplier of TCP/IP applications for Windows."
Home Page: http://www.netmanage.com/

Netscape Communications Corporation

Employment: http://www.netscape.com/people/index.html
Wow! This company is growing and the open positions prove it. Netscape has opportunities for everyone from Administrative Assistant to Server Engineer.
Company Description: Netscape is a provider of open software that enables people and companies to exchange information and conduct commerce over the Internet.
Home Page: http://www.netscape.com

Network Computing Devices (NCD)

Employment: http://www.ncd.com/External/human_resources/jobreq/jobhome.html
NCD's career page lists corporate opportunities, such as Accounting, Human Resources, and Legal; NCD Systems Business Opportunities, such as Finance/Accounting/Order Administration, Sales, MIS, Marketing, Engineering, Tech Support, and

Customer Service; and NCD Software Business Opportunities, such as Sales, Engineering, Technical Support Engineering, and Quality Support Engineering.

Company Description: NCD develops products that provide users access to information in network computing environments.

Home Page: http://www.ncd.com/

Newbridge Networks

Employment: http://www.newbridge.com/marccom/Employment/index.html
Newbridge's Human Resources page lists job offerings in Canada and the U.S. in the areas of Hardware Design, Research and Development, Sales, and Software Design.

Company Description: Newbridge Networks designs, develops, produces, and services a comprehensive family of networking products and systems that deliver the power of multimedia communications to organizations in 80 countries around the world.

Home Page: http://www.newbridge.com/

NeXT Computer, Inc.

Employment: http://www.next.com/NeXTanswers/HTMLFiles/1835.htmld/1835.html
This site gives basic company information, a benefits overview, and relevant contact information. NeXT also lists contract and full-time positions like Product Marketer, Communications Specialist, Technical Support, Trainer, Engineer, Human Resources, and Sales.

Company Description: NeXT develops and markets OpenStep, the first volume object standard for developing cross-platform, object-oriented applications.

Home Page: http://www.next.com/

Novell, Inc.

Employment: http://corp.novell.com/job/
Novell's employment site allows you to search the job category menu, and then the job location menu. Typical positions include both technical and non-technical: Administrative Assistant, Financial Analyst, Product Marketing Engineer, Human Resource Generalist, Internal Communications Manager, Test Engineer, Purchasing Assistant, and Senior Buyer.

Company Description: Novell, Inc. is one of the world's top network software providers, creating products that provide the "distributed infrastructure, network services, and advanced network access required to make networked information and pervasive computing an integral part of everyone's daily life."

Home Page: http://www.novell.com/

Open Market, Inc.

Employment: http://www.openmarket.com/hiring/

Open Market's job page includes company information and lists Boston-area positions such as Engineer, System Administrator, Web Applications Engineer, Customer Support, Technical Lead, Database Administrator, and more.

Company Description: Open Market is a start-up software company that builds technologies for commerce on the Internet, including secure payment transactions, connections between the Internet and financial networks, directory services, authentications, and power tools for creating Internet services.

Home Page: http://www.openmarket.com/

Oracle Corporation

Employment: http://www.oracle.com/corporate/hr/html/index.html

Oracle career opportunities on this page include both technical and non-technical. Typical hires are for Product Development or Management, Consulting, Technical Writing, Technical Support, Education, Corporate Marketing, Sales, Finance, and Administration.

Company Description: Oracle is the world's largest vendor of software for managing information, with more than 14,000 employees worldwide.

Home Page: http://www.oracle.com/index.html

PMC-Sierra, Inc.

Employment: http://www.careermosaic.com:80/cm/pmc-sierra/pmc2.html

This site does not list specific openings, but gives you the information you need to pursue opportunities with PMC-Sierra. You'll get important company and product information, and contact specifics.

Company Description: PMC is owned by Sierra Semiconductor and supplies ATM component solutions.

Home Page: http://www.careermosaic.com/cm/pmc-sierra/

Pacific Communications Sciences, Inc. (PCSI)

Employment: http://www.pcsi.com:80/html/empopps.html

This site lists quite a few openings, including Engineers, MIS Specialists, Technical Writers, Systems Administrators, Inventory Control Managers, and more.

Company Description: PCSI develops innovative communications and internetworking solutions for the rapidly growing telecommunications industry.

Home Page: http://www.pcsi.com/

Paramount Pictures

Employment: http://www.paramount.com/PDEOpp.html

This site features job opportunities for Paramount Digital Entertainment, a new Paramount group specializing in online entertainment products.

Company Description: One of the most active motion picture and television studios in the world.
Home Page: http:.//www.paramount.com

Pencom

Employment: http://www.pencom.com/pencom/careerhome.html
Here you'll find Pencom's complete Career Center, with related career articles, salary survey results, and job listings. You can click on any part of the provided U.S. map to get access to any of the more than 1,000 job postings that were available at the time of this writing.
Company Description: Pencom is a leading professional services provider specializing in software consulting, technical staffing, contract programming, and systems administration.
Home Page: http://www.pencom.com/

PeopleSoft

Employment: http://www.peoplesoft.com/jobs.htm
This is an extensive site, with detailed information on openings and recruiting at various company locations. Typical positions hired for are in Corporate Administration, Professional Services, Sales, Marketing (Channels), Marketing (Communications), Customer Service, Development, Communications Services, Internal Systems, Multimedia Services, Education Services, and Product Strategy.
Company Description: PeopleSoft provides business application software products and services worldwide.
Home Page: http://www.peoplesoft.com/

Perot Systems Corporation (PSC)

Employment: http://www.ps.net/pscdenver.html
PSC's job opportunities site lists tons of openings for Programmers, Software Engineer, Administrative Assistant, Recruiter, Technical Writer, Database Administrator, Security Analyst, LAN Analyst, Systems Programmer, Computer Operator, Staff Accountant, Help Desk Support, and Business Analyst.
Company Description: Perot Systems has become one of the world's fastest-growing information technology services and business transformation companies with more than $300 million in annual revenue.
Home Page: http://www.ps.net/

Philips Semiconductors

Employment: http://www.semiconductors.philips.com/ps/philips19.html
This employment page lists opportunities broken down by geographic locations and gives information on college recruiting and benefits. Typical positions are in the areas

of Design, such as Design Engineer or Manager/Digital Engineering; Product, such as Product Engineer or Product Marketing Manager; Test, such as Test Engineer or Senior Reliability Engineer; Applications, such as Systems Manager or Senior Applications Engineer; Failure Analysis, such as Reliability Engineer or Failure Analysis Engineer; Marketing, such as Marketing Manager; Software, such as Data Systems or 3D Graphics; Information Systems, such as Networks Manager or Business Systems Analyst; Manufacturing, such as Process Engineer or Production Supervisor; Field Sales, such as Regional Manager; and others.

Company Description: Philips is the tenth largest semiconductor supplier in the world, offering advanced proprietary products for high-growth areas.

Home Page: http://www.semiconductors.philips.com/ps/philips1.html

Praegitzer Industries

Employment: http://www.pii.com/EmpOppourtunities/EmpOppsMain.html
This is a short page with a brief description of Praegitzer employment. This company is regularly seeking PCB Designers, Process Engineers, Manufacturing Technicians, Management Staff, and Support Positions.

Company Description: Praegitzer designs and manufactures printed circuit boards (PCBs) for major companies worldwide.

Home Page: http://www.pii.com/

Price Waterhouse LLP

Employment: http://www.careermosaic.com/cm/price-waterhouse/price4.html
This Career Mosaic home and employment page gives important company information and lists current openings in Systems Integration, Open Application Systems, Advanced Systems Engineering, SAP, Manufacturing, Change Integration, and Human Resources.

Company Description: Price Waterhouse is a professional consulting services firm with over 50,000 on staff worldwide.

Home Page: http://www.careermosaic.com/cm/price-waterhouse/

Process Software Corporation

Employment: http://www.process.com/career/employ.htp
This site allows you to apply for specific positions in Software Engineering, Information Systems, Technical Support, Sales, and Administration.

Company Description: Process Software designs, develops, and markets TCP/IP-based networking software solutions and Web server solutions worldwide.

Home Page: http://www.process.com/

Prodigy

Employment: http://www.prodigy.com/contact.htm
This is a straightforward list of jobs like Network Business Planning Analyst, Copywriter, Designer, Programmer/Analyst, Security Systems Administrator, Technical Account Specialist, Project Specialist, and more.
Company Description: Prodigy is one of the top three commercial online services in the U.S.
Home Page: http://www.prodigy.com

QUALCOMM Incorporated

Employment: http://www.qualcomm.com/HR/hr_main.html
This site gives company information, college recruiting information, and job listings for positions like OS/2 Wizard, Analog IC Design Engineer, Unix/Software Engineer, and Digital IC Test Engineer.
Company Description: QUALCOMM develops an application of next generation communications hardware and software.
Home Page: http://www.qualcomm.com/

Quantum Corporation

Employment: http://www.quantum.com/cgi-bin/sirrus.pl/milpitasSIS
This Web page lists job opportunities at Quantum Milpitas, California offices, in the categories of Administration, Application/Customer Support, Engineering, Finance/Accounting, Information Systems, Manufacturing, Marketing, Purchasing/Commodity Engineering, Sales, and Technician.
Company Description: Quantum designs and manufactures storage products designed for today's digitized world.
Home Page: http://www.quantum.com/

R J Pascale & Company

Employment: http://www.ct-jobs.com/pascale/
This employment site lists company information, computer-related job listings, and accounting-related job listings.
Company Description: R J Pascale is a professional search and recruiting firm located in Southwestern Connecticut.
Home Page: http://www.ct-jobs.com/pascale/

Read-Rite

Employment: http://www.careermosaic.com:80/cm/readrite/rr11.html
This site lists opportunities all over the world, including Thailand, Malaysia, Japan, and Singapore. Typical positions include various Engineers, Modeling Designer, and Product Analysis Manager.

Company Description: Read-Rite is an independent supplier of thin film recording heads to the global disk drive industry.
Home Page: http://www.careermosaic.com/cm/readrite/rr1.html

Rockwell Telecommunications

Employment: http://www.rockwell.com/rockwell/careers/
This site gives information on the company and lists open positions in Engineering, Marketing, Manufacturing, Computing, and Technician. You'll also get direct links like the Rockwell Network Systems and the Rockwell Corporate Career site.
Company Description: Rockwell has specialized in communications devices for more than 15 years, with worldwide data and facsimile modem market share of almost 75 percent.
Home Page: http://www.rockwell.com/

Royal Bank of Canada

Employment: http://www.royalbank.com
It's easiest to link to the Royal Bank's job opportunities directly from the home page (URL listed above). Typical positions are Technical Systems Analyst, Business Systems Analyst, Database Analyst, and Software Programmer.
Company Description: Founded 125 years ago, the Royal Bank is Canada's largest financial institution.
Home Page: http://www.royalbank.com

SAS Institute

Employment: http://www.sas.com/corporate/jobs.html
SAS's employment opportunity page has links to positions in the U.S. and Europe. Openings run the gamut from Housekeeper and Security Officer to Account Manager or Technical Training Specialist.
Company Description: SAS Institute is one of the world's top ten software developers, with more than 27,000 sites in 119 countries.
Home Page: http://www.sas.com/

SCO

Employment: http://www.sco.com/Company/Jobs/jobs.htm
SCO's career opportunities page includes a brief company description and job listings in Accounting and Finance, General and Administration, Information Services, Client Integration Product Development, Legal, Manufacturing, Marketing, Server Product Development, Sales, and Support.

Company Description: SCO is the world's leading provider of system software for Business Critical Servers, and a provider of software that integrates Microsoft Windows PCs and other clients with all major Unix servers.
Home Page: http://www.sco.com/

Schlumberger

Employment: http://www.slb.com/recr.dir/index.html
This is a pretty extensive site, complete with frequently asked questions, and information on the company, entry-level positions, mobility within the company, and internship requirements.
Company Description: Schlumberger is an international technical company selling products and services that improve customer productivity. It is a worldwide leader in Oilfield Services and Measurement and Systems, with operations in over 100 countries and 48,000 employees.
Home Page: http://www.slb.com/

 # Seagate Technology

Employment: http://www.seagate.com/hr/hrtop.shtml
Employment: http://www.careermosaic.com/cm/seagate/seagate1.html (Career Mosaic)
You can find employment information and opportunities at both of these sites. You'll get links to international career opportunities, employee benefit information, company news, and more. You'll also find out about college programs and see job listings for positions in the U.S., Canada, Northern Ireland, and Thailand. Most of these opportunities are technical, but you'll also find listings for Financial Analyst, Tax Accountant, Audit Manager, and more.
Company Description: Seagate is a data technology company that provides products for storing, managing, and accessing digital information on the world's computer and data communications system.
Home Page: http://www.seagate.com/

Sears

Employment: http://www.careermosaic.com/cm/sears/sears2.html
This site is for Sears' information systems positions. It gives information on corporate culture, a tour of the corporate campus, employment opportunities and benefit information, a jobs database, and an online response form with contact information. Typical positions are Programmer/Analyst, Database Analyst, Technical Consultant, Project Manager, and LAN Technician.
Company Description: Sears is a diverse company, with money in retail operations, insurance, and more.

Home Page: This is the Career Mosaic home page—http://www.careermosaic.com/cm/sears/sears1.html

Sega

Employment: http://www.segaoa.com/inside/career/index.html

This is a wonderful and extensive site with open positions listed by departments like Sega Software, Finance, Marketing, Product Development, System Integration, Titan (games), Sega Interactive Development, Sega Technical Institute, Sega USA, Fremont Warehouse, and Sega Channel. You can fill out and submit your resume with Sega's online resume form.

Company Description: Sega is a leader in interactive digital entertainment media with operations on five continents.

Home Page: http://www.segaoa.com

Sequent Computer Systems

Employment: http://www.sequent.com:80/public/hr/index.html

This site lists all open positions including technical and non-technical: Administrative Assistant, Systems Technician, Buyer, Planner, Account Executive, Marketing Specialist, Software Engineer, Architect, and hundreds more.

Company Description: Sequent develops and delivers large-scale system solutions for online transaction processing, decision support, and business communications.

Home Page: http://www.sequent.com:80/public/index.html

Figure 4.8 Sega's employment page.

Shiva Corporation

Employment: http://www.shiva.com/corp/hr/index.html
This site lists detailed descriptions of open positions like Technical Communications Engineer, OEM Technical Account Representative, or Systems Engineer. You'll also find contact information.
Company Description: Shiva is the leader in remote access technology, providing access to network resources for remote users, mobile professionals, and remote offices.
Home Page: http://www.shiva.com/

Silicon Graphics

Employment: http://www.sgi.com/Overview/surf_partners.html
SG's employment site allows you to search opportunities by location, division, or title. There are available positions in the areas of Administration, Advanced Systems Division, Corporate Marketing, Customer Support Division, Digital Media Systems, Finance, Interactive Digital Solutions, Interactive Systems Division, Integrated Manufacturing Solutions Division, MIPS Technologies, Inc., Network Systems Division, North American Field Operations, and Silicon Studio, Inc.
Company Description: Silicon Graphics systems are used in industrial design, database analysis, visual simulation, energy exploration, and entertainment.
Home Page: http://www.sgi.com/

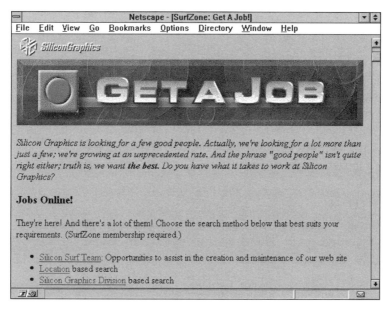

Figure 4.9 The job page for Silicon Graphics.

Sony

Employment: http://www.sepc.sony.com/SEPC/Job/Job.html
Here you'll find employment opportunities at Sony Online and Sony Interactive Entertainment. Typical positions are for Game Programmers, Tools and Technology Managers, and Technical Support Engineers.
Company Description: Sony is an electronics giant specializing in entertainment.
Home Page: http://www.sony.com/

SprintLink

Employment: http://www.sprintlink.net/SPLK/career.html
This site lists a variety of Internet-related career opportunities.
Company Description: SprintLink is a commercial TCP/IP-based service for access to the Internet and communications among native IP networks.
Home Page: http://www.sprintlink.net/

Standard Microsystems Corporation (SMC)

Employment: http://www.smc.com/hr/joblist.html
This employment site lists company locations and job listings (and descriptions) like Quality Manager, Director-Design Automation, Manager-Network Operations, Product Marketing, Public Relations Manager, and various Engineering positions.
Company Description: SMC is one of the world's largest suppliers of products used to connect personal computers over local area networks.
Home Page: http://www.smc.com/

Sun Microsystems

Employment: http://www.careermosaic.com/cm/sun/sun1.html
Sun's site lists career opportunities, benefits, corporate culture, and information on products and services. It also lists a number of places where you can email your resume.
Company Description: Sun is a "major force in enterprise-wide computing."
Home Page: http://www.sun.com/

Sunquest

Employment: http://www.sunquest.com/employment/employment.html
This site lists company information, application instructions, and opportunities in the areas of Software Development, Client Services, Marketing/Sales, Administrative, and Management.
Company Description: Sunquest focuses on the design, development, and installation of clinical information systems.
Home Page: http://www.sunquest.com/

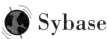 # Sybase

Employment: http://www.careermosaic.com/cm/sybase/sybase6.html

This is a comprehensive job site, giving you the ability to search opportunities by geographic locations (including the U.S., Canada, Hong Kong, or the Sybase business unit). You'll also get descriptions of the business units and job listings for positions like Product Manager, Software Engineer, Technical Writer, Field Support Administrator, Sales Representative, Sales Manager, Consultant, Architect, Business Manager, and Staffing Manager.

Company Description: Sybase specializes in enterprise-wide client/server computing and is the seventh largest software company in the world.

Home Page: http://www.careermosaic.com/cm/sybase/sybase1.html

Symantec

Employment: http://www.careermosaic.com/cm/symantec/

This is the staffing home page, complete with information on the company, benefits, college relations program, educational assistance, and job opportunities. Symantec's typical job openings are for Software Engineer, Product Manager, SQA Analyst, Administrative Assistant, Senior Development Manager, Administrative Specialist, Product Marketing Specialist, Architect, and so on.

Company Description: Symantec is a global software company that creates enterprise-wide software solutions.

Home Page: http://www.symantec.com/

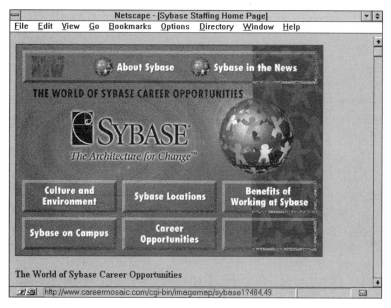

Figure 4.10 Sybase's home page with links to job opportunities.

Symbol Technologies

Employment: http://www.careermosaic.com:/cm/symbol/symbol2.html
Symbol's career listing site gives job openings for New York and California. Typical positions are Software Systems Analyst, Digital Hardware Design Engineer, CCD Engineer, Software Engineer, and more.
Company Description: Symbol is the world leader in bar code-driven data management systems.
Home Page: http://www.careermosaic.com/cm/symbol/

Systems & Computer Technology Corporation (SCT)

Employment: http://www.sctcorp.com/hrhome.html
SCT's employment opportunities site is extensive, with detailed information about the company, employee benefits, and job openings for General Managers, Finance Product Manager, MIS Directors, Sales Representatives, Software Development and Implementation Consultants, Programmers, Database Administrators, and Technical Consultants.
Company Description: SCT develops applications software and computing management services for institutions of higher education, state/local governments, and public/private utilities internationally.
Home Page: http://www.sctcorp.com/scthome.html

TRW

Employment: http://www.trw.com/careers
This page lists openings at TRW's various sections and divisions. Listings here change frequently.
Company Description: TRW provides high technology products and services to automotive, space, defense, and information systems.
Home Page: http://www.trw.com/index.html

Taligent, Inc.

Employment: http://www.taligent.com/job-listing.html
You'll find a lot of job listings here, mostly technical, including various Engineering positions. Typical job openings are for Senior Human Interface Designer, Database Administrator, Product Manager, Public Relations Manager, Account Manager, Technical Writer, and more.
Company Description: Taligent is an independent software company owned by Apple, Hewlett-Packard, and IBM. It develops a new application system based on object-oriented technology.
Home Page: http://www.taligent.com

Tandem

Employment: http://www.careermosaic.com/cm/tandem/tm1.html

This Career Mosaic site gives all kinds of information about Tandem, such as its corporate headquarters; its offices in the Netherlands, Singapore, and Tokyo; company history; university relations; most recent breakthroughs; and its professional opportunities in the areas of Finance, Field Sales, Hardware, Marketing, Technical Education, NT Software Development, MIS, Customer Service, and Technical Writing.

Company Description: Tandem is a leader in high-reliability computing for business-critical applications.

Home Page: http://www.tandem.com

Tangram Enterprise Solutions, Inc.

Employment: http://www.tesi.com/employ.htm

This site describes Tangram's basic work theory and lists job opportunities for offices in the U.S., Paris, London, Amsterdam, Copenhagen/Stockholm, Milano, and Madrid. Typical positions are Technical Manager, Sales Manager, Quality Assurance Test Analyst, Systems Engineer, Programmer, Technical Support Analyst, and Consulting Analyst.

Company Description: Tangram is a leading developer of enterprise network software.

Home Page: http://www.tesi.com

Taos Mountain Software

Employment: http://www.taos.com/contract.html

Taos' jobs site gives you information about talking to a recruiter and why you should work for the company. It also allows you to fill out the provided job applications and search jobs by keyword. Typical listings are for Email Administrator, various System Administrators, Account Manager, PC Network Support Recruiter, Programmer, and Compiler Guru.

Company Description: Taos provides expert Systems Administrators, technical support services, and Unix training to the San Francisco Bay area.

Home Page: http://www.taos.com/

Teknowledge Corporation

Employment: http://www.teknowledge.com/company/job_posting.html

Teknowledge lists positions for Project Leaders, Software Architects, Software Engineers, Distributed Systems Development, Collaborative Command and Control, Configuration Systems, and Intelligent Computer-Aided Instruction for K-12.

Company Description: Teknowledge provides consulting services and software products for commercial and defense applications.

Home Page: http://www.teknowledge.com

Tektronix, Inc.

Employment: http://www.tek.com/Tektronix/Careers/
This site gives you college programs, benefits, information on submitting a resume, and a list of professional opportunities (without descriptions) for Software, Mechanical, Manufacturing, Media, Video Hardware/Software Engineers, Information Systems, Procurement/Commodity Specialist, Accounting and Finance, Human Resources, Technical Marketing, Technicians, and Administrative Support. Also listed are specific, detailed "Hot Jobs of the Week."
Company Description: Tectronix is a global high-technology company based on a portfolio of measurement, color printing, video, and networking businesses.
Home Page: http://www.tek.com/

 ## Texas Instruments (TI)

Employment: http://www.ti.com/recruit/docs/recruit.htm
TI's page lists current job openings and information on university recruiting. To submit a resume, you must use their provided "Resume Builder."
Company Description: One of the world's largest suppliers of semiconductor products, defense electronics, notebook computers, software development tools, calculators, and more.
Home Page: http://www.ti.com/

TransTech

Employment: http://www.interaccess.com/transtech/postpage.html
This site lists regularly updated job opportunities for consultants in the areas of Unix, Oracle DBA, PowerBuilder, C, Visual Basic, and Technical Sales. You'll also get contact information and an overview of the company.
Company Description: TransTech specializes in object-oriented and client/server technologies working on projects throughout the upper Midwestern United States.
Home Page: http://www.interaccess.com/transtech

Tribune

Employment: http://www.tribune.com/employment/index.html
Tribune's "Help Wanted" site lists job openings for all of its newspapers (*Chicago Tribune, Orlando Sentinel*, etc.), such as Art Director, Financial Analyst, Client Service Associate, News Photo Librarian, Marketing Analyst, and more.
Company Description: Tribune is a provider of information and entertainment. It owns business units, establishes partnerships, and makes investments in the publishing, broadcasting, entertainment, new media, and education industries.
Home Page: http://www.tribune.com

Triple-I

Employment: http://www.sky.net/~iii/jobs.html
This site offers job opportunities nationwide for Function Analysts, ABAP Programmers, Basis Consultants, and Document Management/Workflow Programmer/Analysts.
Company Description: Triple-I is a Kansas City-based firm with a nationwide network of offices serving many of America's top corporations.
Home Page: http://www.sky.net/~iii/

Union Bank

Employment: http://www.careermosaic.com/cm/union_bank/ub6.html
This site gives descriptions of its Commercial Financial Services Group, Community Banking, Real Estate Finance, Trust Investments Group, and Specialized Lending. You are also able to search job listings by keyword.
Company Description: Union Bank is the fourth largest bank in California and among the 25 largest banks in the country.
Home Page: http://www.careermosaic.com/cm.union_bank/ub1.html

Figure 4.11 The Career Opportunities page for Union Bank.

Unisys

Employment: http://www.unisys.com/Career/index.html
This page lists Unisys' opportunities categorized by geographical location and job type.
Company Description: Unisys is a worldwide information services company.
Home Page: http://www.unisys.com

US WEST

Employment: http://www.uswest.com/employment/index.html
This site lists openings for US WEST's Enterprise Networking Services, Business, and Government Services. Typical positions are Technical Resource Manager, Technical Design Consultant, Product Marketing Manager, Product Marketing Engineer, and Senior Engineer.
Company Description: US WEST is the leader in frame relay service, which offers users WANs of virtually unlimited size.
Home Page: http://www.uswest.com

United States Cellular

Employment: http://www.uscc.com/corp/hr/scripts/hr_home.html
USC's "Human Resources Online" site lists job openings such as Technical Recruiter, Director-Field Employee Relations, Director of Network Operations, Business Analyst, Systems Architecture Analyst, Programmer Analyst, Assistant Buyer, and more.
Company Description: United States Cellular is the seventh largest cellular company in the U.S. with more than 2,200 employees nationwide.
Home Page: http://www.uscc.com

Utopia

Employment: http://www.utopia.com/jobs/index.html
Utopia's site has various openings for Web designers and includes detailed information about the company.
Company Description: Utopia develops complete Web site solutions for a wide variety of customers.
Home Page: http://www.utopia.com

Vertex Pharmaceuticals Incorporated

Employment: http://www.vpharm.com/job_info/jobopen.html
Vertex lists opportunities in Research, Information Systems, and Research Administration. Look to the home page for company information, press releases, senior management information, and more.
Company Description: Vertex is a drug discovery and development company that

has pioneered the application of structure-based rational drug design.
Home Page: http://www.vpharm.com/

WAIS, Inc.

Employment: http://www.wais.com/newhomepages/jobs.html
At the time of this writing, the job listings at this site were for WAIS' commercial Internet publishing systems. Positions include Production Services Project Managers, Information Engineers, Senior Systems Administrator/Unix Guru, Development Engineers, and Human Interface Engineers.
Company Description: WAIS provides interactive online publishing systems and services to organizations that publish information.
Home Page: http://www.wais.com/newhomepages/default.html

 # Wal-Mart

Employment: http://www.wal-mart.com/cgi-bin/htm/disp?ci:1
Wal-Mart's job page lists corporate and information systems professional positions.
Company Description: "The nation's leading retailer."
Home Page: http://www.wal-mart.com/

 # Walgreens

Employment: http://www.walgreens.com/wg-2.html
Walgreens' site includes detailed company information, and lists technical job openings such as Lead Computer Telephone Programmer Analyst, MVS Lead Computer Operator, Unix Support Administrator, Programmer Analyst, TPF Lead Operator, ORACLE Database Administrator, and Data Communications Technician.
Company Description: Walgreens is America's leading drugstore chain, with nearly 2,100 stores in 31 states.
Home Page: http://www.walgreens.com/

Wayne Memorial Hospital

Employment: http://www.wmh.org/events/employment.html
This site lists openings for Family Practice Physicians, OB/GYN Physicians, and Nurse-Midwifes.
Company Description: Wayne Memorial Hospital is a community health resource serving Wayne and Pike Counties in northeastern Pennsylvania.
Home Page: http://www.wmh.org/

 # Wells Fargo

Employment: http://wellsfargo.com/ftr/jobs/
Opportunities are listed by bank division (consumer, checking, legal, etc.) or by the

categories Technical, Sales/Service, Finance, Product Development, Marketing, and Law.
Company Description: Wells Fargo is the seventh largest bank in the United States.
Home Page: http://wellsfargo.com

Wolfram Research

Employment: http://www.wri.com/wri/wrijobopenings.html
This site lists technical and non-technical positions like Technical Editor, Technical Support Engineer, Sales Account Executive, Programmers, and Marketing Manager. You'll get detailed descriptions and contact information for each position.
Company Description: Wolfram Research developed Mathmatica, a comprehensive mathematical productivity tool for scientists.
Home Page: http://www.wri.com

The World Wide Web Consortium (WC3)

Employment: http://www.w3.pub/hypertext/WWW.Consortium/Recruitment/
This site gives general organization information and lists job openings for positions like Protocol Designer, System Designer, System Manager, Software Engineer, and more.
Company Description: WC3 is made up of various companies that have invested significant resources into the Web by developing software products or information products.
Home Page: http://www.w3.org/pub/WWW/

Xicor

Employment: http://www.xicor.com/xicor/menulink/ink9.htm
Xicor's career opportunities site lists relevant company and contact information. Open positions are in the areas of Design, Wafer Fab, Development, Administration, Facilities, Product Quality, Safety and Environmental, Technical Sales, and Marketing.
Company Description: Xicor is an established leader in the area of field alterable technologies and in pioneering the application of this technology in new markets such as linear, DSP, and microcontroller peripherals.
Home Page: http://www.xicor.com

Zenith Data Systems (ZDS)

Employment: http://www.zds.com/htdocs/zds/jobs/zjobs.htm
This site lists open positions in Customer Service, Engineering, Manufacturing, Marketing, Sales, and more.
Company Description: ZDS offers a full range of personal computing products. The products vary from high-performance servers and network-ready desktops to a line of notebook and subnotebook computers.
Home Page: http://www.zds.com

How to Create a Killer Electronic Resume

Chapter 5 Topics

If you've spent some time reviewing Chapter 4, and if you've taken a look at the job opportunities offered by some of the company sites we listed in that chapter, you may have already found a few jobs that you'd like to take a crack at. That's great, because now is as good a time as any to get started! This chapter is intended to help change your mindset about resumes and standard resume formats so that you can create a unique, yet professional resume that will make you marketable in the 90s: a resume that you can email to a company or post on the Internet.

Out with the Old, In with the New

You probably already have a resume, and you may think that it's perfect for all of your job-hunting needs. But you're probably wrong. Your resume is probably designed to be placed in an envelope and sent through the mail. That's great if you want to rely on snail mail for your job seeking efforts, but you don't have to rely on the post office nor should you want to. More and more companies today are jumping onto the electronic resume bandwagon because it saves them time and money, and ultimately helps them find more-qualified candidates. If you don't have a resume that is tailored for a company's electronic searches, your resume may be skipped over altogether—especially if a company places priority on resumes that they receive electronically.

As we mentioned in an earlier chapter, there is an increasing possibility that some human resources or staffing people may never actually look at a paper resume. Many companies today, especially if they pride themselves on being technologically advanced, will do most of their job-candidate selection using electronic resumes. There are several ways your resume can become electronic:

- You email your resume. If you email your resume to an employer, it is already in electronic form, and therefore can be imported directly into a database or other electronic medium.

- You send your resume on a diskette.

- You send a paper resume to a company. The company uses OCR (Optical Character Recognition) software to scan your resume into an electronic form.

- Your resume is posted on the Internet and is downloaded by a company, and then is converted to an acceptable format or font, if necessary.

How OCR Works

Optical Character Recognition software has been around for more than a dozen years. It's an offshoot of the same scanning technology used to read bar codes in the supermarket or the department store. But it can also be used to read text documents. The basic premise is simple. For instance, the letter "Q" has certain characteristics, regardless of which font is used. But that's a bit simplistic. Some stylistic fonts create letters that are highly stylized. For instance, consider these two characters:

Q

2

The first "Q" character is in a font called Garamond. The second "Q" character is in a font called Brush Script. The first character is easily recognized by OCR software, but the second character can be difficult for OCR to identify because its physical features are similar to other characters—chiefly "S" and "Z." This is an important point. You might be tempted to submit your resume in a stylized font because it appears very attractive and sets your resume apart from others. But if you are submitting a paper resume to a company that will be scanning it into an electronic format, that could prove to be deadly. Instead, use a font that has a "basic" look. Otherwise, your resume might become unreadable online, and you'll be automatically disqualified for an interview simply because your resume can't be read. Variations of Times, Courier, Palatino, Arial, and Bookman are all fonts that can easily be deciphered by OCR software.

Here's how the OCR process works: To convert your paper resume into a company's electronic database, they'll use a scanner and OCR software. The resume is scanned and then interpreted by the OCR software and converted to ASCII text, which is the most common, and most simple, text language used by computer software. After the resume is converted to ASCII, it can be accessed by all kinds of software programs: spreadsheets, databases, word processors, and more.

There are tons of different kinds of OCR software, with different degrees of sophistication, and you'll never know what kind of software a company will have. Not all kinds of OCR software can recognize all of the hundreds of existing fonts. This makes OCR an imperfect science. Depending on what fonts are used in a document, and the level of sophistication of the software, OCR can misread certain letters and sometimes garble the resume that you've spent hours pondering. So we need to reiterate this point: *Send a resume that is as simple and standard as possible.* Resist the impulse to create a unique-looking resume, at least where the font is concerned. Why disqualify yourself from a job simply because your resume looks too good for OCR software to decipher?

For instance, if after being scanned and converted, your resume comes out looking like a garbled mess, one of two things can happen:

- Many companies have a person specifically assigned to check electronic resumes against the masters to correct any strangeness that may have occurred. If a couple of letters don't translate, these people will correct them.

- Some companies think it's enough trouble just feeding the resumes through a scanner. If your resume doesn't translate well, it's tossed into the "forget about it" stack.

Bottom Line

- Don't be one of the people whose resume is ignored simply due to something as trivial as a font choice. Stick to very common fonts on your resume and cover letter.

- Don't use a tiny point size. Anything less than a 10 point size is unacceptable and difficult to scan. Keep your font size between 10 and 14 point.

- Don't use anything but plain white or ivory paper. Scanners have a difficult time with grays, mauve, and other colors.

- Don't use borders because border characters often appear as garbage when an OCR scanner converts them to ASCII.

- Send your resume in a 9"×12" envelope, and don't fold it. Scanners have problems with creases in the paper.

What Do Companies Do with Your Electronic Resume?

Let's assume that the company now has your resume in an electronic form, either because you sent it that way or because they scanned and converted it. Now what happens to it? In most cases, it goes into the company's job database. The database automatically generates a "Thank You for Your Interest. We'll Keep You in Mind" letter. If you get one of these letters, don't assume that it's an instant rejection or that they already gave someone else the job. You may get one of those letters before a human has actually read the submitted resume.

Next, the electronic resumes are sorted into several groups depending on how many of the desired criteria you meet for open positions (see keywords below). If your resume doesn't fit into any of the open positions, the company will usually continue to store it in the job database for up to six months.

Therefore, it's a good idea to send your updated resume to the same company about every six months. Or ask someone in Human Resources how long they store resumes and use this as a benchmark for resubmitting your resume.

The Keyword Search: Don't Be Overlooked

What is a keyword search? In the case of electronic resumes, keywords can be specific skills, titles, or other terms that a Human Resources person looks for in a candidate's resume and/or cover letter. The most important fact to remember is: *Keywords are almost always nouns!* This is an important point because it goes against most of the advice you've probably heard about resumes in the past.

You may have been told to use action verbs such as *led, earned, solved, supervised, increased,* and *coordinated* in your resume to explain some of the things you have achieved in the past. While this may work for you if a real person is reading resumes one by one, you might be overlooked if the employer uses electronic searching techniques.

After a keyword search is performed, your resume is sorted into one or more job categories based on several things in your resume: skills, education, job titles, schools, companies, buzzwords, and so on. After your resume is sorted, it can be placed in more than one job category if your keywords indicate that you are qualified for more than one job. The more categories your resume is placed in, the better your chances for getting a job!

Never send more than one resume to the same company, thinking that you can tailor them differently depending on the job you want. Since all resumes are stored in the same database, it will be painfully obvious that the same person is trying to apply for a variety of jobs instead of being focused on one area. Besides, you don't need to send more than one resume since, in most cases, your resume will be automatically considered for *all* open positions.

What Kind of Keywords Does Someone Look For?

That depends on the company, the type of open position, and the person in charge of choosing the keywords. Of course, if you're responding to a description from an advertised position, you already have a good idea about what the staffing people are looking for. In that case, you should include many words from the ad and job description, without boasting of skills that you don't have. The best way to decide what keywords to use is by conducting research. Surf the Internet and scan the newspaper classifieds for help-wanted ads. Make a list of the words and terminology that are used by the companies you're interested in applying to.

The following list includes the kinds of keywords that an employer might look for, and some examples of each.

Skills: The skills section is probably the broadest category of keywords. You can list skills that you have experience in (10-key), the kinds of duties that you perform at your current job or have performed in a previous job, the kinds of skills that you obtained in your education, and so on. Here are some examples:

word processing

data entry

technical writing

customer service

problem solving

financial analysis

administrative

database use

telephone

desktop publishing

telephone

accounting

spreadsheet use

Education: This category is self explanatory. If you have a degree or any other kind of post-secondary training, list it in the education section of your resume. If you have only a high school diploma, list the high school and grade point average. Here are some examples:

Bachelor of Science, Marketing

B.A., Finance

Masters Degree (fill in your area of education)

English

Job Titles: You'll, of course, want to list any job titles of relevant positions that you've held in the past, but you can also list the title of the job that you want in your resume objective. Some examples:

Human Resources Manager

Vice President, Sales

Interactive Media Specialist

Sales Representative

Customer Service Specialist

Schools: It's not likely that someone will conduct a keyword search for specific schools, but it does happen. If you're dealing with a hiring manager who graduated from a university that's local to the company you're applying to, he or she may want to give special consideration to other people who went to, or are currently attending, that same university. So some example school keywords are:

Harvard

Monroe High School

St. Andrew's Preparatory

Arizona State University

Companies: A hiring manager may be looking for someone who has experience with a certain company, often a competitor. Or he or she may be looking for companies that you may have had a working relationship with. Let's say that the manager is looking for an advertising executive who has had some big-name accounts. He or she may conduct a keyword search for:

PepsiCo

Proctor and Gamble

Nintendo

Budweiser

Industry
Buzzwords
and Jargon: In traditional resume creation, you were probably told never to use jargon, but in electronic resumes, jargon that is used industry-wide can be chosen for a keyword search. Especially in the technical field, using industry buzzwords can be a definite advantage. Here are a few examples:

virtual media

interactive

Webmaster

Here is a sample resume from the World Wide Web Resume Bank (http://www.careermag.com/resumes/resumebank.html). We've highlighted words and phrases that could be considered keywords by a recruiter.

```
John Smith

                    Computer Science Experience
4/93 to present

Managed Mapping Software Library project (see One Call
Concepts, below). Developed fast-food delivery applications
for Fortune 500 company. Managed various smaller development
and support projects for local companies.


8/93 to 12/93

Instructed CS-680 Introduction to Software Engineering class
and laboratory.  Developed lectures, handouts, homework
and examinations.  Solely responsible for lecturing,
grading.

7/90 to 8/93

Specified, designed and managed project for mapping software
library (MSL).  Supervised and scheduled 5 staff members
for 5 major project components, and 3 major applications.
Library is written in the C++ programming language for Unix
SVR4 platforms running X Window X11R5 and Motif 1.2.
Library contains Abstract Data Type, Geometric, Graphical
User Interface, Overlay and Mapping components.  Software
was written with strict adherence to Object Oriented
Development principles and was selected as one of top 19
object oriented projects in the contest held by 1992 Object
World Conference, Computerworld, and the Object Management
Group (see Paul Harmon and David A. Taylor Objects in
Action, Addison-Wesley, Reading, MA, ISBN 0-201-63336-1).
The software is used in 14 states, in Canada, and in Asia.

Designed and implemented complete interactive mapping system
for utility notification system. System takes an address,
street or intersection, generates a polygon around address
points and performs evaluation against stored polygon data
to determine which utility to notify.  Also designed and
implemented a similar non-interactive system.  Designed and
implemented polygon on polygon evaluation subsystem.
Designed and implemented software for digitizing subsystem,
including device driver, user interface and processing
components. Digitizing system allows utilities to enter
linear and polygonal data for comparison during interactive
mapping phase.  Designed and implemented software for
plotting subsystem, including device driver and user
interface.  Software was implemented for Unix SVR3 platforms
running X Window X11R4, using the ANSI C programming language.
```

1/90 to 8/90

Instructed CS-215 Ada Language class and laboratory.
Developed lectures, handouts, homework and examinations.
Solely responsible for lecturing, grading.

Instructed CS-105 Introduction to Computers class and
laboratory. Solely responsible for lecturing, grading.
Supervised 3 teaching assistants who conducted laboratories
for the class.

1/89 to 6/89

Designed and developed flight simulation software in Ada on
a large military project. Involved converting Defense
Mapping Agency satellite data for real time 3D flight
simulation display. Specific responsibilities included
designing and implementing software to handle data
violations of digital image generator physical limits;
designing and implementing algorithm to perform convex
decomposition of polygonal data.

9/87 to 1/90

Wrote quality control and analysis software in development of
world map database for military applications. Involved
designing and implementing algorithms for reentrancy checking,
polygon filling, spherical deprojection, rectangular
"rectification", and polygon clipping and subdivision.

Lead team in design and development of in-house Computer
Aided Software Engineering environment to increase
productivity. Obtained extensive knowledge of VAX/VMS
system programming. Supervised three entry-level engineers,
and was put in charge of main component development.
Designed and developed man-machine interface for in-house
Software Reuse tool in VAX/VMS Ada.

5/87 to 8/87

Developed software to translate waveforms generated by
YM2151 FM Synthesizer chip to MIDI and RS232 signals. Used
Zilog Z80 microprocessor for control. Designed transmission
protocol.

EDUCATION

Master of Science/Computer Science from M.I.T., 1/90 to 5/94

Components of a Resume

Even if you tailor your resume for electronic search capabilities, you can't just popu-
late your resume with pages full of nouns. You must have a real resume that shows

specifically what your capabilities are and why you're the right person for the company, and for the job. But as we've explained, keywords are important.

Let's take a look at what a resume should accomplish besides having it appear within a keyword search.

Contact Information

First, every good resume should have your name and contact information at the top. Include your physical address, a phone number, and an email address if you have one. Also, if you have your own home page (see Chapter 7), include its URL.

Objective

On your resume, after your contact information, you should list a definite and specific career objective. The career objective is one of the most important parts of a resume and should be given extra consideration. It tells the prospective employer what direction you're moving in, and what your work preference is.

Your career objective should be clearly stated, brief, and should be consistent with the skills and accomplishments listed in the remainder of your resume. We've found that the more specific you are with your career objective, the better. This is easy if you are submitting your resume to one specific company and you can say something like "I'm seeking a challenging position as Executive Assistant with AT&T." But what if you're posting your resume on the Internet and you don't know who will see it? Still try to be specific. "A challenging position as Executive Assistant with a large telecommunications company" is a good bet.

Summary

A new approach, and one that's expected by many companies, is to include a summary instead of a career objective. A summary is simply a sentence or two explaining who you are and why you are the perfect candidate for the job in question.

Take a look at Figure 5.2, the resume of Jim Barber, which was posted at the JobCenter on the World Wide Web. Jim summarizes his background and experience, and he has put his most important keywords at the beginning of his resume. Here is an example of a resume with a summary at the beginning.

```
WEBMASTER
 Name: Jim Barber
 Company: AudioPro Network
 E-mail: jbarber@ix.netcom.com
 Phone: (500) 367-3550
 Location: Anywhere
 Keywords: Webmaster, Internet, Web Site Administrator, WWW, HTML, web
```

JIM BARBER
Phone: (500) 367-3550
e-mail: jbarber@ix.netcom.com

SUMMARY: Experience in web site development and management, entrepreneurial business management, marketing, customer service, technical support in audio applications, university level teaching, film and video production, music recording, and writing.

-EXPERIENCE

**May 1995-present:

Principal, AudioPro Network, New York, New York. Web publishing in the fields of professional audio and multimedia. As webmaster, I develop, program, and maintain the site, create content, do the HTML authoring and graphic design. As principal in the company, I market the site to advertisers and cultivate client relationships. The AudioPro web site is located at http://www.panix.com/~audiopro.

**November 1992-May 1995:

General Manager, Professional Sound Services, Inc., New York, New York. I served as an entrepreneur, general manager, and corporate secretary of this start-up company from its inception in Manhattan in December of 1992. PSS specializes in providing professional audio equipment to motion picture productions, broadcast networks, theatrical venues, recording studios, hotels, video producers, universities, theme parks, and government agencies. In addition to equipment sales, the company offers rentals, service, and consulting.

My responsibilities as general manager included overseeing the daily operations of the company, supervising up to 14 employees, writing monthly management and financial reports, periodically updating our profit plan, securing dealerships with manufacturers, obtaining an FCC license, attending trade shows (principally NAB and AES), setting up and administering the in-house computer network (IS), hiring new employees, conducting employee reviews, writing articles for the company newsletter, devising and executing marketing strategies, preparing a plan for the acquisition of the assets of another company, organizing the company's presence at trade shows such as ShowBiz Expo and AES, conducting our professional seminar series featuring presentations by well-known sound mixers, providing technical support on music videos, and consulting on Diehard III.

My marketing responsibilities included collecting and maintaining a marketing database, and conducting numerous direct mail campaigns. I also coordinated the New York City roll-out of the Yamaha ProMix01 mixer, co-hosting a professional audio clinic at the Manhattan Center Studios with the support and participation of Yamaha Corporation.

I coordinated the activities of our sales force, and personally handled several of our most important accounts, notably CBS and Capital Cities/ABC.

As a result of effective marketing, excellent customer service, and the well-attended professional seminar series, the gross annual revenues of Professional Sound Services, Inc. grew from zero in 1992 to $1.8 million in 1994.

**September-December 1993:

Adjunct Professor, Hunter College, New York, New York. Taught semester-long class "Production Audio for Film and Video."

**May 1990-November 1992:

Adjunct Professor, Valencia Community College, Orlando, Florida. Institute of Entertainment Technology, Production Technology Training Program (sponsored by Disney-MGM Studios and Universal Studios Florida). I taught "Introduction to the Film Process." I also held the staff position of film/video/computer Technical Specialist.

**May 1972-October 1992:

Freelance film/video production, Los Angeles, New York, and Florida. Some selected credits:

"Get Published!", Peter Miller Agency - co-producer/director/editor
"VSDA Show ", MCA Home Video - video editor
"Moongoddess", Lion Entertainment - associate and screenplay editor
"Suzuki Motorcycle videos", Martin Brinkerhoff Assoc's - video editor
"Automatically Natural", James Barber Productions - producer/director/camera
"Victoria Estates promos", Coastal Video - lighting
"The Walk-In", Michael McDonough Productions - writer
"The Shaping of America", Meta-4 Productions - video editor
"CA$H", Corbett Productions - unit production manager
"VCC promos", Valencia Community College - producer/director
"Home Savings of America promos", Presentation Arts - video editor
Produced music recordings with the band "Fury" at studios in Los Angeles.

**August 1970-April 1972:

Film Department, Maryland Center for Public Broadcasting, Owings Mills, Maryland. Staff positions as film cameraman and supervisory film editor. I directed the half-hour documentary "A-rab Summer" and several new station promos.

**February-June 1968:

Filmmaker, WJZ-TV Channel 13, Baltimore, Maryland. Created weekly film segments for the "Weekend" show , including a music video featuring singer Tom Rush performing "Urge For Going."

**March-June 1967:

Production Intern, Westinghouse Broadcasting in association with WJZ-TV, Baltimore, Maryland. I received much of my initial production and post-production training as an assistant to director Julian Krainen

```
(Krainen/Sage Productions) on his Emmy-winning documentary "The Other
Americans."

-EDUCATION

1983-1986            California Institute of the Arts (MFA-Live Action
                     Film/Video)
1964-1968            Johns Hopkins University (BA-Arts & Sciences)

Other training:     Computer animation class at West Coast University
                    (Los Angeles) and production seminars at UCLA and USC.

Other teaching:

**December 1995:

Guest lecturer, New York Institute of Technology, New York, New York.
Presentation: "A Private Industry Perspective on Marketing."

Awards:

1980 Houston International Film Festival, Bronze Award for 35mm short film
"Automatically Natural" - a fictional portrait of rock 'n' roll lifestyle.
```

Education

After your objective, you should include either your education or your experience section. This depends on which is more important to you and which is more impressive. Notice in Jim Barber's resume (Figure 5.2) that extensive experience is Jim's strength. Therefore, experience is what he lists first in his resume, and he includes education toward the end.

If you are a recent graduate and have little or no work experience, highlight your education. Include your degree, major, institution or institutions that you attended, date of graduation, minors or concentrations, academic awards, and any related coursework, seminars, projects, or workshops. Also include your GPA if it is 3.0 or higher.

Experience

This is usually what determines the length of a resume. The standard "all resume information should fit one page" rule does not necessarily apply in the world of electronic resumes. The standard for electronic resumes: Keep it at one to two pages if you are a recent graduate with limited job experience, and if you're a professional with five-plus years experience, take the space you need, up to four pages. Some job or resume banks and other places where you can post your resume online will not allow resumes of more than two pages, so have on hand a short and long version of yours.

The experience section of your resume is critical, even if you are directly out of school. All significant work experience should be listed in reverse chronological order, with your most recent work experience appearing first. Some important elements that you should include in your experience entries:

- The title of your position: for example, Corporate Communications Manager

- Name of the organization: for example, Microsoft Corporation

- Location of work (city, state): for example, Redmond, WA

- Dates of service (month, year): for example, June 1993 to July 1995

- Work responsibilities and duties with an emphasis on nouns for keyword searches: For example—Responsible for the layout, design, and content of the corporate newsletter on a Macintosh platform using PageMaker.

If you have a lot of experience in a wide variety of areas, be sure to emphasize the experience that is relevant to the job you are interested in.

We Thought You Should Know...

If you don't have any paid work experience, include volunteer work, internships, student teaching, or other work-like experience. And you can include experience that may not be related to the desired position to prove that you can hold a job, that you contributed to your college expenses, and so on.

Keyword Summary

Keyword summaries are becoming increasingly important—especially for online-distributed resumes. We've already told you that you must include important keywords in your resume. But if your resume is full of keywords and is pages long, chances are that the database used will only return a certain number of keywords. If you have 150 keywords in your resume, and the computer only uses the first 50, something will be left out.

That's why you should always place your most important keywords near the beginning of your resume. One way to do this is in a *keyword summary*, which is simply an additional category (like Education or Experience) that gets to the point and lists only keywords. A keyword summary is also helpful if a human will be reading your resume because you'll peak his or her interest immediately.

If you decide to include a keyword summary, we recommend that you place it after your career objective. Figure 5.3 contains a resume posted at the JobCenter on the Web. You'll notice that it contains a keyword summary at the beginning. This resume uses its keyword summary in place of its career objective. While we don't recommend omitting an objective altogether, keep in mind that some resume banks are very structured and specific, and may not allow an objective.

Here is an example of a resume with a keyword summary.

```
Public relations/affairs professional

 Name: Bill R. Adams
 E-mail: minister@sirius.com
 Phone: 415.467.8215
 Location: San Francisco, Bay Area, Peninsula
 Keywords:  public relations, public affairs, government affairs, public
            information, publication, publishing, media, public agencies,
            editorial, desktop publishing, public, affairs, relations,
            free-lance

William "BILL" R. ADAMS
21 Alvarado St., #7
Brisbane, CA  94005
415.467.8215

EXPERIENCE:
1986-1995          Public Information Officer, City of Santee, California.
Duties:  Newsletter production, City & Redevelopment promotional publication;
media affairs, copywriting, headline and caption writing, interviewing,
research, biographies, layout, design, photography; public affairs; press
conferences, media advisories, news releases; public service announcements;
booklets; bulletins; consultant supervisor; op-ed articles; ghostwriting;
community liaison; troubleshooter; special projects; presentations.  Member
of disaster-preparedness team.

1985-1986          Reporter, Carlsbad Journal, Carlsbad, California.  City Hall
beat, including coverage of City Council, committees, commissions, boards,
court cases, city organizations.  Also responsible for features, profiles,
photo assignments.

1984-1985          Reporter, La Mesa Courier, La Mesa, California.  City Hall
beat, including coverage of City Council, committees, commissions, boards,
court cases, city organizations.  Also responsible for features, profiles,
photo assignments, layout and paste up.

1982-1984          Freelance editor, writer, proofreader, indexer, abstracter,
Washington D.C.  Worked through Creative Options, which acted as agent to
procure consulting jobs with private and public agencies.

1980-1982          Press Officer, National Organization for Women (national
office), Washington D.C.  Duties included press releases, media relations,
proofreading, pamphlets, fund-raising.
EDUCATION:              B.A., University of Maryland, College Park, MD:  Government &
```

```
Politics; Journalism
COMPUTERS:           IBM Personal Computer: DOS 6.0, Microsoft Windows, PageMaker
5.0 Desktop Publishing; Wordperfect 6.0; Internet Literate

MEMBERSHIPS:         California Association of Public Information Officials; San
Diego Press Club.

REFERENCES:          Available upon request.
```

Additional Information

Additional information that you include in your resume, if any, is at your discretion. Our recommendation is to spend considerable time on the Internet, looking at the resumes of other people in your field. Try to identify what these resumes include that yours does not. Here are some of the common categories that we've seen from online resumes:

SPECIAL SKILLS:

I always include a special skills section in my resume, and you probably should, too, especially if you decide not to use the keyword summary. It's just another opportunity to list keywords, but it's also the perfect place to mention skills that are beneficial in your field, and that not everyone else has.

I got my first job as an editor because my resume was the only one whose Special Skills section mentioned a "thorough knowledge of English grammar and usage." This seems like a given, but it piqued someone's interest.

COMPUTER KNOWLEDGE:

If computer use is necessary for your job, this section is a good place to highlight your experience. You can subdivide this category into Software (WordPerfect, Access databases, Excel, Lotus,etc.) and Hardware (IBM, PC, Macintosh, Unix, etc.).

ACTIVITIES, HONORS, AND LEADERSHIP:

This is a good place to list any professional organizations you belong to now or have belonged to in the past, any awards you've won for work or service, and any committees or offices you've served in.

REFERENCES:

We don't recommend that you always list references on your resume, but you can state that references are available upon request. If your references are particularly impressive,then go ahead and include two or three.

The Resume Standard

After you've decided what you want to include in your resume, you need to put it into a format that can be read by several different types of computers and operating systems. If you want to email a resume or post it, the standard format is ASCII. Unfortunately, ASCII, which stands for American Standard Code for Information Interchange, is text only, as you'll see in all the figures in this chapter. This means that it doesn't allow any text formatting—such as bold, italics, underlining, or graphics.

If you send your electronic resume in another format, such as Word for Windows, without converting it, the company's software could perform the Word-to-ASCII conversion itself, which will probably transform your wonderfully important resume into a mess.

Since your resume will probably be read on a screen, you must be especially conscientious about readability. This means you should include plenty of white space, which might be difficult with a paper resume's limitations (one page only), but is perfectly acceptable with electronic resumes.

To save your resume in ASCII text, you'll first type your resume into your word processing program using a monospaced font like Courier. ASCII text is always monospaced, so it's not a good idea to use proportionally spaced fonts (where there's different space between letters to account for the different widths of letters) like Times, Arial, or Helvetica. If you use a proportionally spaced font, the proportions will change when you convert the file to monospaced ASCII—destroying any brilliant centering, spacing, or tabs that you might have added to improve the appearance of your resume.

Remember too that you can't use any special formatting features—other than tabs and spacing. So boldfacing, italicizing, special indents, and margin adjustments are all worthless in ASCII. Also—and this is very important—you must keep your individual lines to less than 70 characters in case those who read your resume have different email programs and different sized screen widths.

When you are finished, save the file in ASCII by opening the File menu in your word processing program. Choose the Save As option, and then name your file. When you choose the Save As option, you should be able to choose from a variety of formats. If your word processing program is WordPerfect, you will choose DOS text, which means ASCII. In Word for Windows, you will choose Text Only.

Making ASCII Look Good

After what we've told you, the following advice may seem like a contradiction, but it's really not: ASCII text can be made to look quite attractive, despite its formatting limitations. There are two ways to highlight your category headings. First, you can left-align them with text directly underneath:

```
EDUCATION
B.S. in Finance with an emphasis in Mathematics, 1994, University of Texas at
Tyler, 1994, 3.34/4.00 GPA
```

Or you can left-align the headings and indent and align the rest of the text, with at least five spaces between the heading name and text:

```
EDUCATION    B.S. in Finance with an emphasis in
             Mathematics, 1994, University of Texas at
             Tyler, 1994, 3.34/4.00 GPA
```

You can also use hyphens, asterisks, and the lowercase letter 'o' for bullet points. But always leave a space between your bullet and a word so the bullet will not interfere with the keyword search. Below is an example of three different kinds of ASCII bullets. Though we've used a variety of bullets in the same list to show you the different styles, *do not* do this in your actual resume:

```
EXPERIENCE
9/95-Present
            CORPORATE COMMUNICATIONS MANAGER
            Microsoft Corporation, Redmond, WA

            o Created all internal and external marketing
              materials and newsletters.
            o Conducted market research for several
              products in a variety of test groups.
            o Acted as team leader and group manager for
              several media projects.
```

Feel free to get a little creative. Put a box of asterisks around your name, centered at the top of your resume:

```
             ***********************
              John Henry Smith, III
             ***********************
```

The following three formats provide some good examples of online resumes and demonstrate some of the acceptable techniques to use in creating attractive ASCII documents.

John's resume is, in our opinion, in the easiest-to-read format, with headings aligned left and text on the right side. John also includes a background summary instead of an objective.

```
        JOHN T. CRISWELL
        URH 337 Allen
        1005 West Gregory Drive
        Urbana, IL 61801
        (217) 332-3205
```

BACKGROUND SUMMARY

PROGRAMMER with seven years experience and two years Internet experience.

Programming Languages: BASIC, Pascal, C, 65C02 assembly language, and VAX assembly language

Operating systems: ProDOS, MacOS, MS-DOS, VAX/VMS, and UNIX

WORK EXPERIENCE: Programmer
                    Open Port Technology, Inc.
                    676 North Saint Clair
                    Suite 900
                    Chicago, IL 60611
                    July 1995 to present
                    Duties: Writing programming tools in the UNIX
                    environment

                    Tutor
                    Ripon Middle School
                    651 Metomen Street
                    Ripon, WI 54971
                    October 1992 to May 1995
                    Duties: Helped students in all subject areas and kept
                    records on students required to attend the After School
                    Study Program

EDUCATION: Ripon Senior High School
                    850 Tiger Drive
                    P.O. Box 991
                    Ripon, WI 54971
                    Graduated May 1995

                    Successfully completed three computer science courses at
                    Ripon College during senior year of high school:

                    CS213-VAX Assembly Language
                    Learned VAX assembly language. Topics included
                    arithmetic, handling overflow, addressing modes,
                    floating point numbers, and microcode.

                    CS300-Compiler Writing
                    Learned how to write compilers using Lex and Yacc.
                    Topics included lexical analysis, syntax analysis,
                    code generation, finite state machines, pushdown
                    machines, and grammars.

                    CS452-Operating Systems
                    Learned theories and algorithms used in implementing
                    multiprocessing operating systems. Topics included
                    CPU scheduling, disk scheduling, memory management,
                    virtual memory, process synchronization, and

```
                        deadlock.  Also read journal articles written by
                        authors such as Peter Denning and E. W. Dijkstra.

ACCOMPLISHMENTS:        Scored a 3 on the AP Pascal AB Exam in 1994.
                        Earned a national honorable mention in the SuperQuest
                        competition in 1994.  SuperQuest is a national computer
                        programming competition for high school students. Ripon's
                        four student team earned one of fifteen honorable
                        mentions.

REFERENCES:             Martin T. Wegner
                        Open Port Technology, Inc.
                        676 North Saint Clair
                        Suite 900
                        Chicago, IL 60611
                        Office: (312) 664-1800

                        Kristine J. Peters
                        Associate Professor
                        Ripon College
                        Department of Mathematics and Computer Science
                        300 Seward Street
                        P.O. Box 248
                        Ripon, WI 54971
                        Office: (414) 748-8363
                        Home:   (414) 833-7155
                        E-mail:  petersk@acad.ripon.edu
```

The following is the resume of Owen Lynn. Notice that the objective has a good number of keywords. Also notice the use of lines to separate information. The "Force recalcitrant SCSI hard drives to cooperate" line is a tasteful yet subdued and professional use of humor—guaranteed to get positive attention.

```
Owen Lynn

                        101 Ann Street #A41
                        Auburn, AL 36830
                        (334) 826-8654
                        lynn@physics.auburn.edu
                        http://mainstream.physics.auburn.edu/~lynn

Objective: To find a job administrating UNIX boxes. Extensive
experience with SunOS; some experience with HP-UX.
_____


Experience

                        Unix system administrator, Auburn University - 9/92 to
                        present
                        Install/configure hardware
                        Started with two Sparcstations, now administrate eight
                        Force recalcitrant SCSI hard drives to cooperate
```

```
                       Install CPUs and SIMMs
                       Make purchases for new equipment
                       Install/configure/hack software
                       Started with SunOS 4.1.x, now manage Solaris 2.x
                       Started with NIS, now manage NIS+
                       Configure NCSA httpd
                       Design World Wide Web pages
                       Hack Berkeley popper to run under Solaris 2.x
                       Program in C
                       Write shell scripts
                       Program in Bourne
                       Program in Perl
                       Write TeX-formatted documents (including this one)
                       Summer research assistant at Lawrence Livermore
                       National Laboratory,
                       Livermore, California - 6/92 to 9/92.


                       Wrote numerical integration software for Cray Supercomputers
                       Programmed in Fortran

     Education

                       Auburn University, Auburn, Alabama - 9/90 to present
                       Physics major, graduating in June 1995
                       3.26/4.0 GPA
                       Phi Eta Sigma Honor Society
                       Sigma Pi Sigma Physics Society
                       Auburn Presidential Scholarship
                       Auburn National Merit Scholarship
                       High School: Shades Valley Resource Learning Center,
                       Birmingham, Alabama

                       National Merit Finalist
                       National Honor Society
                       Alabama Youth Symphony

     References

                       Available upon request
```

The next resume is that of Jennifer Rexford. This is a great example of how you can tailor a resume if you are still in school or have recently graduated. Her format is easy on the eyes, and includes bullet points for emphasis and clarity.

```
                          JENNIFER REXFORD
                        jrexford@eecs.umich.edu

Work Address                            Home Address
2220 EECS Building                      Apartment 150-C
1301 Beal Avenue                        3645 Green Brier Ave.
Ann Arbor, MI  48109-2122               Ann Arbor, MI  48105
(313) 763-5363                          (313) 995-5054
```

Resume and publications available at
  http://www.eecs.umich.edu/~jrexford
  ftp://rtcl.eecs.umich.edu/outgoing/jrexford

Research interests
  Real-time communication; network performance evaluation;
  parallel/distributed computing

Education
  University of Michigan, Computer Science and Engineering,1991-
  Ann Arbor, MI
  MSE 1993, PhD expected in Spring 1996 (GPA: 8.4/8.0, 9=A+,
  8=A, ...
Thesis: Tailoring router architectures to performance requirements
  in cut-through networks
Advisor: Professor Kang G. Shin

Princeton University, Electrical Engineering, 1987-91, Princeton, NJ
  BSE 1991, with highest honors (GPA: 4.0/4.0)

Academic recognition and honors
  o Intel Foundation graduate fellowship (1995-1996)
  o Distinguished Achievement Commendation for U. Michigan CSE graduate
       student (1995)
  o Rackham graduate fellowship for U. Michigan graduate students (1994-1995)
  o Co-author of publication chosen as ''best paper'' in (1993)
  o Office of Naval Research graduate fellowship (1991-1994)
  o National Science Foundation graduate fellowship, awarded (1991)
  o AT&T Graduate Research Program for Women grant (1991)
  o Pyne Honor Prize for Princeton University senior (1991)
  o James Hayes-Edgar Palmer Prize in Engineering graduation award (1991)
  o Computer Engineering Excellence graduation award (1991)
  o Tau Beta Pi, Sigma Xi, and Phi Beta Kappa

Work experience
  AT&T Bell Laboratories, Network Services Research Lab, June
  & October 1995

  AT&T Bell Laboratories, Mathematics Center, Summer 1994
  Murray Hill, NJ
  Design and evaluation of efficient hardware
  architectures for traffic shaping and link scheduling in
  high-speed ATM (asynchronous transfer mode) networks.

  AT&T Bell Laboratories, Mathematics Center, Summer 1991
  Murray Hill, NJ
  Development of parallel algorithms for evaluating circuit
  switched networks, with implementation on the MasPar MP-1.

  Princeton University, Electrical Engineering Dept., Fall
  1990 Princeton, NJ
  Teaching assistant for "Computer Structures and
  Organization" (EE317).

AT&T Bell Laboratories, Mathematics Center, Summer 1990
Murray Hill, NJ
Creation of a quadruple precision floating-point library
in C++.
Naval Research Laboratory, Plasma Physics Lab., Summer 1989
Washington, D.C.
Design of FORTRAN computer simulations for the VAX and Cray
XMP.

Professional societies

IEEE, IEEE Computer Society, ACM
Collaborative graduate research projects
Link-scheduling architectures
Design of efficient link-scheduling architectures to support
time-constrained communication in multicomputer routers and
high-speed network switches.
Point-to-point message simulator (pp-mess-sim)
Development of an object-oriented simulation environment for
evaluating multicomputer router architectures under a
variety of routing algorithms, switching schemes, network
topologies, application workloads, and performance metrics.
Programmable routing controller (PRC)
Design and implementation of a programmable router chip for
flexible communication in point-to-point networks.
Window-consistent primary-backup service
Design and prototype implementation of a primary-backup
protocol for maintaining fault-tolerant data repositories
for real-time control applications.

Educational experiences

Representative on departmental committees, 1995-96
University of Michigan
Officer in the computer science and engineering graduate
student organization (CSEG), serving as the student represen
tative on the faculty committee and the graduate
committee.
Mentor for undergraduate projects, Summer/Fall 1995

University of Michigan
Coordination of undergraduate research projects on the
design of a router chip for real-time parallel machines and
on efficient hardware architectures for high-speed link
scheduling.

Student in "Teaching Engineering" (ChE697), winter 1995
University of Michigan
Study of learning styles and teaching techniques, coupled
with creation of syllabus, assignments, exams, and lecture
for an undergraduate logic design course.
Co-editor of "She's an Engineer? Princeton Alumnae Reflect,"
1993 Princeton U.
Publishing of a book, edited with a colleague, on engineering
education and women in engineering, addressing under graduate
curriculum, student retention, and teaching styles.

Emailing Your Resume

Most organizations that advertise jobs online will allow, and even welcome, you to email your resume. But take care that you follow directions closely. A company may tell you to include a special code that indicates which job you are applying for or where you read the ad. You may also need to email your resume to a specific person's attention. Don't embarrass yourself by overlooking the obvious.

When you email your resume, include a subject line that's interesting and eye-catching. If you only put "Resume" in the subject line, you're basically telling a potential interviewer, "I'm really an uninteresting person." Feel free to be a little intriguing—even boastful. Remember, you're selling yourself, and there's no reason you can't use the subject line of an email to help do this. For instance, you might enter something like, "Resume showing 14 years of sales success."

How you email your resume will depend on the email software you're using and whether you're using an online service. Many online services allow you to attach a file (in this case, the file that contains your resume) by specifying the directory it's in on your hard drive. If your software won't let you attach an ASCII file, simply paste it in the text (message) area of your email, and send it.

The Cover Letter

Include a cover letter with your resume. Although the letter usually won't be read until you are considered to be a viable candidate (after a keyword search), providing a cover letter is always important. When you email your resume, place the cover letter in the same document, before the resume.

Use the cover letter to:

- explain why you are the person for the job/what you can do for the company.

- tell the reader how you found out about the open position or company.

- provide your salary requirements, if salary requirements were mentioned in the advertisement.

Since the cover letter will be scanned along with the resume, include keywords! Also, keep your electronic cover letter short and sweet.

The following example is a resume with cover letter:

```
Name: Paul DuBose
Address: 25 Pitman Road
E. Hampstead, NH 03826
Daytime Phone: 603 772-1500x3651
Evening Phone: 603 382-3553
```

Email: dubose_p@apollo.hp.com
Date: Fri Dec 9 11:25:28 EST 1994
To: Hiring manager

Dear Sir/Madam:

As you may be aware, the operational structure at Hewlett-Packard's Manufacturing operations in the U.S. are going through some major changes. These changes will be taking place over the next 18 months. While I am enthusiastic about the future of the company under this evolving structure, I have elected to take this opportunity to investigate my options for change and professional growth.

My unique position as a Senior Supplier Quality Engineer has afforded me the opportunity to work closely with some of the best suppliers in the world. I have had the responsibility of evaluating and managing different approaches to manufacturing with the goal of optimizing quality, reliability, and cost.

I would like to meet with you and demonstrate that along with these credentials, I have the personality that makes for a successful team player.

Yours truly,

Paul DuBose

RESUME

Skills:
Team Leader; Excellent communication and interpersonal skills written and verbal; Strong negotiator; High degree of initiative; Demonstrated ability to work with people from the manufacturing floor to the President and CEO; Extremely computer literate having used computers for over 17 years (PCs, Mini-computers, Mainframes, and workstations); Detailed knowledge of all aspects of electronics manufacturing; Thorough knowledge of the principles and implementation of various quality and reliability systems (ISO 9000, Strife Test, FMEA, DFR, ect...).

From 10/87 - Present

Hewlett-Packard Co., Sr. Supplier Quality Engineer - 7 yrs

Commodity responsibilities have included: Power Supplies; Monitors; Input/Output devices; Vendor built surface mount memory boards.

Successful commodity team leader contributing towards 400% volume growth in 7 years as well as introducing more than 25 new products. This team currently manages purchases exceeding $20 million annually and is a strong contributor to the corporation's strategic commodity management worldwide.
Direct efforts have resulted in reduced field and in-process failure rates of 73% and 72% respectively over a 5 year period. In this same time frame, cost has been reduced 64%,development time 67%, and lead times have been shortened 67%.

Special projects successfully completed include: Development and implementation of a strife test program (1994); Led effort to re-engineer corporate wide supplier quality metrics (1993 1994); Represented division at corporate procurement strategy board; Team leader for make/buy decision for high volume entry level workstation; Developed guidelines for establishing quality and reliability goals for new products (1993).

Project engineer responsible for evaluating and selecting suppliers, and awarding business. Work closely with suppliers during the development phase to ensure functionality goals are met and that quality and reliability are assured.

Developed and implemented various test and inspection strategies, processes, and equipment for incoming inspection and functional test.

From 12/84- 10/87
Apollo Computer Co., Test Engineer - 1 yr
(note that Hewlett-Packard acquired Apollo Computer in 1989)

Printed Circuit Assembly Functional Test - Led team that devised test strategies, which reduced the amount of capital equipment needed during the test process and reduced maintenance costs.

Apollo Computer Inc., Advanced Manufacturing Engineer - Systems Design / Assembly - 2 yrs

Worked closely with R&D ensuring that new designs were optimized for volume manufacturing. Coordinated prototype and pre-production builds. Developed manufacturing plans and procedures. Led effort to transition products into volume manufacturing.

From 05/82- 12/84

Compugraphic Corp., Manufacturing Engineer - Printed Circuit Assembly - 2 1/2 yrs
Project engineer responsible for the evaluation, justification and successful implementation of automated printed circuit assembly equipment.

Worked closely with R&D to ensure that all new printed circuit assembly designs were optimized for volume manufacturing.

Education:
BSME - Minor in CS, University of Lowell, 1982

Currently attending NH College towards an MBA

Specialized training:

Program Management
Statistical Process Control
ISO 9000
Strategic Cost Management
Frontline leadership: Basic Principals; Taking Corrective

```
Action; Managing Change.
Procurement Strategies and Negotiation Techniques
International Procurement
Principles of Power Electronics
```

Following Up

Feel free to follow up about four days after you email your resume. You can send a simple message indicating that you'd like to verify receipt of your resume. If there were any problems at all with the format of your resume, or if it somehow got "lost in cyberspace," you'll want to know as soon as possible.

Check your email regularly after you send your resume. If you've been sent mail indicating that there is interest in you, and someone wants to set up an interview, you don't want it to seem like you're ignoring them.

Posting Your Resume Online

When you email your resume, it goes to one person or organization. When you post your resume to an Internet or bulletin board site, it's available to everyone interested in reading it. Most of the time, you will email your resume, but there are a few instances in which a posting will be requested. Once again, follow directions.

You can post your resume to a variety of places, many of which are listed in Chapter 10. These include resume banks, which are accessed directly by employers, employment newsgroups, and bulletin boards. Before you post your resume, you should make sure that you want to go public with the fact that you're looking for a job. If you are currently working, do you want your employer to know that you are exploring your options?

Resume Banks

If you post your resume to a bank, you should first find out if it costs money to do so. If there is no initial cost, find out if there is a fee for you to update it. It may not be worth it to pay $25 dollars to correct a typo. Also, most good resume banks will delete a resume after three to six months if it is not updated. So, if you don't want yours to be nuked, update it regularly.

Newsgroups

We discussed newsgroups in Chapter 2. You should only post your resume to a newsgroup if it is acceptable for that particular newsgroup. Find out what the rules are before blindly posting your resume to every newsgroup you can find. Nothing will prevent you from getting a job quite like offending large groups of people at one time.

In some cases, you will be posting to a newsgroup using Trumpet Newsreader or another similar newsgroup program. In this case, you can post your resume by following these steps:

1. Log onto the Internet using your connection software, and run your newsreader software.

2. Choose "Group" from the menu bar, and then choose "Sub scribe."

3. The newsreader will then check for new groups. Double click on the name of the newsgroup you are interested in.

4. After you double click, you will be in the group. You will see the group's messages (articles).

5. At this point, you can either read articles or post a message. Click on "Post."

6. A new screen will appear with blanks for you to fill out. In the first blank, Newsgroups, enter the names of the newsgroups you want to post your resume to. You can post to more than one newsgroup by inserting commas between the newsgroup names.

7. Fill out the subject line similar to the subject message of an email. Be descriptive.

8. Paste in a short version of your resume (keep it at two computer screens or less) in ASCII text.

9. Click on "Post" and you're finished!

If you are using Netscape as opposed to Trumpet Newsreader, you will type, in the Open Location box, "news:" followed by the name of the newsgroup that you would like to post to. Then just click the "Post Message" button, and begin with step 6 above.

A Summary of Important Points to Remember

- An electronic resume must be filled with, and must focus on, keywords.

- Place the most important keywords toward the beginning of the resume.

- Use a simple, monospaced font and format for paper resumes that might be scanned and converted with OCR software.

- If you submit a paper resume, don't fold it, and use only white or ivory paper.

- When you save your resume in ASCII text, make sure to re-open the file to verify that it looks good.

- Always provide good contact information at the top of your resume, and include an email address if you have one.

- When using bullets in your ASCII resume, make sure to insert a space between each bullet and text so that the bullet doesn't interfere with a keyword search.

- Keep your resume and cover letter to no more than 65 to 70 characters per line.

- Include a short cover letter or introduction when emailing your resume unless you receive instructions indicating otherwise.

- When you email or post your resume, always enter something in the subject line (something interesting, preferably). Never leave the subject blank.

- If you want to post to a newsgroup, become familiar with the rules of that group before assuming that it's acceptable to post your resume.

- Always read instructions provided by a company or job database specifying how they want to receive resumes.

Great Resume Resources

While this chapter touched on some important rules in electronic resume creation, creating a resume of any kind is a difficult undertaking. If you are starting from scratch, consider taking a look at some of the resources listed below.

Online

Several resources on the Web offer hints on resume formatting and creation. Some of them cost money, so watch out! If you want to see what resources are available, use a search engine, and enter words like "resume creation."

Here are some of the resources we found and enjoyed:

Achieving Your Career
http://www.dnai.com~upsoft/achieving.html

Hot Resume How To's
http://www.monster.com:80/resumehows.html

How to Survive in a Resume Databank
http://www.webcom.com/~resumes/keyword.html

Movin' On: Tips for Resumes
http://www.wm.edu/catapult/resmdir/contents.html

Purdue's "Your Resume"
http://owl.trc.purdue.edu/Files/35.html

Quick Guide to Resume Writing
http://www.wm.edu/catapult/guenov/sampleres.html

What Do Employers Really Want in a Resume?
http://www.wm.edu/catapult/enelow-r.html

Books

Spend a few minutes at your local bookstore browsing the business or career sections. There may be a book specifically designed to help someone in your profession with a resume. But keep in mind that while the general concepts may be true, you must use what you've learned in this chapter for your electronic resume.

HTML Resumes

HTML resumes are resumes that you create on the World Wide Web and that can be read by a Web browser. Chapter 7 explains how to create your own HTML document.

Schmoozing Online: Meet the Right People, Make the Right Impression

CHAPTER 6 TOPICS

YOUR SCHMOOZING GOALS

YOUR FIRST TIME ONLINE

NEWSGROUP RULES AND "NETIQUETTE"

The Internet is an incredible place to meet people, from first graders to brain surgeons. But since schmoozing a first grader probably won't help you get a job, how do you meet the brain surgeon or other professionals?

As we mentioned earlier, Usenet newsgroups are the perfect place to join in on discussions on specific topics. Of course, you can participate in job and resume newsgroups (a list of those is provided in Chapter 2), but if you want to meet people who can help you find a job, or who can hire you themselves, you'll want to branch out, hang out where they hang out, and, well, schmooze.

Schmoozing is an art. Officially, to schmooze means "to chat informally," but in marketing and related fields, it's come to mean more: meeting people and making friends for a specific purpose—in your case getting a job. To successfully schmooze, you can't sound as if you're selling yourself like a used car. You should always be a valued contributor to a discussion, and you should follow the already established rules of the discussion.

Your Schmoozing Goals

Before you embark on your schmooze quest, you should decide what it is you hope to accomplish. By this time, you should know not only what your career goal is, but what kind of people you would like to interact with. Also, be aware of current trends and topics in your field so you can be a valuable contributor to newsgroups. If you've been out of your desired industry for awhile, read some industry trade magazines, or simply watch related newsgroups for awhile, and observe what some of the most common topics are.

There are several angles you can take in your search for good networking contacts. What will your online networking goals be? You can:

- Find someone in your profession or area of expertise who might be willing to share ideas about your search for a job and your qualifications, and who might know someone who is hiring.

- Find someone who works for the company you are interested in. It's helpful to know someone on the inside.

- Find someone who will be willing to tell you how you can be more competitive in your field.

- Get your name out there, in front of the people who count. Just by participating in newsgroups, your name will become recognizable to people. Of course, you don't want it easily remembered as a result of something embarrassing you've said.

- Find out about other important and related newsgroups and organizations where you can meet even more networking contacts.

- Find someone who is in your situation or a similar job-search situation and may have discovered some hot leads in the job-hunting process.

- Find someone in your geographical area or the area where you would like to work.

You'll probably be amazed at some of the helpful people you'll meet in an online discussion group. For instance, if you're in a newsgroup for writers, you'll probably find yourself in the company of editors with award-winning magazines, authors, and even publishers.

And with Usenet newsgroups, approximately 25 percent of the 4 million members are in countries other than the United States. Where else would you be able to discuss geology with a top scientist in Germany?

Your First Time Online

When you decide to participate in a newsgroup—and although we've emphasized this already, we want to stress its importance—you must follow the already established and sometimes unwritten rules of the group.

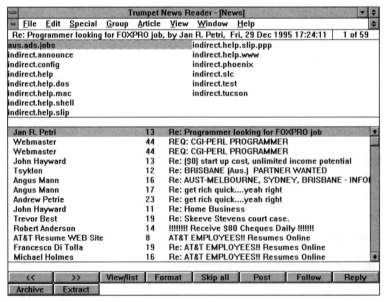

Figure 6.1 An Australian employment newsgroup: aus.ads.jobs.

1. First, you should subscribe to the group, as discussed earlier in the book.

2. Then, search the posted articles for some FAQs (Frequently Asked Questions) relating to the specific group and its members.

3. After reading the FAQs, read some of the articles and their threads. *Threads* are strings of discussions. Observe the relationships among the newsgroup members. Is the writing style formal or informal? Which members are discussing which topics? Who is the friendliest, most receptive person on the board? Take at least five hours or more of online time just to observe.

After you've followed these first three rules, you may be ready to post a message, but before you do, here's some newsgroup terminology you should be aware of:

Posting: sending a message to a newsgroup.

Follow-up: otherwise known as a reply, this is a response to someone else's post. A reply adds another message to a thread.

Thread: strings of discussions. Figure 6.2 shows a thread titled "<<BE FIRST>> BE FIRST<<This Time!!!!!>>."

Flame: to be avoided! A flame is a rude comment or response to a discussion or email

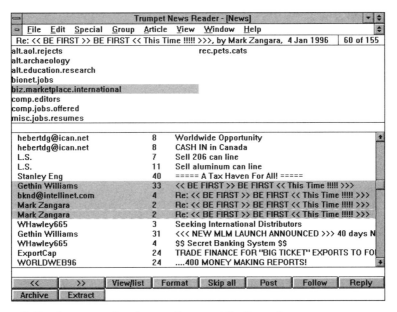

Figure 6.2 *An example of a posting and its thread.*

message. (See Figure 6.4 later in this chapter.) To avoid being flamed, take a look at "Newsgroup Rules and Netiquette" below.

Header: the "subject" part of an email or newsgroup message.

Newsgroup Rules and Netiquette

The Internet is open to anybody, and you're allowed to say virtually anything, but if you want to be accepted into a newsgroup, you need to follow some "netiquette" rules. If you don't follow these rules, you will be viewed by other newsgroup partici-pants as either rude or inexperienced.

Posting Versus Emailing

When you choose to respond to someone's posting in a newsgroup, you can either reply within the newsgroup, or you can send that person an email. You should email a comment or response when the information in your response would not be of great value to the entire membership of the group. If your reply to a posting would only be of interest to one person, you are wasting other people's time and money. Remember that some people pay for the time they spend reading their newsgroup information.

Let's say that Bob has posted an article discussing the overall worth of trade shows to a particular industry, and you know of an upcoming trade show in Bob's area. You want Bob to know about the show and to find out if he's already planning to attend. Should you send an email to Bob, or should you reply to the posting?

Definitely send an email directly to Bob. Not only will most other people not care about the time and place of a trade show that they cannot attend, but remember that there is international participation in newsgroups. People in other countries may be offended that you wasted their time discussing trade shows that they can't possibly attend.

Be Culturally Sensitive

Even if you have found an informal and fun-loving newsgroup, you should avoid using slang, abbreviations, or acronyms, if for no other reason than to appeal to the international participation. If you talk about the fact that you live in NY, study PhysEd, or belong to the NRA, who's to say whether someone from Zambia is going to know what the heck you're talking about? Exceptions to this are the acronyms commonly used as shorthand in email messages, such as:

- IMHO- in my humble/honest opinion
- FYI- for your information
- BTW- by the way

Also avoid references to television shows, movies, current events in your country, and so on. Be patient with other people's writing. Many newsgroup participants are just learning English or have a very basic knowledge. Don't flame someone for misspelling what you consider a common word.

Watch Your Spelling and Grammar

As is the case with formal written correspondence, typos and bad grammar reflect poorly on your professionalism. One of the wonderful things about newsgroups and email is that you can ponder what you write, reread it, and even have it proofed before you send it. Take advantage of this fact, and make your writing as error-proof as possible.

Certain typos, such as misspelling the word "writing" or "grammar" in the subject line of a posting expressing interest in a writing job (Figure 6.3) can be fatal.

Use proper capitalization and punctuation in your online writing. If you use all caps in your email or postings, it is interpreted as shouting, which is rude:

```
HEY! I WANTED YOU TO READ THIS!
```

If you need to emphasize a word, and since you can't use italics in ASCII text, use asterisks:

```
I don't think that virtual reality is the technology of tomorrow.
I think it's the technology of *today*.
```

Likewise, you can't italicize the titles of books in email, but it is acceptable to place the underscore symbol before and after the title, like this:

```
Have you ever read _Dolores Claiborne_ by Stephen King?
```

Be Careful of Misinterpretation

Written communication is entirely different from face-to-face communication because you don't have the luxury of facial expressions, body language, or tone of voice. Because all you have are words on a screen, you should be careful that your witticisms and comments are not taken the wrong way. Read and reread your messages and make sure your writing cannot be misinterpreted.

Be Brief

As we mentioned above, many people pay for the time they spend reading their newsgroup messages. Be brief in your postings and responses. No one has time to read a book online. The usual limit for a posting or reply is about half a screen.

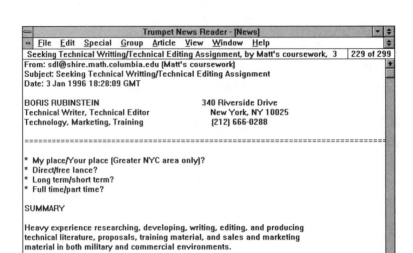

Figure 6.3 An example of a fatal typo in a newsgroup posting's header.

Don't Post Irrelevant Information

Again, the one thing you don't want to gain a reputation for is wasting other people's time or money. If you belong to a writers' newsgroup, don't take up space by posting an article about crochet. That sounds obvious, but you'd be amazed how many people get caught up in message threads that really have nothing to do with the main topic of the newsgroup. If you and another member want to talk about something else, use email. Likewise, if someone is discussing the literary aspects of Stephen King's *Dolores Claiborne*, and you want to discuss the movie, you should switch to a movie newsgroup.

Also, be careful not to join in the middle of a conversation (thread) when you haven't read the entire thread. You may be bringing up ideas long since discussed and abandoned. As shown in Figure 6.4, an inappropriate posting could get you flamed.

Don't Blatantly Sell Yourself

Networking and schmoozing don't mean saying "Hi! I'm great! Give me a job!" Be subtle. You want to become part of the group rather than be considered as an unwanted outsider. There's nothing wrong with posting a message to the professional writers' newsgroup, like the one below:

```
Hi. I'm a recent graduate of the journalism program at the University of Texas.
I'm trying to break into news writing, and I wondered if anyone has any advice
about how to begin.
```

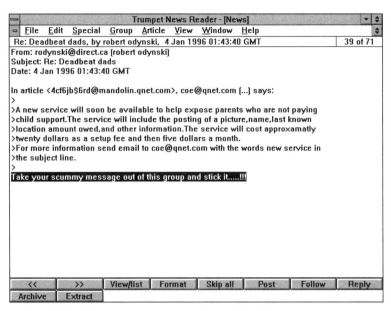

Figure 6.4 *An example of a flame in response to an inappropriate posting.*

Perfectly acceptable. Another way to become involved is to watch discussions and form personal, one-on-one relationships. For instance, you could respond to a posting with this email:

```
I read your posting yesterday regarding newswriting in the 90s, and I completely
agree with you. I'm a recent graduate, and I wondered how you first broke into
newswriting. Do you mind telling me how you got your start?
```

One thing's almost always true: People like to talk about themselves. Asking somebody about his or her experience and background is a great way to build an online relationship.

Be a Giver, Not Just a Taker

Don't just take, take, take. It's okay to ask for advice and opinions, but people will grow tired of you if you always "want" and never "give." Make sure to contribute as much if not more than other subscribers. If someone offers you advice or help, thank them. Also, if there are other job searchers whom you might be able to help with your job-hunting experience, share with them.

Don't Slam Your Employer (or Previous Employer)

You never know who's going to read newsgroup articles. If you publicly complain about your employer, or even former employer, that's not only unprofessional, but it could damage your reputation or even get you into legal trouble.

Refer to Previous Postings When You Reply

When you respond to someone's posting, or when you email someone about his or her posting, always specifically reference the initial article. If you email someone and simply say

```
I completely agree with you!
```

and that person has been away from his or her computer for a few days and hasn't checked email, he or she may not know what you're referring to. You can even include parts of the initial posting in your response and address specific parts, but when quoting someone, edit out what isn't directly applicable to your reply.

Figure 6.5 shows a response to a posting in the rec.pets.cats newsgroup. The person who is replying has included part of the original posting. The original posting is indicated by the carets (>) on the left-hand side.

Be Descriptive in Your Header

The header (subject line) of your posting helps people decide whether they should spend their time reading it. Keep your header to 40 characters or less, and make it interesting, specific, and descriptive, like the posting in Figure 6.6.

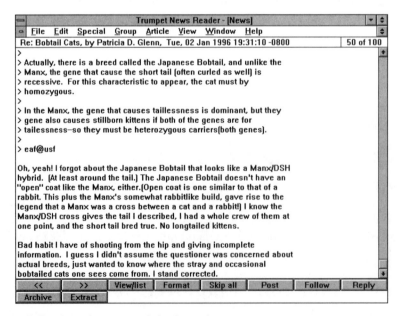

Figure 6.5 A reply to an original posting.

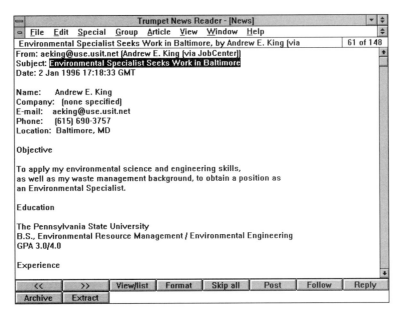

Figure 6.6 A descriptive header.

Be Patient

Remember that, while your job hunt may be the most important and time-consuming priority for you, it almost certainly isn't for the people you're sending messages to. Don't become impatient or rude.

Remember Your Audience

When you post an article, keep in mind who you're trying to reach. Asking about computer programming positions in an auto mechanic newsgroup probably won't get you very far. Post instead to a computer programming newsgroup. Try to get the most appropriate, not necessarily the widest, audience for your message. If your message is limited to a specific geographic area, restrict the distribution to newsgroups for that area.

Respect Copyrights and Licenses

Once something is posted on the network, it's usually considered public domain unless someone owns the appropriate rights and it is posted with a valid copyright. If you borrow something, cite your source.

Include a Signature

Include your signature at the end of all your postings, with your full name, address, and other relevant contact information, including email address. For newsgroup postings, keep your signature to four lines or less, with 65 to 70 characters per line.

Some other important netiquette to keep in mind:

- Limit line length of your message to around 65 to 70 characters.

- Focus on one subject per message.

- Check your email regularly.

Crossposting

Avoid posting a message to more than one newsgroup unless you are sure it is appropriate for all newsgroups. If you do post to multiple newsgroups (known as crossposting), do not post to each group separately. Instead, specify all the groups on a single copy of the message. You can do this by placing the names of all the groups you want to post to in the "Newsgroups" area, separated by commas (with no space), as shown in Figure 6.7.

Adding Emotion to Your Writing

Emoticons, also known as smileys, are symbols people add to online communication to show emotions like sarcasm or humor that can be lost in the translation from oral

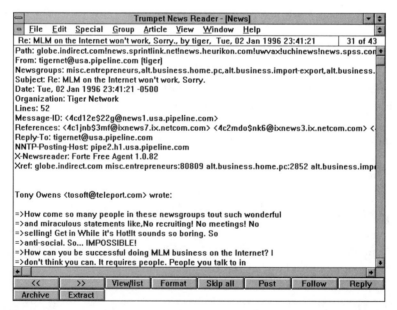

Figure 6.7 An example of crossposting. Note the "newsgroups" section of the header.

speech to written text. Smileys are perfectly acceptable in a less formal discussion group, or when a message may be confusing without them. But don't overuse smileys; they can seem "too cute." And don't use smileys for any kind of formal online communication, such as submitting a resume by email.

Below is a list of the most common emoticons you can use in your online communication. To see them better, you can turn this book sideways:

:-)   basic smiley; denotes humor or happiness

:-0   indicates surprise

:-(denotes unhappiness

:->   sarcastic smiley

:-@   screaming smiley

:-P   smiley sticking his tongue out at you

;^)   smirking smiley

;-(crying smiley

'-0   winking smiley

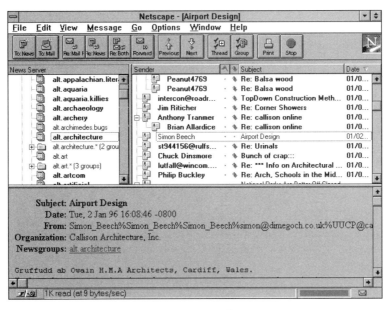

Figure 6.8 Netscape's built-in newsreader.

If you're interested in discovering or interpreting smileys other than those listed above, check out "helwig's smiley dictionary" on the World Wide Web (http://www.cg.tuwien.ac.at/~helwig/smileys.html) or conduct a Web search on "smileys."

Getting Together in Realtime

If you meet some people online and realize that you live or do business in the same area, why not get together, face to face? Maybe you'll be attending some of the same conferences or trade shows. Face-to-face meetings will make your networking relationships even stronger. Encourage local online members to meet with you in person.

Using Netscape to Use Newsgroups

The Netscape browser allows you to read and post to newsgroups from within the browser itself instead of using a separate newsreader like Trumpet Newsreader. For instruction on how to use Netscape's newsreader, refer to Netscape's Handbook "Mail, News, and Bookmarks," which can be found on the Web at http://home.mcom.com/eng.mozilla/2.0/handbook/.

CHAPTER **7**

Market Yourself on the Web: Create Your Own Home Page

CHAPTER 7 TOPICS

Creating your own Web page is a great way to represent yourself to the millions of would-be employers who spend time on the Internet. By now, you've probably traveled to many company home pages. One of the most important purposes of a company's home page is to market the company's products and services and to create awareness. Some companies even directly sell their products on the Web. If Web pages are so successful for companies, wouldn't this same marketing approach work for a job hunter? It can and does.

By creating your own home page, you will be marketing yourself to some of the most sophisticated and creative organizations and people in the world. And you can often demonstrate your skills directly on the Web. For instance, if you are seeking employment in a creative arts field, you will be able to show off some of your best work, such as photographs, paintings, published works, or Web page creation samples. The Web is the place to get your work noticed worldwide without ever having to leave home.

What's the best part about marketing yourself on the Web? It's easy, and almost anyone can do it. You don't even need to have any experience in programming. All you need is a little creativity, the willingness to learn a few HTML (Hypertext Markup Language) commands, and a place to store your document.

Watch and Learn

There are as many ways to design home pages as there are home pages. The best way to prepare yourself for writing HTML documents is to look at what other Web publishers are doing. By browsing other authors' home pages, you can examine and learn different techniques for organizing and presenting information. Many Web browsers allow you to view the source code of any Web page. When you find a home page that you really like and would like to use as a model for your own home page, you can simply view the HTML source code used to create it. For instance, in Netscape, if you want to view the HTML codes for a Web page currently being displayed, just click on View|Source. You can even save the source code to a text file. You can read the file at any time from directly within your favorite word processing program.

What are the characteristics of a good home page? You might think that quality is subjective, and that different Web pages will appeal to different people. After all, isn't it just a matter of taste? To a very small extent, yes. But some Web sites get more traffic than others. The reason for their popularity is usually easy to identify, because all good Web pages share some common traits. In particular, outstanding Web pages have the following characteristics. They:

- Are simple
- Are concise

- Are well organized

- Are functional

- Have accurate information

Simplicity and Conciseness

The most important consideration in designing any home page is to keep it simple—and simplicity and conciseness go hand in hand. Put most of your effort into presenting the content of your Web pages as clearly and concisely as possible. You want to grab readers' attention and invite them to further explore your home page. Don't bog down your Web page with lots of different fonts, links to every topic under the sun, or excessive graphics. Viewers will become confused and will probably decide to surf elsewhere.

Organization and Functionality

Organizing the information presented in a Web page is the key to creating a simple, eye-pleasing design. If your Web page is disorganized or difficult to navigate, your message will be lost.

Also, do not use extremely large graphics or distracting colors. Some of your visitors may have slow modem connections, so you should keep your images as small as possible and limit the number of images in your document. There is nothing more annoying than having to wait five to ten minutes for images to load.

If you do plan on using several images, you should indicate this at the beginning of your document to warn the reader of the slow load time. It's a good idea to provide a link at the top of your page that says something like "text version" or "text only." This link takes viewers to a different HTML file that contains no graphics.

Your Web pages should present the main focus of your site within a single viewing window at the top of the home page. In-depth information on any particular subject should be presented on separate pages through hyperlinks. Functionality goes hand-in-hand with good organization. In particular, the text and graphics at the top of your home page should be relevant to the message you want to convey. You don't want to mislead viewers the first time they visit your Web page.

For example, it would be irrelevant to have a large image of your cat Scooter at the start of your home page, especially if the purpose of your page is to find employment. You want to begin immediately by selling yourself, not your cat. On the other hand, an image of Scooter might be relevant if you include it on a separate, linked Web page that provides personal information about your hobbies and personal interests. The bottom line: The information that you present in your home page and the various links you provide should directly relate to the main theme of your page. Make sure you include an interactive element to your home page—for example, an email link that makes it easy for prospective employers to communicate with you.

Accuracy

You might think it would be difficult to provide inaccurate information about yourself, since you supposedly know yourself better than anybody else. But it's surprisingly easy to misrepresent yourself by "stretching the truth." Don't. Represent your skills honestly. Don't provide any information on your Web page that you can't later back up during a job interview or through references.

Probably the single biggest category of inaccurate information on the Web stems from Web page authors who create lists of links to related sites and then fail to keep the links up to date. Because the Web is changing so rapidly, it is important to monitor the validity of your hyperlinks and other information contained on your home page and make appropriate updates on a regular basis. It's frustrating to click on a link that just results in an error message. If you have several links that are out of date, that tells a prospective employer that you lack diligence. It's tantamount to turning in shoddy work on the job.

We Thought You Should Know...

Before we tell you what a Web page is, you should understand some basic Web terminology. Some of this was discussed in Chapter 2, so we'll just give you a refresher. There are several Web terms that sound like they mean the same thing, but in truth refer to very different concepts. On the other hand, some terms sound different yet actually do mean the same thing. Here are a few of the important terms and concepts you should understand before you begin planning your first Web page.

Web Site: First, anything that you see published on the Web is physically stored somewhere in the world on someone's computer's hard disk. This location is known as the *Web site.* For a Web site to *be* a Web site, it has to be connected to the Internet.

So basically you can send information *to* or get information *from* the Web site. If you want to get a picture of Shamu, the killer whale, you would have to go to Sea World's Web site. At this Web site, there may be a picture of Shamu that you can download onto your computer. For another scenario, let's assume that you want to join the Shamu fan club. Everyone in the fan club sends a letter to

Shamu telling him why he or she is a fan. This letter can be posted at the Sea World Web site.

Web Server: Before you can download that picture of Shamu, the communication has to be processed and transmitted from the Web site via a *Web server*. The Web server is software that makes all the information at a site Web-readable and transmits it to you. When you access a location on the Web using your Web browser (such as Netscape), your browser is sending a message to the Web server asking it for information. The server sends files and other documents that your Web browser can read and display.

Web Pages: All documents that are published on the Web are known as *Web pages*. A Web page is simply a document consisting of regular text along with special formatting and instructions called *HTML tags*. HTML, or Hypertext Markup Language, has two basic components—first is the hypertext component, which allows a Web page to contain direct references to other Web pages or other Web locations. With a simple click of your mouse button, you are immediately transported to the referenced location. This is also known as *hyperlinking*.

The second component is the markup language itself. This is simply a way to specify the format of text in your Web page. For example, unlike word processors, which allow you to highlight text and click on a button to make the text italicized, you must explicitly *mark* the beginning and end of text that you would like to have displayed in italics. This is done using HTML commands enclosed in brackets called *tags*. For example

```
<I>This will be in italics when displayed by a browser.</I>
```

would actually show up in a browser as

This will be in italics when displayed by a browser.

In this chapter, we'll explain all of the HTML tags you'll need to create great-looking Web pages.

Home Pages: Some pages serve a very specific purpose in Web publishing. The home page is the first Web page that a Web server will transmit when you access a Web site, unless you ask for a specific file. A home page is like the cover of a book. Its goal is to interest the reader and invite him or her in for further exploration.

Jump in with Both Feet

The best way to learn how to create Web pages is by jumping in and getting your feet wet. To create an HTML document, all you need is a text editor, such as the Windows Notepad, or one of the many special-purpose HTML editors, like Web Spinner (included in the CD-ROM with this book). Again, we encourage you to surf the Web to examine some good home pages so you can get ideas for your own. And by applying the HTML examples that we'll provide in the next few sections, you'll be able to create a great-looking home page literally in a matter of hours.

HTML 101

As we mentioned earlier, all HTML documents are composed of text with tags that describe the way in which the text should be displayed by a Web browser. HTML documents do not follow the WYSIWYG (What You See Is What You Get) rule used by most word processors, since HTML does not recognize *white space* (spaces, tabs, and line breaks). It simply displays text with a single space between each word, even if you have multiple spaces or a hard return.

The text in an HTML document normally is wrapped to fit the browser's window and screen. You need to take this into account when you create your Web pages. Text might wrap perfectly on your 15-inch screen, but might wrap much differently on a 14-inch monitor. Plus, users might be displaying their Web browser in a window that's smaller than the full size of the screen. As the size of a browser window is increased or decreased, the browser automatically rewraps text. Figure 7.1 shows a Web page in a Netscape window that's open to 17 inches. Figure 7.2 shows this same Web page after the window has been reduced in size a few inches. Notice how the text has been rewrapped. If you design your Web pages carefully, they'll look good at any size. If you design your pages with one particular screen and window size in mind, text might look strange or even disorganized when it's viewed on a different-sized screen.

HTML commands are enclosed in brackets called tags, and most tags are inserted in pairs. A beginning tag marks the start of the text or graphics you wish to format, and an ending tag tells the Web browser where to terminate the formatting. The ending tag typically has the same content as the beginning tag, except that it has a forward slash in front of the command name. For example, the title of your first HTML document, which we will brilliantly call "My First HTML Document," would look like this:

```
<TITLE>My First HTML Document</TITLE>
```

Note: HTML is *case insensitive*, so **<TITLE>** and **<title>** mean exactly the same thing.

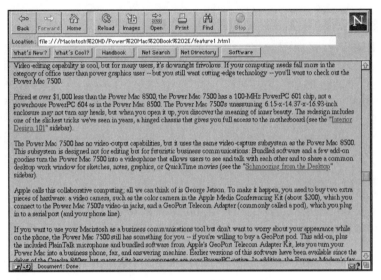

Figure 7.1 A Web page displayed on a 17″ monitor.

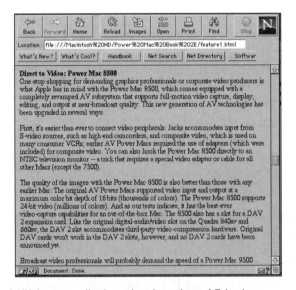

Figure 7.2 A Web page displayed at less than 15 inches.

The Basic HTML Document Template

The basic structure of an HTML document is quite simple. The following HTML provides a basic template we recommend as a starting point for all of your HTML documents.

```
<HTML>

    <HEAD>
            <TITLE>This is where the title of your document goes.</TITLE>
    </HEAD>

    <BODY>
            <H1>This is where the major document heading goes.</H1>

            <A HREF="A URL goes here.">Description of anchor</A>

            <ADDRESS>
                    Author of document and email address goes here.
            </ADDRESS>
    </BODY>
</HTML>
```

Although HTML is case insensitive, it is standard practice to type HTML tags in uppercase, which makes them easier to read and helps keep your documents organized. Take a quick look at the meaning of the codes shown in the template:

- The template begins with an **<HTML>** tag. Every HTML document must begin with this tag and end with the **</HTML>** tag. Everything enclosed between this pair of tags is recognized and interpreted by the Web browser. If you place text outside of the **<HTML>** tags, the text will be ignored by the browser. Outside the tags is where you can put notes to yourself for future reference, or special information concerning the Web page. However, keep in mind that these notes can still be read by most other users, simply by viewing the HTML source file. So don't put anything in an HTML document that you aren't willing to have the entire world read.

- Next, notice the **<HEAD>** tag in the template. This tag indicates the header section of the document. Within the **<HEAD>** and **</HEAD>** tags is the title of the document. Every HTML document should have a title. This title is displayed separately from the document. The title will usually appear in the browser's heading bar. Browsers also use the title to create bookmarks (also called hotlists by some browsers).

- The next main section of an HTML document is placed between the **<BODY>** and **</BODY>** tags. This is the meat and bones of the document and is where you will add all your text, images, any hyperlinks, and even sound files.

A Quick Tour of a Sample Home Page

Now that you have an understanding of the basic template, let's take a quick tour of a sample home page to demonstrate some HTML basics. Figure 7.3 shows you a Web page that we've created as an example for your review. Figure 7.4 shows you the actual

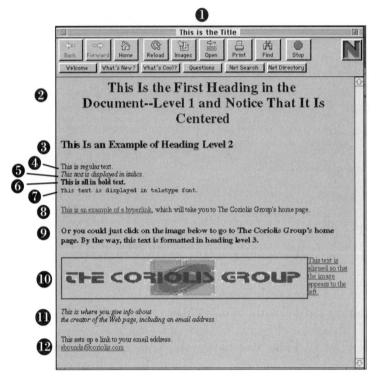

Figure 7.3 A sample HTML document.

HTML source document, and shows you all of the tags we used.

Next, we'll explain the steps we took to create the Web page, with numbers that correspond to Figure 7.3.

1. **<HTML>** Again, every HTML document must begin with the **<HTML>** tag and end with **</HTML>**.

   <HEAD> This tag marks the beginning of text that will be displayed at the top of the page. It differentiates between the heading and the body of the document.

   <TITLE> The title of the document must go between the **<HEAD>** and **</HEAD>** pair. The title is very important, but does not actually appear in your document. Instead, it will appear in the title bar of your Web browser, and is used by the browser to create bookmarks. All of your HTML documents should have a title that gives a good description of your home page.

   </TITLE> This tag marks the end of the title.

   </HEAD> This tag marks the end of the header.

2. **<BODY>** This marks the beginning of all the good stuff—the body of your document.

```
<HTML>
     <HEAD>
              <TITLE>This is the Title</TITLE>
     </HEAD>

     <BODY>

              <CENTER>
              <H1>This Is the First Heading in the Document—Level 1
              and Notice That It Is Centered</H1>
              </CENTER>

              <H2>This Is an Example of Heading Level 2</H2>

              This is regular text.
              <BR>
              <I>This text is displayed in italics.</I>
              <BR>
              <B>This is all in bold text.</B>
              <BR>
              <TT>This text is displayed in teletype font.</TT>
              <BR>
              <P>
              <A HREF="http://www.coriolis.com">This is an example of a hyperlink</A>,
              which will take you to The Coriolis Group's home page.
              <P>

              <H3>Or you could just click on the image below to go to The Coriolis Group's
              home page. By the way, this text is formated in heading level 3.</H3>

              <P>

              <A HREF="http://www.coriolis.com"><IMG SRC="newlgosm.gif" ALIGN=LEFT>This text
              is aligned so that the image appears to the left.</A>

              <P>
              <P>
<P>

              <ADDRESS>
              <I> This is where you give info about<BR> the creator of the Web page,
              including an email address.<I>
              </ADDRESS>

              <P>

              This sets up a link to your email address.<BR>
              <A HREF="mailto:sbounds@coriolis.com">
              sbounds@coriolis.com</A>


     </BODY>
```

Figure 7.4   The HTML source code for the Web page shown in Figure 7.3.

<CENTER> This tag works with most browsers and enables you to center your text. Use this tag when it's important to have the text centered regardless of the window size of the browser. The browser will wrap the text and create as many lines as necessary to center the text. In our example, the **<CENTER>** tag used three lines to center the text in the browser's window.

<H1> HTML offers six levels of headings, numbered 1 through 6. Level 1 has the largest font size, and should be used as your major heading.

</H1> This is the end of the heading 1 tag.

</CENTER> This marks the end of the centering tag.

3. <H2> This, of course, starts a second-level heading.

    </H2> And this marks the end of a second-level heading.

4. **No tag** This is just regular text. In other words, a Web browser defaults to regular text if the text is not surrounded by tags. You can have plain text anywhere in a document.

 This tag is used to insert a line break (carriage return). The <BR> tag does not have a closing tag.

5. <I> This is the tag used to display text in italics.

    </I> And this tag ends an italic display.

6. <B> This is the tag used to display bold text.

    </B> And this tag ends a boldface display.

7. <TT> This is the tag used to display the teletype font, which is a monospaced version of Courier.

    </TT> And, as you've no doubt figured out by now, this tag ends the display of the teletype font.

    <P> This tag creates a new paragraph. It is important to note that this tag *does* have an ending tag, </P>, but it is rarely needed. Why? When a browser sees the <P> tag, it knows that it must end the previous paragraph if it is to begin a new one. The paragraph tag is very useful because it's the best way to create a blank line.

8. <A HREF="http://www.coriolis.com">This is an example of a hyperlink.</A>

    This is your first exposure to a hyperlink, also known as an anchor. It will probably look a bit strange to you at first, but it's really quite simple. In our example, we are setting up a link to The Coriolis Group's home page (http://www.coriolis.com). It is important to note that you can use any URL to link to, or a directory location on your hard drive. For instance, you may have your HTML resume located on the same hard drive as your home page document. If you labeled this document "myresume.html," you could have done this

    ```
    <A HREF="myresume.html">My Resume</A>
    ```

    which would have created a hyperlink to your HTML resume document.

    Whether it is a URL or an HTML file on your hard drive, a hyperlink must be enclosed in quotation marks. The next step is to assign a name to your anchor, which will appear in your document. Typically the anchor text will be displayed in a different color and will be underlined to let the user know that it is a hyperlink. We chose to use "This is an example of a hyperlink" as our anchor text (and described where it will take you, in a plain text description). It's a good idea to make your anchor text the actual description of the location that it is anchored to. Remember, keep it simple!

9. **<H3>** This tag marks the start of a third-level heading.

    </H3> And obviously this tag marks the end of a third-level heading.

10. **<A HREF="http://www.coriolis.com"><IMG SRC="newlgosm.gif" ALIGN=LEFT>This text is aligned so that the image appears to the left </A>**

    This is an example of how you can set up an image as a hyperlink. It is very similar to the hyperlink we examined earlier but adds new life to our home page using a graphical representation of a hyperlink. The **<IMG SRC="filename">** tag is used to add an image to your Web document. The filename is the actual filename of the image and must be either in GIF (Graphics Interchange Format), JPEG (Joint Photographics Experts Group), or XBM (X Bitmap) format and must have an extension of either .GIF, .JPG, or .XBM. XBM is a Unix format, so you'll probably never use it. GIF and JPEG are the most common formats.

    In the sample home page, we used a file called "newlgosm.gif," which is The Coriolis Group graphic that appears near the bottom of our sample page. **ALIGN=LEFT** is used to tell the browser where to place the anchor text with respect to the image. Note that "LEFT" means to the left of the image. There are several other ways to use the **ALIGN=** tag. This is just one example.

11. **<ADDRESS>** This is an important part of each document. It is customary to separate the address section from the rest of the document with a horizontal line **<HR>** (which stands for horizontal "rule"—a graphic arts term for "line"—go figure). This is where you, as the author of the home page, will put your signature: your name and relevant contact information. You can also put your email address here; however, we recommend setting up an automatic email link (discussed below).

    </ADDRESS> This marks the end of the address section.

12. **<A HREF="mailto:sbounds@coriolis.com">sbounds@coriolis.com</A>**

    This sets up a link to your email address. By setting up this link to your email address and by adding the mailto URL, users can simply click on the link to get a blank email form with your email address filled in. Use the above format and simply insert your own email address in place of sbounds@coriolis.com.

More HTML

Up to this point, we've provided an HTML example that includes some of the most basic and most frequently used tags (some, like <HTML> and <BODY>, are essential). Now we'll expand on what the tags mean, and give you additional tips to help you to create a dynamite home page. Along the way, we'll introduce some additional tags that we think you'll find useful.

Normal Text

Most HTML documents are composed of plain, or normal, text. Any text not appearing between format tag pairs is displayed as normal text.

Normal text, like every other type of paragraph style except the preformatted style, is wrapped at display time to fit in the user's window. A larger or smaller font or window size will result in a totally different number of words on each line, so don't try to change the wording of a sentence to make the line breaks come at appropriate places. It won't work.

 Tag

If line breaks are important, as in postal addresses or poetry, you can use the <BR> command to insert a line break. Subsequent text will appear one line down, on the left margin.

The general format for this tag is:

```
<BR CLEAR=[Left|Right]>
```

The section listed between the [] is optional. This is an HTML 3.0 enhancement; it's supported by newer versions of Netscape (1.0 and later) and several other browsers.

Let's look at an example of how <BR> is used. To keep

```
Coriolis Group Books
7339 East Acoma Drive, Suite 7
Scottsdale, Arizona 85260-6912
```

from being displayed as

```
Coriolis Group Books 7339 East Acoma Drive, Suite 7 Scottsdale, Arizona 85260-
6912
```

you would use these tags:

```
Coriolis Group Books<BR>
7339 East Acoma Drive, Suite 7<BR>
Scottsdale, Arizona 85260-6912<BR>
```

The extended form of the **
** tag allows you to control how text is wrapped. The **CLEAR** argument allows text to be broken so that it can flow to the right or to the left around an image. For example, this tag shows how text can be broken to flow to the left:

```
This text will be broken here.<BR CLEAR=Left>
```

This line will flow around the right edge of an image displayed with the IMG tag.

<NOBR> Tag

This tag stands for No Break. This is another HTML 3.0 extension supported by Netscape and several other browsers. To keep text from breaking onto a new line, you can include the **<NOBR>** tag at the beginning of the text you want to keep together.

<WBR> Tag

This tag stands for Word Break. If you use the **<NOBR>** tag to define a section of text without breaks, you can force a line break at any location by inserting the **<WBR>** tag, followed by the **
** tag.

<P> Tag

The **
** tag causes a line break within a paragraph, but more often we want to separate one paragraph from another. We can do this by enclosing each paragraph in a **<P>** tag pair, starting with **<P>** and ending with **</P>**. The actual appearance of the paragraphs will depend on the user's Web browser: Paragraph breaks may be shown with an extra line or half line of spacing, a leading indent, or both.

The **</P>** tag is optional; most people include a single **<P>** at the beginning of each paragraph, at the end, or alone on a line between two paragraphs.

Physical and Logical Attributes

The character attribute tags allow you to alter the appearance of your text within a paragraph. HTML supports two different types of character attributes: *physical* and *logical*. Physical attributes include the familiar bold, italic, and underline, and the TT attribute, which we've demonstrated in Table 7.1 and 7.2.

Logical attributes are different. They let you describe what sort of emphasis you want to place on a word or phrase, but leave the actual formatting up to the browser. That is, where a word marked with a physical attribute like **<B>bold</B>** will always appear in bold type, a word marked with the logical attribute **<EM>emphasized</EM>** may be italicized, underlined, bolded, or displayed in color.

Web style guides suggest that you use logical attributes whenever you can, but there's a slight problem: Some current browsers only support certain physical attributes, and few or no logical attributes. Since Web browsers simply ignore any HTML tag that they don't recognize, when you use logical tags, you run the risk that your readers will not see any formatting at all! Table 7.1 shows a list of physical attributes. The standard format for using any of the physical attribute tags is as follows:

```
<tag>text goes here</tag>
```

You can nest attributes, although the results will vary from browser to browser. For example, some browsers can display bold italic text, while others will only display the innermost attribute. (That is, **<B><I>bold italic</I></B>** may show up as bold italic.) If you use nested attributes, place the end tags in reverse order of the start tags; don't write something like **<B><I>bold italic</B></I>**! This may work with some browsers, but may cause problems with others. Table 7.2 shows a list of logical attributes.

Keep in mind that, even if current browsers arbitrarily decide that <EM> text will be displayed as italic and <KBD> text will be displayed as Courier, future browsers will probably defer these attributes to a setting controlled by the user.

<BLINK> ... </BLINK>

This is a new enhanced tag supported by Netscape. Text placed between this tag pair will blink on the screen. This feature is useful as an attention getter, but using it too much could get rather annoying. The format for this tag is:

```
<BLINK>This text will blink</BLINK>
```

<CENTER> ... </CENTER>

This HTML enhancement makes some Web page authors feel like they have died and gone to heaven. Any text (or images) placed between this tag pair is centered between the left and right margins of the page. The format for this tag is:

Table 7.1 Physical HTML Attributes

Attribute	Tag	Sample	Effect
Bold	<B>	Some <B>bold</B> text	Some **bold** text
Italic	<I>	Some <I>italicized</I> text	Some italicized text
Underline	<U>	Some <U>underlined</U> text	Some underlined text
TT	<TT>	<TT>monospaced</TT>	Some monospaced text

Table 7.2 Logical HTML Attributes

Attribute	Tag	Use of Interpretation	Typical Rendering
Citation	<CITE>	Titles of books and films	Italic
Code	<CODE>	Source code fragments	Monospaced
Definition	<DFN>	A word being defined	Italic
Emphasis	<EM>	Emphasize a word or phrase	Italic
PRE	<PRE>	Used for tables and text	Preformatted text
Keyboard	<KBD>	Something the user should type word-for-word	Bold monospaced
Sample	<SAMP>	Computer status messages	Monospaced
Strong	<STRONG>	Strong emphasis	Bold
Variable	<VAR>	A description of something the user should type, like <filename>	Italic

```
<CENTER>This text will be centered between the left and the right margins
</CENTER>
```

<FONT> ... </FONT>

This HTML tag enhancement allows you to control the sizes of the fonts displayed in your documents. The format for this tag is:

```
<FONT SIZE=font-size>text goes here</FONT>
```

where font-size must be a number from 1 to 7. A size of 1 produces the smallest font. The default font size is 3. Once the font size has been changed, it will remain in effect until the font size is changed by using another **<FONT>** tag.

<BASEFONT>

To give you even greater control over font sizing, a new HTML tag has been added so that you can set the base font for all text displayed in a document. The format for this tag is:

```
<BASEFONT SIZE=font-size>
```

Again, font size must be a number from 1 to 7. A size of 1 produces the smallest font. The default font size is 3. Once the base font size has been defined, you can display text in larger or smaller fonts using the "+" or "-" sign with the **<FONT>** tag. Here's an example of how this works:

```
<BASEFONT SIZE=4>
```

This text will be displayed as size 4 text.

```
<FONT SIZE=+2>
```

This text will be displayed as size 6.

```
</FONT>
```

This text will return to the base font size: size 4.

Headings

HTML provides six levels of section headings, **<H1>** through **<H6>**. While these are typically short phrases that fit on a line or two, the various headers are actually full-fledged paragraph types. They can even contain line and paragraph break commands.

You are not required to use an **<H1>** before you use an **<H2>**, or to make sure that an **<H4>** follows an **<H3>** or another **<H4>**.

The standard format for using one of the six heading tags is illustrated by this example.

```
<H1>Text goes here</H1>
```

Lists

HTML supports five different list types. All five types can be thought of as a sort of paragraph type. The first four list types share a common syntax, and differ only in how they format their list elements. The fifth type, the description list, is unique in that each list element has two parts—a tag and a description of the tag.

All five list types display an element marker—whether it be a number, a bullet, or a few words—at the left margin. The marker is followed by the actual list elements, which appear indented. List elements do not have to fit on a single line or consist of a single paragraph—they may contain **<P>** and **
** tags.

Lists can be nested, but the appearance of a nested list depends on the browser. For example, some browsers use different bullets for inner lists than for outer lists, and some browsers do not indent nested lists. However, Netscape and Lynx, which are probably the most common graphical and text mode browsers, do indent nested lists;

the tags of a nested list align with the elements of the outer list, and the elements of the nested list are further indented. For example,

- This is the first element of the main bulleted list.
  - This is the first element of the nested list.
  - This is the second element of the nested list.
- This is the second element of the main bulleted list.

The four list types that provide simple list elements use the list item tag, **<LI>**, to mark the start of a list element. The **<LI>** tag always appears at the start of a list element. Thus, all simple lists look something like this:

```
<ListType>
```

```
<LI>
```

There isn't really any ListType list; however the **OL**, **UL**, **DIR**, and **MENU** lists (which we'll describe later) all follow this format.

```
<LI>
```

Since white space is ignored, you can keep your source legible by putting blank lines between your list elements.

```
<LI>
```

(If we hadn't used the ampersand quotes in the previous list element, the "<li>" would have been interpreted as the start of a new list element.)

```
</ListType>
This tag ends a list.
```

Numbered List

In HTML, numbered lists are referred to as ordered lists. The list type tag is **<OL>**. Numbered lists can be nested, but some browsers become confused by the close of a nested list, and start numbering the subsequent elements of the outer list from 1.

Bulleted List

If a numbered list is an ordered list, what else could an unnumbered, bulleted list be but an unordered list? The tag for an unordered (bulleted) list is **<UL>**. While bulleted lists can be nested, you should keep in mind that the list nesting may not be visible; some browsers indent nested lists; some don't. Some use multiple bullet types; others don't.

Netscape List Extensions

Netscape has added a useful feature called **TYPE** that can be included with unordered and ordered lists. This feature allows you to specify the type of bullet or number that you use for the different levels of indentation in a list.

Unordered List with Extensions

When Netscape displays the different levels of indentation in an unordered list, it uses a solid disc (level 1) followed by a bullet (level 2) followed by a square (level 3). You can use the **TYPE** feature with the <UL> tag to override this sequence of bullets. Here's the format:

```
<UL TYPE=Disc|Circle|Square>
```

For example, here's a list defined to use circles as the bullet symbol:

```
<UL TYPE=Circle>
<LI>This is item 1
<LI>This is item 2
<LI>This is item 3
</UL>
```

Ordered List with Extensions

When Netscape displays ordered (numbered) lists, it numbers each list item using a numeric sequence—1,2,3, and so on. You can change this setting by using the **TYPE** modifier with the <OL> tag. Here's how this feature is used with numbered lists:

```
<OL TYPE=A|a|I|i|1>
```

where TYPE can be assigned to any one of these values:

A—Mark list items with capital letters

a—Mark list items with lowercase letters

I—Mark list items with large roman numerals

i—Mark list items with small roman numerals

1—Mark list items with numbers (default)

But wait, there's more! You can also start numbering list items with a number other than 1. To do this, you use the **START** modifier

```
<OL START=starting-number>
```

where starting-number specifies the first number used. You can use this feature with the **TYPE** tag. For example, the tag

```
<OL TYPE=A START=4>
```

would start the numbered list with the Roman numeral IV.

Using Modifiers with List Elements

In addition to supporting the **TYPE** modifier with the <UL> and <OL> tags, Netscape allows you to use this modifier with the <LI> tag to define list elements for ordered and unordered lists. Here's an example of how it can be used with an unordered list:

```
<H2>Useful Publishing Resources</H2>
<UL TYPE=Disc>
<LI>HTML Tips
<LI>Web Page Samples
<LI TYPE=Square>Images
<LI TYPE=Disc>Templates
</UL>
```

In this case, all the list items will have a disc symbol as the bullet, except the third item, Images, which will be displayed with a square bullet.

The **TYPE** modifier can be assigned the same values as those used to define lists with the <UL> and <OL> tags. Once **TYPE** has been used to define a style for a list item, all subsequent items in the list will be changed, unless another **TYPE** modifier is used.

If you are defining <LI> list elements for ordered lists <OL>, you can also use a new modifier named **VALUE** to change the numeric value of a list item. Here's an example:

```
<H2>Useful Publishing Resources</H2>
<OL>
<LI>HTML Tips
<LI>Web Page Samples
<LI Value=4>Images
<LI>Templates
</UL>
```

In this list, the third item would be assigned the number 4 and the fourth item would be assigned the number 5.

Directory and Menu Lists

The directory and menu lists are special types of unordered lists. The menu list, **<MENU>**, is meant to be visually more compact than a standard unordered list; menu list items should all fit on a single line. The directory list, **<DIR>**, is supposed to be even more compact; all list items should be less than 20 characters long, so that the list can be displayed in three (or more) columns.

We're not sure if we've ever actually seen these lists in use, and their implementation is still spotty; current versions of Netscape do not create multiple columns for a **<DIR>** list, and while they let you choose a directory list font and a menu list font, they do not actually use these fonts.

Description List

The description list, or **<DL>**, does not use the **<LI>** tag the way other lists do. Each description list element has two parts, a tag and its description. Each tag begins with a **<DT>** tag and each description with a **<DD>** tag. These appear at the start of the list element and are not paired with **</DT>** or **</DD>** tags.

The description list looks a lot like any other list, except that instead of a bullet or a number, the list tag consists of your text. Description lists are intended to be used for creating formats like a glossary entry, where a short tag is followed by an indented definition, but the format is fairly flexible. For example, a long tag will wrap, just like any other paragraph, although it should not contain line or paragraph breaks. (Netscape will indent any **<DT>** text after a line or paragraph, as if it were the **<DD>** text.) Further, you needn't actually supply any tag text; **<DT><DD>** will produce an indented paragraph.

Compact and Standard Lists

Normally, a description list puts the tags on one line, and starts the indented descriptions on the next:

Tag 1
    Description 1.
Tag 2
    Description 2.

For a tighter look, you can use a **<DL COMPACT>**. If the tags are very short, some browsers will start the descriptions on the same line as the tags:

Tag 1   Description 1.
Tag 2   Description 2.

However, most browsers, except Netscape 2, do not support the compact attribute, and will simply ignore it.

More on Inline Images

As we have shown in the previous examples, the **<IMG>** tag is a very useful HTML feature. It lets you insert images into your text. This tag is rather different from the tags that are used to format text. This is an empty tag that always appears alone; it has a number of parameters between the opening **<IMG>** and the closing. Some of the parameters include the image filename, as mentioned earlier, and some optional modifiers, which we will take a close look at here. The basic format for this tag is:

```
<IMG SRC="URL" ALT="text"
    ALIGN=top|middle|bottom
    ISMAP>
```

Since HTML 3 has emerged and additional Netscape extensions have been added, this tag has expanded more than any other HTML feature. Here is the complete format for the latest and greatest version of the **<IMG>** tag:

```
<IMG SRC="URL" ALT="text"
    ALIGN=left|right|top|texttop|middle|absmiddle|
            baseline|bottom|absbottom
    WIDTH=pixels
    HEIGHT=pixels
    BORDER=pixels
    VSPACE=pixels
    HSPACE=pixels
    ISMAP>
```

The extended version allows you to specify the size of an image, have better control of the image and text alignment, and specify the size of an image's border.

Every **<IMG>** tag must have an **SRC=** parameter. This specifies a URL, or Uniform Resource Locator, which points to a GIF or JPEG image file. When the image file is in the same directory as the HTML document, the filename is an adequate URL. For example, **<IMG SRC=MySmilingface.gif>** would insert a picture of a smiling face.

Some people turn off inline images because they have a slow connection to the Web. This replaces all images, no matter what size, with a standard graphic. This isn't so bad if the picture is ancillary to your text, but if you've used small inline images as bullets in a list or as section dividers, the placeholder graphic will usually make your page look rather strange. For this reason, some people avoid using graphics as structural elements; others simply don't worry about people with slow connections; still others include a note at the top of the page saying that all the images on the page are small, and invite people who keep inline images turned off to turn them on and reload the page.

Keep in mind that a few people use text-only browsers, like Lynx, to navigate the Web. If you include a short description of your image with the **ALT**=parameter, text-only browsers can show something in place of your graphic. For example, <**IMG SRC=MySmilingFace.gif**> could be supplemented by the code <**ALT**="**A picture of the author**">, so that no one feels left out.

Since the value assigned to the ALT parameter has spaces in it, you have to put it within quotation marks. In general, you can put any parameter value in quotation marks, but you *need* to do so only if it includes spaces.

Mixing Images and Text

You can mix text and images within a paragraph; an image does not constitute a paragraph break. However, some Web browsers, like earlier versions of Netscape, did not wrap paragraphs around images; they displayed a single line of text to the left or right of an image. Normally, any text in the same paragraph as an image would be lined up with the bottom of the image, and would wrap normally below the image. This works well if the text is essentially a caption for the image, or if the image is a decoration at the start of a paragraph. However, when the image is a part of a header, you may want the text to be centered vertically in the image, or to be lined up with the top of the image. In these cases, you can use the optional **ALIGN**=parameter to specify **ALIGN=top**, **ALIGN=middle**, or **ALIGN=bottom**.

Using Floating Images

With the extended version of the <**IMG**> tag, you can now create "floating" images that will align to the left or right margin of a Web page. Text that is displayed after the image will either wrap around the right-hand or left-hand side of the image. Here's an example of how an image can be displayed at the left margin with text that wraps to the right of the image:

```
<IMG SRC="limage.gif" ALIGN=left>
```

Text will be displayed to the right of the image.

Specifying Spacing for Floating Images

When you use floating images with wraparound text, you can specify the spacing between the text and the image by using the **VSPACE** and **HSPACE** modifiers. **VSPACE** defines the amount of spacing in units of pixels between the top and bottom of the image and the text. **HSPACE** defines the spacing between the left or right edge of the images and the text that wraps.

Sizing Images

Another useful feature that has been added to the **<IMG>** tag is image sizing. The **WIDTH** and **HEIGHT** modifiers are used to specify the width and height for an image in pixels. Here's an example:

```
<IMG SRC"logo.gif" WIDTH=250 HEIGHT=310>
```

When a browser like Netscape displays an image, it needs to determine the size of the image before it can display a placeholder or bounding box. If you include the image's size using **WIDTH** and **HEIGHT**, a Web page can be built much faster. If the values you specify for **WIDTH** and **HEIGHT** differ from the image's actual width and height, the image will be scaled to fit.

Using Multiple Images per Line

Since an image is treated like a single (rather large) character, you can have more than one image on a single line. In fact, you can have as many images on a line as will fit in you reader's window! If you put too many images on a line, the browser will wrap the line and your images will appear on multiple lines. If you don't want images to appear on the same line, place a **
** or **<P>** tag between them.

Defining an Image's Border

Typically, an image is displayed with a border around it. The border is set to the color blue when the image is part of an anchor. Using the **BORDER** modifier, you can specify a border width for any image you display. Here's an example that displays an image with a five-pixel border:

```
<IMG SRC="logo.gif" BORDER=5>
```

Table 7.3 shows the summary of **<IMG>** parameters.

ISMAP Parameter

The optional **ISMAP** parameter allows you to place hyperlinks to other documents in a bitmapped image. This technique is used to turn an image into a clickable map. (See the section *Using Many Anchors in an Image* for more detail.)

Table 7.3   <IMG> Parameters

Parameter	Required?	Settings
SRC	Yes	URL
ALT	No	A text string
ALIGN	No	top, middle, bottom, left
		right, texttop, absmiddle,
		baseline, absbottom
HEIGHT	No	Pixel setting
WIDTH	No	Pixel setting
BORDER	No	Pixel setting
VSPACE	No	Pixel setting
HSPACE	No	Pixel setting
ISMAP	No	None

Horizontal Rules

The <HR> tag draws a horizontal rule, or line, across the screen. It's fairly common to put a rule before and after a form, to help set off the user entry areas from the normal text.

Many people use small inline images for decoration and separation, instead of rules. Although using images in this manner lets you customize your pages, it also takes longer for them to load—and it may make them look horrible when inline images are turned off.

The original <HR> tag simply displays an engraved rule across a Web page. A newer version of the tag has been extended to add additional features including sizing, alignment, and shading. The format for the extended version of <HR> is:

```
<HR SIZE=pixels
    WIDTH=pixels|percent
    ALIGN=left|right|center
    NOSHADE>
```

The **SIZE** modifier sets the width (thickness) of the line in pixel units. The **WIDTH** modifier specifies the length of the line in actual pixel units or a percentage of the width of the page. The **ALIGN** modifier specifies the alignment for the line (the default is center), and the **NOSHADE** modifier allows you to display a solid line.

As an example of how some of these new features are used, the following tag displays a solid line, five pixels thick. The line is left justified and spans 80 percent of the width of the page:

```
<HR SIZE=5 WIDTH=80% ALIGN="left" NOSHADE>
```

Hypermedia Links

The ability to add links to other HTML documents or to entirely different sorts of documents is what makes Web browsers so powerful. The special sort of highlight that your reader clicks on to travel to another location is called an anchor, and all links are created with the anchor tag, **<A>**. The basic format for this tag is:

```
<A HREF="URL"
     NAME="text"
     REL=next|previous|parent|made
     REV=next|previous|parent|made
   TITLE="text">

text</A>
```

Links to Other Documents

While you can define a link to another point within the current page, most links are to other documents. Links to points within a document are very similar to links to other documents, but are a little more complicated, so we'll talk about them later. (See the section *Links to Anchors*.)

Each link has two parts: The visible part, or anchor, which the user clicks on, and the invisible part, which tells the browser where to go. The anchor is the text between the **<A>** and **</A>** tag pair, while the actual link data appears in the **<A>** tag.

Just as the **<IMG>** tag has a **SRC=** parameter that specifies an image file, so does the **<A>** tag have an **HREF=** parameter that specifies the hypermedia reference. Thus, **<A HREF=SomeFile.Type>click here</A>** is a link to SomeFile.Type with the visible anchor click here.

Browsers will generally use the linked document's filename extension to decide how to display the linked document. For example, HTML or HTM files will be interpreted and displayed as HTML, whether they come from an http server, and FTP server, or a gopher site. A link can also be to any sort of file—a large bitmap, sound file, or movie.

Images as Hyperlinks

Since inline images are in many ways just big characters, there's no problem with using an image in an anchor, as we've shown in the sample home page. The anchor can include text on either side of the image, or the image can be an anchor by itself. Most browsers show an image anchor by drawing a blue border around the image (or around the placeholder graphic). The image anchor may be a picture of what is being linked to, or for reasons we'll explain shortly, it may even just point to another copy of itself:

```
<A HREF=image.gif><IMG SRC=image.gif></A>
```

Thumbnail Images

One sort of picture of a link is called a thumbnail image. This is a tiny image, perhaps 100 pixels in the smaller dimension, which is either a condensed version of a larger image or a section of the image. Thumbnail images can be transmitted quickly, even across slow communication lines, leaving it up to the reader to decide which larger images to request. A secondary issue is aesthetic: Large images take up a lot of screen space; smaller images don't.

Linking an Image to Itself

Many people turn off inline images to improve performance over a slow network link. If the inline image is an anchor for itself, these people can then click on the placeholder graphic to see what they missed.

Using Many Anchors in an Image

The <IMG> tag's optional **ISMAP** parameter allows you to turn rectangular regions of a bitmap image into clickable anchors. Clicking on these parts of the image will activate an appropriate URL. (A default URL is also usually provided for when the user clicks on an area outside of one of the predefined regions.) While forms (a new feature of Netscape) let you do this a bit more flexibly, the **ISMAP** approach doesn't require any custom programming—just a simple text file that defines the rectangles and their URLs—and this technique may work with browsers that do not support forms.

Links to Anchors

When an HREF parameter specifies a filename, the link is to the whole document. If the document is an HTML file, it will replace the current document and the reader will be placed at the top of the new document. Often this is just what you want. But sometimes you'd rather have a link take the reader to a specific section of a document. Doing this requires two anchor tags: one that defines an anchor name for a location (specific section of the document), and one that points to that name. These two tags can be in the same document or in different documents.

Defining an Anchor Name

To define an anchor name, you will need to use the **NAME** parameter: **<A NAME=AnchorName>**. You can attach this name to a phrase, not just a single point, by following the **<A>** tag with an **</A>** tag.

Linking to an Anchor in Current Document

To then use this name, simply insert an **<A HREF=...>** tag as usual, except that instead of a filename, use a # followed by an anchor name. For example, **<A HREF=#AnchorName>** refers to the example in the previous paragraph.

Names do not have to be defined before they are used; it's actually fairly common for lengthy documents to have a table of contents with links to names defined later in the document. It's also worth noting that, while tag and parameter names are not case sensitive, anchor names are; **<A HREF=#anchorname>** will not take you to the AnchorName example.

Linking to an Anchor in a Different Document

You can also link to specific places in any other HTML document, anywhere in the world—provided, of course, that it contains named anchors. To do this, you simply add the # and the anchor name after the URL that tells where the document can be found. For example, to plant a link to the anchor named "Section 1" in a file named complex.html in the same directory as the current file, you could use **<A HREF="Complex.html#Section 1">**. Similarly, if the named anchor was in http://www.another.org/Complex.html, you'd use **<A HREF="http://www.another.org/Complex.html#Section 1">**.

Using URLs

Just as a complete DOS or Windows filename starts with a drive letter followed by a colon, so a full URL starts with a resource type—HTTP, FTP, GOPHER, and so on—followed by a colon. If the name doesn't have a colon in it, it's assumed to be a local reference, which is a file name on the same file system as the current document. Thus, **<A HREF=Another.html>** refers to the file "Another.html" in the same directory as the current file, while **<A HREF=/html/File.html>** refers to the file "File.html" in the top-level directory html. One thing to note here is that a URL always uses "/" (the Unix-style forward slash) as a directory separator, even when the files are on a Windows machine, which would normally use "\", the DOS-style backslash.

Local URLs can be very convenient when you have several HTML files with links to each other, or when you have a large number of inline images. If you ever have to move them all to another directory, or to another machine, you don't have to change all the URLs.

It is very important to remember, that unlike HTML tags, some URLs are case sensitive. This will only have an impact on your home page creation if you will be including hyperlinks to locations where the Web server is run on a Unix system, which is case sensitive. A good rule of thumb when adding hyperlinks to your home page is: **Always** type in the URL exactly the way it appears in your browser's location or status bar.

We Thought You Should Know...

If you're using Netscape 1.0 or later, you don't need to type in "http://" or any other protocol name when you type in a URL. If you omit the "http://", Netscape assumes the address is to a Web site. If no Web site can be found, Netscape assumes that the address is to a Gopher address. If the address begins with "ftp" (as in ftp.coriolis.com), Netscape assumes the address is to an FTP site. So Netscape can almost always find the correct address even when you omit the protocol type at the start of the address.

<BASE> Tag

One drawback of local URLs is that, if someone makes a copy of your document, the local URLs will no longer work. Adding the optional **<BASE>** tag to the **<HEAD>** section of your document will help eliminate this problem. While many browsers do not yet support it, the intent of the **<BASE>** tag is to provide a context for local URLs.

The **<BASE>** tag is like the **<IMG>** tag, in that it's a so-called empty tag. It requires an **HREF** parameter—for example, **<BASE HREF=http://www.imaginary.org/ index.html>**—which should contain the URL of the document itself. When a browser that supports the **<BASE>** tag encounters a URL that doesn't contain a protocol and path, it will look for it relative to the base URL, instead of relative to the location from which it actually loaded the document. The format for the **<BASE>** tag is:

```
<BASE HREF="URL">
```

Table 7.4 summarizes the <A> tag syntax.

Preformatted and Other Special Paragraph Types

HTML supports three special "block" formats. Any normal text within a block format is supposed to appear in a distinctive font.

Table 7.4 **<A>** Tag Syntax Options

To	Use
Link to another document	<A HREF="URL">highlighted anchor text</A>
Name an anchor	<A NAME="AnchorName">normal text</>
Link to a named anchor in this document	<A HREF="#AnchorName">highlighted anchor text</A>
Link to a named anchor in another document	<A HREF="URL#AnchorName">highlighted anchor text</A>

<BLOCKQUOTE> ... </BLOCKQUOTE> Tag

The block quote sets an extended quotation off from normal text. That is, a **<BLOCKQUOTE>** tag pair does not imply indented, single-spaced, and italicized; rather, it's just meant to change the default, plain text font. The format for this tag is:

```
<BLOCKQUOTE>text</BLOCKQUOTE>
```

<PRE> ... </PRE> Tag

Everything in a preformatted block will appear in a monospaced font. The **<PRE>** tag pair is also the only HTML element that pays attention to the line breaks in the source file; any line break in a preformatted block will be treated just as a **
** elsewhere. Since HTML tags can be used within a preformatted block, you can have anchors as well as bold or italic monospaced text. The format for this tag is:

```
<PRE WIDTH=value>text</PRE>
```

The initial **<PRE>** tag has an optional **WIDTH=** parameter. Browsers won't trim lines to this length; the intent is to allow the browser to select a monospaced font that will allow the maximum line length to fit in the browser window.

<ADDRESS> ... </ADDRESS> Tag

The third block format is the address format: <ADDRESS>. This is generally displayed in italics, and is intended for displaying information about a document, such as creation date, revision history, and how to contact the author. Official style guides say that every document should provide an address block. The format for this tag is:

```
<ADDRESS>text</ADDRESS>
```

Many people put a horizontal rule, **<HR>**, between the body of the document and the address block. If you include a link to your home page or to a page that lets the reader send mail to you, you won't have to include a lot of information on each individual page.

Using Tables

Features like lists are great for organizing data; however, sometimes you need a more compact way of grouping related data. Fortunately, some of the newer browsers like Netscape have implemented the proposed HTML 3 specification for tables. Tables can contain a heading and row and column data. Each unit of a table is called a cell, and cell data can be text and images.

<TABLE> ... </TABLE> Tag

This tag is used to define a new table. All of the table-specific tags must be placed within the pair **<TABLE> ... </TABLE>**, otherwise they will be ignored. The format for the **<TABLE>** tag is:

```
<TABLE BORDER>table text</TABLE>
```

Leaving out the **BORDER** modifier will display the table without a border.

Creating a Table Title

Creating a title or caption for a table is easy with the **<CAPTION>** tag. This tag must be placed within the **<TABLE> ... </TABLE>** tags. Here is its general format:

```
<CAPTION ALIGN=top|bottom>caption text</CAPTION>
```

Notice that you can display the caption at the top or bottom of the table. By default, the caption will be displayed at the top of the table.

Creating Table Rows

Every table you create will have one or more rows. (Otherwise, it won't be much of a table!) The simple tag for creating a row is:

```
<TR>text</TR>
```

For each row that you want to add, you must place the **<TR>** tag inside the body of the table, between the **<TABLE> ... </TABLE>** tags.

Defining Table Data Cells

Within each <TR> ... </TR> tag pair comes one or more <TD> tags to define the table cell data. You can think of the cell data as the column definitions for the table. Here is the format for a <TD> tag:

```
<TD  ALIGN=left|center|right
     VALIGN=top|middle|bottom|baseline
     NOWRAP
     COLSPAN=number
     ROWSPAN=number>
text</TD>
```

The size for each cell is determined by the width or height of the data that is displayed. The **ALIGN** parameter can be used to center or left- or right-justify the data displayed in the cell. The **VALIGN** parameter, on the other hand, specifies how the data will align vertically. If you don't want the text to wrap within the cell, you can include the **NOWRAP** modifier.

When defining a cell, you can manually override the width and height of the cell by using the **COLSPAN** and **ROWSPAN** parameters. **COLSPAN** specifies the number of columns the table cell will span and the **ROWSPAN** specifies the number of rows to span. The default setting for each of the parameters is 1.

Defining Headings for Cells

In addition to displaying a table caption, you can include headings for a table's data cells. The tag for defining a heading looks very similar to the <TD> tag:

```
<TH  ALIGN=left|center|right
     VALIGN=top|middle|bottom|baseline
     NOWRAP
     COLSPAN=number
     ROWSPAN=number>
 text</TH>
```

Here's an example of HTML used to create a table:

```
<TABLE BORDER>
          <CAPTION ALIGN=top>Table example</CAPTION>
          <TH ALIGN=left>Column 1</TH>
          <TH ALIGN=left COLSPAN=2>This column spans two column
    widths</TH>
          <TR>
               <TD>row 1 column 1 </TD>
               <TD ROWSPAN=2>spans rows 1 and 2 in column 2</TD>
```

```
                    <TD>row 1 column 3</TD>
        <TR>
                    <TD>row 2 column 1</TR>
                    <TD>row 2 column 3</TR>
    </TABLE>
```

Figure 7.5 shows how this table looks when it's displayed in Netscape.

Helpful HTML Resources

In this section, we've provided several Web sites that can help you learn HTML and create killer Web pages.

Creating Net sites
http://www.netscape.com/assist/net_sites/index.html

A Guide to HTML and CGI scripts
http://snowwhite.it.brighton.ac.uk/~mas/mas/courses/html/html.html

HTML Authoring Guides
http://www.chem.uidaho.edu/html-info.html

Introduction to HTML (a Nice Tutorial)
http://www.cwru.edu/help/introHTML/toc.html

HTML Guides
http://www.sbcc.cc.ca.us/web/htmlinfo.html

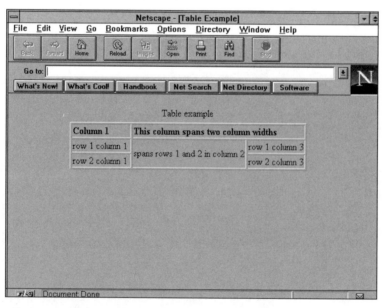

Figure 7.5 A sample table as it appears in Netscape.

Getting Your Home Page Published on the Web

Now that you've learned how to create Web pages, you're ready to publish your work on the Web. Most service providers provide publishing services through the use of a Unix shell account that can be accessed from your computer through a terminal emulation session using a Telnet utility. Another alternative is the use of an independent Web space provider.

Most service providers will supply you with the necessary instructions for getting your home page placed on their system. You may even be able to find information on the provider's home page. If you can't find the information you need, give your provider a call.

More than likely, your service provider will charge you a monthly fee based on the space that your HTML documents take up on their computer and the traffic volume or number of times your home page is visited. That's another good reason why you should avoid using extremely large image files.

Typically, getting your HTML documents on your provider's computer is a three-step process:

1. You need to create a directory under your home directory (on your provider's computer) to store your documents. This directory might have a name like *public_html*. This is the directory where the Web server goes to retrieve your files. Your service provider will give you the details on how to properly set up this directory and how to set the permissions.

2. You will need to name your home page using a predetermined name. Remember that Unix uses different filename conventions than DOS and Windows. Unix is case sensitive.

3. Upload your home page and other documents to your newly created directory.

Registering Your Home Page

A home page isn't much good if no one can find it. In addition to including the URL of your home page on your resume and in your email, you'll need to submit the URL of your home page to various search engines so that, when people search for keywords (such as "resume"), they will retrieve a link to your page.

You can do this by going to the home pages of each of the search engines, such as Lycos, Infoseek, and WebCrawler (you can get to these by clicking on "Net Search" in Netscape), or you can use a service that does it for you.

Several services are available for submitting your pages to search engines. Some of them will charge you, but we recommend using a service like "Submit It!" With Submit It!, a free service, you'll be asked to fill out the provided form with such information as the title of your site, the URL, a search category, keywords, your email address, and a brief description of your page. Spend some time deciding which keywords to use, as they will determine when your URL will be retrieved in response to a user's Net search. For more information on keywords, refer to Chapter 5.

Submit It! can be found on the Web at http://www.submit-it.com/.

8

Bulletin Board Systems: Hidden Job Opportunities

CHAPTER 8 TOPICS

Schmoozing online doesn't have to be limited to the Internet. Thousands of privately run bulletin board systems are in operation around the world, and they provide a great way to meet people and exchange job information.

What are BBSes?

A Bulletin Board System (BBS) is basically a computer connected to a phone line that runs special BBS software. The person who owns the computer and maintains the BBS is referred to as the *sysop* (slang for system operator). The BBS software allows the sysop's computer to accept modem calls from other people, and allows people to log onto the sysop's computer just as if they were logging onto the Internet or an online service.

We Thought You Should Know...

While certain online services, such as Prodigy, call their special interest groups "bulletin boards," when we use that term, we mean actual bulletin board systems operated by private parties.

BBSes were around long before the Internet became popular, and are often run out of the homes of computer hobbyists who maintain their BBSes because they enjoy doing so, not because they're trying to make a profit. So most BBSes are a bargain (usually free) for users.

What Do BBSes Have to Offer?

What a specific BBS has to offer depends on what the sysop wants to provide, what kind of BBS it is (job BBS, adult BBS, etc.), and what kind of software the sysop uses. Some BBSes offer pictures and sound files, and others offer email and Internet access.

Below, we've listed some of the BBS features that will matter most to job hunters. We won't waste your time by giving you specific instructions on how to use these features because they will be different on different systems. Don't worry that you'll be lost and confused when you call up a BBS for the first time. One of the benefits of BBSes is that they are graphical, although not as colorful as Web sites, and in most cases self-explanatory. You just have to follow instructions.

Free Software

Many BBSes are excellent distribution channels for free software. Did you know that Doom, id Software's wildy popular shoot-'em-up computer game, was first made available on a BBS? It's true, but how does this tidbit help you as a job hunter? Doom certainly won't help you find a job, but knowing that professional-grade software is available from BBSes *can* help. You might find software that you can use to improve your resume, improve your knowledge of your career field, or simply improve productivity in your everyday life.

News and Information

General information available on BBSes can include stock prices, community calendars, weather forecasts, and more. If, for example, you are interested in local PRSA (Public Relations Society of America) conferences, you might be able to find dates and times in a particular BBS's news and information section. You might also discover information about local job fairs, local company information, and more.

Public Forums and Chat Areas

These are the most useful BBS areas for job hunters because they provide another way to schmooze online. Public forums are the equivalent to Usenet newsgroups on the Internet. You can choose to enter into certain topics of conversation, and then participate in conversations by posting messages and responding to other participants' messages.

When you "chat" on a BBS, you're actually carrying on a real-time conversation with someone else over the modem line. They see your words as you type them, and you see theirs. It's similar to making a phone call, except you use the keyboard instead of your voice.

Electronic Mail

Most BBSes provide email, at least to the extent that you can send messages to other users of the BBS. So, just because a BBS sysop says his or her service provides email, don't assume this means Internet email. It usually doesn't—at least not if it's *free* email.

Internet Access

Some BBSes offer limited Internet access for a fee, typically email-only access or access to newsgroups. If you want to get your feet wet using email or newsgroups, using a BBS that offers these features is a good place to start.

Why Care about BBSes When You Have the World Wide Web?

True, BBSes are not quite as popular as the Web or other online services. They aren't as glitzy and they don't usually advertise on TV during the Super Bowl. And, frankly, they won't offer you as many resources for your job search as the Web, but there are several reasons you should consider trying a few bulletin boards.

Local Interest

First, most BBSes cater to the local community (although they certainly will allow out of state or even international access to callers who are willing to pay the long-distance charges). If you're interested in finding a job in your area, dial up your neighborhood BBS. If it has a job opportunities or help wanted area, you're literally in business. Also, most BBSes have public forums and chat capabilities, so you can communicate with other people in your area. You can schmooze, network, and generally have a good time.

What if you're interested in working in a different city? Let's say that you've always wanted to live in San Francisco. You could then go to the newsstand and buy the current issue of *Boardwatch*, a magazine specifically dedicated to bulletin board systems. Look up San Francisco, find a BBS, and dial it up. Yes, you'll be paying long distance charges, but now you have instant access to San Francisco's community news, people who live there, and more. It's like using newsgroups, but with BBSes you can specifically target your audience within the city of your choice.

Job Boards

Some bulletin board systems, which we'll list later in this chapter, exist solely to help people find jobs. Some offer toll-free numbers, although this is an exception rather than a rule, but most offer job postings and allow you to email or post a resume. Most job postings include a postal address for resumes and cover letters.

Finding a BBS That Matches Your Needs

As we mentioned earlier, you can find lists of bulletin board systems in special BBS magazines such as *Boardwatch*, which you can pick up at your local bookstore or newsstand. *Computer Shopper Magazine*, also found on newsstands, also publishes lists of BBSes. For more information, or if all else fails, you can also get lists of BBSes from:

- *The Internet.* Use one of the Web's search engines (see Chapter 2) and search for specific BBS information. For instance, you could conduct a search for "Texas bulletin boards" or "BBS software development."

- *Your local computer newspaper or magazine.* If your city (or the city that you're interested in) has a local computer magazine or a computer section in the local newspaper, you'll probably be able to find BBS numbers and information there.

- *Your local computer society or users group.* The sysops of local BBSes are usually members of their local users group, so give the group a call or attend a meeting or two, and ask around.

Connecting to a BBS

Connecting to a BBS is simple. To do so, you need a modem and communications software (Figure 8.1), which usually comes with the modem. In most BBS listings in magazines and newspapers, you'll also see what appears to be a strange code next to each BBS name. These are the log on *communications parameters*, a fancy way to describe the way two modems "handshake" so they can exchange information. Parameters usually include the number of data bits, the parity bit (even, odd, or none), and the number of stop bits.

Don't worry about the meaning of these terms: a few examples should help you get the hang of this. For instance, 8-N-1 means 8 data bits, no parity, and 1 stop bit (this is rapidly becoming the standard set of modem parameters). If you see 7-E-1, that means 7 data bits, even parity, and one stop bit. Your communication software will include a menu option and a dialog box for setting these parameters. Many BBS listings will also include a maximum modem speed, but since most BBS host computers today have at least a 14.4 Kbps modem, this maximum speed usually won't be important. On the other hand, if *you're* still using a 2400 Kbps or 9600 Kbps modem, you really should upgrade to a faster modem.

After you've set your communication parameters, you're ready to connect. To log on, follow these steps:

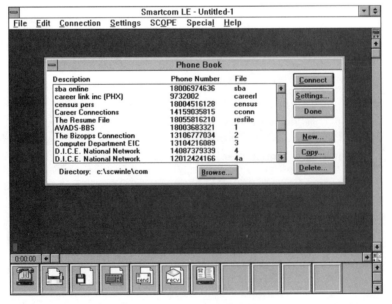

Figure 8.1   Smartcom LE for Windows' Phone Book.

1. Make sure your telecommunications software is open and active.
2. Open its dialing directory.
3. If the phone number you want to dial is not already in the dialing directory's phone book, add the number.
4. Highlight the number and click on the dial or connect command. With some software, the dial command will be an icon; with other communications software, you might simply highlight the number and press Enter.

After your computer dials and connects to the BBS host computer, you'll be asked to type your name and give your password (or to choose a password if it's your first time on the board). If the BBS charges a usage fee, you'll be requested to provide a credit card number. It's up to you to decide whether you want to do this.

After you've entered a password and have been admitted, you'll be taken to the Welcome Screen (Figure 8.2), which is similar to a home page on the Web. This screen identifies the BBS with things like logos, announcements, recent changes, or maybe the BBS's mission.

When you've finished reading the Welcome Screen, you'll go to the Bulletin Menu, which is where you'll find the information about the BBS: frequently asked questions, who uses the BBS, rules of conduct, and more. The Bulletin Menu may also list the files that have changed since the last time you logged on.

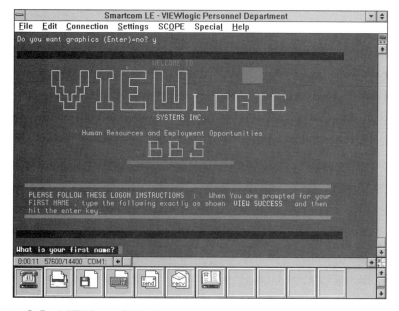

Figure 8.2 VIEWlogic BBS' Welcome Screen.

From the Bulletin Menu, you'll be able to go to the Main Menu, which is where you'll make most of your navigation decisions (Figure 8.3). When you type in a command, usually a letter or a symbol displayed in the Main Menu, you'll be taken to the BBS area of your choice.

Speed

When you connect to a BBS, the maximum baud rate will depend not only on the speed of *your* modem, but on the speed of the sysop's modem, too. For instance, if you have a 14,400 bps modem, but the sysop has a 2,400 bps modem, you'll connect at 2,400 bps.

Job BBSes

Now that you know some BBS basics and how to log on, it's time to try a few of the job-related BBSes we've found. Some of these BBSes offer more than one phone number; so use the number that will be the least expensive for you, or if the main number is busy, try the alternate. Keep in mind that BBSes can change as often as Web pages, so some of the information in this chapter may have changed by the time you read this.

Before dialing a BBS for the first time, set your communications parameters to 8-N-1, or to "Zmodem" if you have this option (Zmodem detects and adjusts parameters automatically).

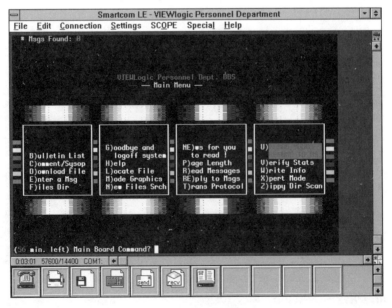

Figure 8.3 The Main Menu of VIEWlogic BBS.

Access America
Modem: 918-747-2542

Access America BBS in Tulsa, Oklahoma, has job-related Usenet newsgroups and Internet email, and it allows you to upload your resume. There is no fee.

The Ad Connection
Modem: 804-978-3927

This BBS in Charlottesville, Virginia, contains classified ads and federal job listings. There is no fee.

Advanced R&D's Pipeline
Modem: 407-894-0580

Located in Orlando, Florida, Advanced R&D's Pipeline contains job listings for the Midwest and Southeast. You can also upload your resume, and there is no fee.

Analysts International Corp.
Modem: 214-263-9161

The AIC BBS contains computer job listings for contract positions in the Dallas/Ft. Worth area. There is no fee.

AVADS-BBS
Modem: 800-366-3321

This is the Automated Vacancy Announcement Information Center, which lists jobs for the Department of the Interior. You'll get information on job vacancies for up to ten bureaus without having to pay a fee.

The Bizopps Connection
Modem: 310- 677-7034

This information service has a searchable database of business listings and franchise opportunities, venture capital sources, and money-making opportunities. There is a charge for this BBS.

Bust Out BBS
Modem: 510-888-1443

Bust Out BBS in Hayward, California, is an echo of JobNet, which has nationwide job listings. There is a fee.

CapAccess Career Center
Modem: 202-785-1523

This is the National Capital Area Public Access Network in Washington, D.C. A free BBS, it contains job information for the National Institutes of Health, National Science Foundation, Federal Government, and more. To access, log in as "guest" and use "visitor" as the password.

Career Connections
Modem: 415-903-5815
         415-903-5840

This Los Altos, California, BBS lists worldwide job opportunities and does not charge a fee. You can also Telnet to career.com.

Career Connections
Modem: 414-258-0164

Career Connections BBS, in Wauwatosa, Wisconsin, offers employment opportunities for job seekers and employers. There is no fee.

Career Systems Online
Modem: 413-592-9208

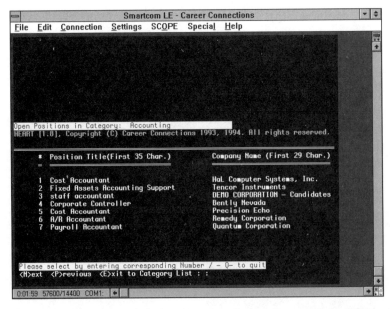

Figure 8.4 *Accounting job listings on the Career Connections BBS in California.*

This Chicopee, Massachusetts, BBS lists a variety of job openings and allows you to upload your resume. There is no fee.

Careers BBS
Modem: 305-828-5697

Careers BBS includes national forums, Internet email, and local and national areas for reading and posting employment classifieds. There is no fee.

Careers First, Inc. of NJ
Modem: 609-786-2666
         609-786-2667
         215-676-5528

This New Jersey BBS lists employment opportunities for computer and miscellaneous positions. You can upload your resume and get job-hunting tips. There is no fee.

Careers On-line
Modem: 508-879-4700

Careers On-line is the job BBS for the Framingham, Massachusetts-based *Computer World* newspaper. There is no fee, and the BBS includes an online resume board.

Census Personnel Board
Modem: 800-451-6128

This board is operated by the U.S. Department of Commerce Bureau of the Census. Job listings are for Suitland, Maryland only.

Chicago Syslink
Modem: 708-795-4442
         708-795-4485
         708-795-4456

Chicago Syslink lists Help Wanted-USA job listings nationwide and offers Internet email. There is a fee.

City of Fort Worth Information Center
Modem: 817-871-8612

This Texas BBS contains job openings in various areas and miscellaneous information about the Fort Worth area. There is no fee.

Computer Careers
Modem: 704-554-1102

Computer Careers, in Charlotte, North Carolina, specializes in computer, and specifically data processing, jobs nationwide.

Computer Department EIC
Modem: 310-677-7034

This California BBS provides information on computer consulting and secretarial jobs. There is no fee.

Computer Jobs BBS
Modem: 817-268-2193

This BBS is operated by Data Processing Careers, Inc. in Bedford, Texas and lists Texas jobs only. There is no fee.

Condell Online
Modem: 803-686-3465

Condell Online, based in Hilton Head, South Carolina, has job listings for people in the title insurance industry. It also offers free access to the Employment Exchange section.

Contractors Exchange
Modem: 415-334-7393

Contractors Exchange in San Francisco lists construction-type contractor jobs, and doesn't charge a fee.

Delight the Customer
Modem: 517-797-3740
　　　　　616-662-0393

This BBS in Hudsonville, Michigan, focuses on customer service, training, and the help desk profession. It has job information for the manager level and above. There is a fee.

Detroit Service Center
Modem: 313-226-4423

The Detroit Service Center BBS is operated by the U.S. Office of Personnel Management in Detroit, Michigan. It lists jobs and job information for the Detroit area.

DICE National Network
Modem: 201-242-4166
        214-782-0960
        408-737-9339
        515-280-3423
        708-782-0969

DICE specializes in nationwide contract and permanent jobs, and allows you to fill out a keyword-searchable questionnaire. There is no fee.

Digital X-Connect BBS
Modem: 214-517-8443
        214-517-8315

Digital X is based in Dallas, and lists opportunities nationwide. It also has a BBS listing of all other BBSes that carry the JobNet echo nationwide.

We Thought You Should Know...

An *echo* is a duplication of an original newsgroup or listing. For instance, imagine that EmployNet is a group of job listings that resides on the NewJob BBS. If other BBSes get permission from the NewJob BBS to also carry EmployNet, the EmployNet is an echo. An echo is basically the same as a *mirror* site on the Internet.

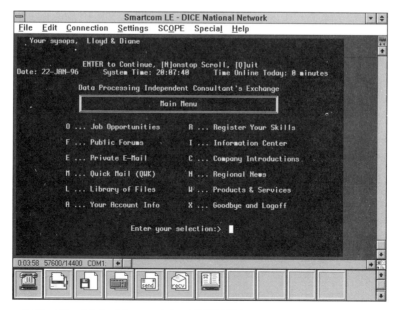

Figure 8.5 *The Main Menu of the DICE BBS.*

Doc's Place
Modem: 309-682-6560

Located in Illinois, this BBS lists employment opportunities in various fields in the medical technical area.

DP NETwork (Toner Corp.)
Modem: 415-788-7101
           415-788-8663

DP NETwork is a good source of desktop publishing jobs in the San Francisco and Sacramento areas of California. There is no fee.

ECCO BBS
Modem: 212-580-4510
           312-404-8685

This BBS offers East Coast Consulting Opportunities for technical positions, does not charge a fee, and offers Internet email.

Employer's Network
Modem: 206-475-0665
           206-471-7575

Based in Tacoma, Washington, Employer's Network has Internet job listings, federal job listings, local job listings, resume programs, and a resume database. There is no fee.

Employment Board
Modem: 619-689-1348
           619-993-9319

The Employment Board includes a job opportunities database, which lists openings mostly in the San Diego area, and an employment database that gives you employment statistics.

Employment Connection
Modem: 508-537-1862

The Employment Connection lists various job positions in Leominster, Massachusetts, and other areas on the East Coast.

The Employment Line BBS
Modem: 508-865-7928

In Sutton, Massachusetts, this BBS lists various job opportunities in all areas, mostly on the East Coast. There is a fee.

Enginet
Modem: 513-858-2688

This is a referral service for engineers in Fairfield, Ohio. It has an online job placement system that helps engineers and employers in meeting job needs. It also includes Internet email and Usenet newsgroups.

Environet
Modem: 415-512-9108
         415-512-9120

Environet is a free BBS that lists job openings with Greenpeace. Most jobs are in the U.S. The second number above supports 28.8 Kbps.

Exec-PC BBS
Modem: 414-789-4210
Exec-PC BBS in Wisconsin provides E-Span job search access and a large variety of job listings in all areas. There is no fee.

Executive Connection
Modem: 214-306-3393

This Dallas BBS gives information about careers, employment, and business management. It also lists local and national job openings in all occupations.

Federal Jobline
Modem: 818-575-6521

Los Angeles' Federal Jobline is for the Federal Job Information Center, operated by OPM. It contains federal job listings and information for the Western region. There is no fee.

FedWorld
Modem: 703-321-8020

Fedworld lists job openings all over the world for the National Technical Information Service. It also has a gateway to more than 100 other government BBSes. There is no fee. You can also find FedWorld on the Web at http://www.fedworld.gov.

FirstStep
Modem: 404-642-0665

FirstStep is an Atlanta BBS with an employment database, Telnet capability, and links to Usenet newsgroups. It contains job listings for approximately 100 occupations. There is no fee.

Figure 8.6 The Main Menu for the Fedworld BBS.

FJOB BBS
Modem: 912-757-3100

This is the Macon, Georgia, Federal Job Information Center BBS. It contains federal job listings and information for all of the U.S. There is no fee. On the Internet, you can also Telnet to fjob.mail.opm.gov.

FORTUNE Consultants of Orlando
Modem: 407-875-1028

This Maitland, Florida, BBS is free and includes job listings for various occupations. You can also upload your resume.

Georgia Online
Modem: 404-591-0777

Operated by Foster Employment Services in Atlanta, Georgia, Online features job listings, resume databases, Help Wanted-USA service, Internet email, and newsgroups. There is a fee.

Global Trade Net
Modem: 415-668-0422

Global Trade Net is an international trade forum and offers help for starting a new business. There is no fee.

hi-TEC BBS
Modem: 512-475-4893

This Austin BBS has the Governor's Job Bank, which includes information on job placement services, unemployment compensation, and employment law. It also lists job openings within several Texas state agencies. There is no fee.

Index Systems TBBS
Modem: 404-591-8414
          404-924-8474
          706-613-0566

Located in Atlanta, Georgia, Index Systems TBBS provides high-tech job listings, job hotlines, job hunting software, and networking information. There is a fee.

INFO-Line
Modem: 908-922-4742

INFO-Line is an Oakhurst, New Jersey, BBS that contains job information, primarily from pharmaceutical companies. You can also upload your resume at no charge.

InfoMat BBS
Modem: 714-492-8727

InfoMat, in San Clemente, California, lists job opportunity and franchise information. It also carries echoes for JobNet and job forums. There is no fee.

J-Connection
Modem: 813-791-0101
          703-379-0553
          404-662-5500

This BBS lists jobs in data processing and allows you to post your resume and download job files.

Job & Opportunity Link
Modem: 708-690-9860

The Winfield, Illinois-based Job & Opportunity Link is the home of JOB-LINK and RESUME-LINK. You can download all job listings posted here. There is no fee.

Job Bulletin Board
Modem: 214-612-9925

This Plano, Texas, Job Bulletin Board lists data processing job openings. There is no fee.

JOBBS!
Modem: 707-992-8937

JOBBS! lists jobs from thousands of potential employers in the Southeastern United States, and resumes from about 33,000 job seekers. For $10 a month, you can have your cover letter and resume posted and can access the job listings database. Here, you'll find both technical and non-technical jobs.

JOBS-BBS
Modem: 503-281-6808

Based in Portland, Oregon, the JOBS-BBS lists thousands of open positions all over the U.S. It is regularly updated and is free.

Job Search
Modem: 416-588-9690

This is a free Canadian BBS with job-related information, job postings, and a place to post your resume.

Job Trac BBS
Modem: 214-349-0527

Job Trac, based in Dallas, Texas, provides job listings, resume uploads, and job forums for the Dallas/Fort Worth area. There is no fee.

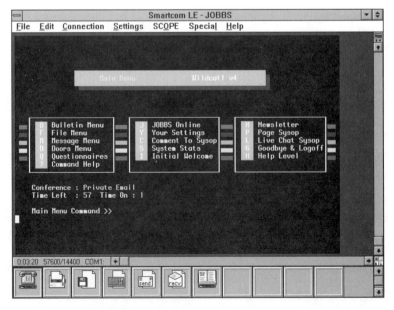

Figure 8.7 The JOBBS! BBS Main Menu.

Kasta, James and Associates BBS
Modem: 612-536-0533

This board lists jobs for MIS and engineering in the Minneapolis metro area. There is no fee.

Lee Johnson International BBS
Modem: 510-787-3191

Based in Crockett, California, this BBS represents a search firm specializing in employer-paid recruiting and placement. There is no fee.

Logikal Career Connection
Modem: 708-420-0424

Logikal Career Connection is an Illinois BBS for data processing professionals. To use the BBS, you need special software, which is downloadable upon your first call.

Matrix Resources
Modem: 214-239-5627

This Dallas BBS has various computer job listings for permanent and contract positions, and allows you to upload your resume. There is no fee.

Mushin BBS
Modem: 619-278-8137

Mushin contains job listings for the San Diego, California, area. There is no fee.

NFB Net
Modem: 410-752-5011

NFB Net, in Baltimore, Maryland, is sponsored by the National Federation for the Blind. It provides information and training materials to assist the blind, and offers services that are designed to help both the job seeker and employer. There is no fee.

National Software Employment
Modem: 800-860-7860

NSE in Burlington, Vermont, contains a job database of more than 15,000 listings for over 17 U.S. cities. There is no fee.

National Technical Search
Modem: 413-549-8136

This BBS is operated by Allen Davis & Associates in Amherst, Massachusetts. It has national job listings, forums, and career guides. There is no fee.

Nebraska Online
Modem: 800-392-7932

Nebraska Online includes jobs for the State of Nebraska and other state-related information. There is no fee.

Network World Online
Modem: 508-620-1178

This BBS is operated by *Network World Magazine*. It contains job listings and information and advice on career and job-related issues. There is no fee.

Online Info Services
Modem: 206-253-5213

Online Info Services BBS is in Vancouver, Washington, and has job listings from FIDONET, ESN (Enterprise System Network), and Usenet. It also has a job broker profile database. There is no fee.

Online Opportunities
Modem: 610-873-7170

This BBS allows you to post your resume, but you have to pay to access job openings. It provides access to Help Wanted-USA, carries career information, program, and job hotlines. You can post your resume free here to the Philadelphia Tri-State area (Pennsylvania, Delaware, and New Jersey).

OPM Atlanta
Modem: 404-730-2370

OPM Atlanta is for the Federal Job Information Center in Atlanta. It includes an online job search facility and downloadable files for all regions. There is no fee.

OPM FEDJOBS- Philadelphia
Modem: 610-580-2216

This BBS is operated by the Office of Personnel Management and is the source for open federal government jobs and training schedules. There is no fee.

OPM Mainstreet
Modem: 202-606-4800

Based in Washington, D.C., OPM Mainstreet is operated by the Office of Personnel Management. It contains information for government employees, but also has a gateway to other federal job information centers. There is no fee.

ouT therE BBS
Modem: 408-263-2248

ouT therE lists contract and permanent jobs for the San Francisco Bay area. There is no fee.

Pacific Rim
Modem: 619-278-7361

Pacific Rim has job listings from Usenet newsgroups and offers Internet email. There is a fee.

Praedo BBS
Modem: 609-953-0769

This New Jersey BBS has federal job listings and job listings for senior executives and CEOs. It also features tips on resume writing. There is no fee.

Project Enable
Modem: 304-759-0727

Project Enable, in Cross Lanes, West Virginia, is sponsored by the President's Committee on Employment of People with Disabilities. It has job information and help guides for the disabled. There is no fee.

RadioComm
Modem: 708-518-8336

This Park Ridge, Illinois, BBS is for people in the radio broadcasting field. It includes job information and industry news. There is a fee.

The Resume File
Modem: 805-575-6521
        805-581-6210

In Simi Valley, California, this BBS is a comprehensive list of thousands of job postings nationwide. It also has job-related areas with job hunting information and tips, and government job information. There is no fee.

RHost
Modem: 404-392-9164

This BBS is operated by Robert Half in Atlanta, Georgia, and contains job listings in all areas. There is no fee.

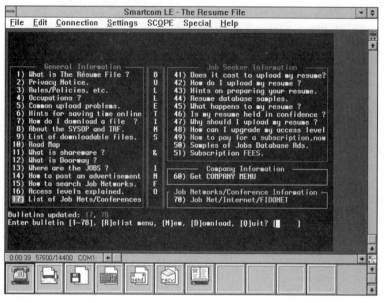

Figure 8.8   The Main Menu for the Resume File BBS.

SAK Consulting BBS
Modem: 703-715-1016

SAK is a Reston, Virginia, BBS with lists of federal job openings, specialized search programs, and national and overseas job listings. There is a fee.

SBA-Online
Modem: 800-697-4636

This is the Small Business Administration BBS, which is free and provides Internet email. You can also access this BBS through the Internet gopher (gopher:// www.sbaonline.sba.gov).

Society for Technical Communications
Modem: 703-522-3299

Located in Washington, D.C., this board is for technical writers only. It is a free service that lists job opportunities for STC members only.

TAG On-Line Career Bank
Modem: 610-969-3845

This BBS is in Philadelphia and includes information on more than 40 job-oriented conferences, nationwide job listings (and some from Japan), employment help, an online resume area, and more. There is a fee.

Techtips BBS
Modem: 615-662-5712

Techtips, in Nashville, Tennessee, has a biomedical/imaging service forum with job-related files. It also provides Internet email and newsgroup access. There is a fee.

Turning Point
Modem: 512-219-7848
        512-703-4400

This BBS is based in Austin, and carries job listings from the Usenet newsgroups, Internet email, and more. There is no fee.

Unicom Info Services
Modem: 614-538-9250
        614-538-0548

Based in Columbus, Ohio, this BBS serves as an information exchange for entrepreneurs, managers, and business professionals. It's a networking tool that also provides Internet email and Usenet newsgroups. There is a fee for expanded access.

U.S. Department of Labor
Modem: 212-219-4784

In Washington, D.C., this BBS allows you to download federal job opportunity files at no charge.

Vanguard Chronicle Network
Modem: 305-524-4411

This Florida BBS lists jobs for hospital positions in nursing, administration, and more. You can also upload your resume, and you can get information on business employment, the community, and health in general. To use this BBS, you have to download special software, which you can obtain upon your first call.

VIEWlogic Personnel Department
Modem: 508-480-8769

Located in Marlboro, Massachusetts, this BBS lists VIEWlogic System, Inc.'s human resources and employment opportunities. It contains career opportunities for California and Massachusetts, allows you to upload your resume, and gives you benefits and contact information. There is no fee.

Virginia Employment Comm.
Modem: 804-371-6521

Virginia Employment has military, federal, state, international, and regional job openings in all occupations. There is no fee.

WASNET
Modem: 202-606-1113
              202-606-1848 (voice number)

This is a Washington-state BBS with federal and recruitment-related information. Before you can use the BBS, you must call the voice number. There is no fee.

Window on the State Government BBS
Modem: 800-227-8392 (in Texas only)

Window on the State is operated by the Texas State Comptroller's office, and contains a variety of information and a gateway to other state BBSes. There is no fee.

9

Been There, Done That: Straight Talk from Job-Hunting Experts

CHAPTER 9 TOPICS

CORPORATE RECRUITERS TELL IT LIKE IT IS

RECRUITERS' PET PEEVES

COVER LETTER HELP

EXPERIENCES OF A REAL JOB HUNTER

RESEARCHING THE COMPANY

This chapter is kind of a grab bag of job-hunting information and do's and don'ts. Actually, we could easily have devoted several chapters that explain what we think companies are looking for in employees, and what kinds of experiences you'll probably have while you're looking for a job. But why take our word for it? Instead, we'll provide you with information straight from the people who are actually doing the hiring, and from people who have made it their full-time business to advise job hunters.

In particular, we'll give you important advice and inside information directly from the human resources people at top companies. Plus, you'll get online and general job-hunting tips from industry experts like Bradley Richardson, author of *JobSmarts for Twentysomethings* and president of BGR Group Inc., a training and consulting firm that helps corporations and colleges incorporate JobSmarts™ skills among their employees and students. You'll also get valuable advice from Terry Devlin, a career counselor at Career Management International, and from Damir Joseph Stimac, the Internet's first syndicated career columnist. We'll also list resume and cover-letter writing tips from two top university writing centers, and describe the real-life experiences of an online job hunter.

Corporate Recruiters Tell It Like It Is

We sent questionnaires to more than 100 of the top companies on the Web, asking them about their online hiring practices, and what they think about online job hunting and job seekers in general. Some of what they told us confirms what we may have mentioned in earlier chapters, but some of their advice surprised even us. No information is more valuable than the suggestions of the people who actually are responsible for hiring.

Will I Be Able to Find "Regular" Jobs Online?

"Interestingly enough," said John Jamieson, Personnel Manager at Blueridge Technologies, "we've had greater response from the marketing position listings at our Web site than the technical position listings." Figure 9.1 shows one of Blueridge's non-technical job postings.

In Chapter 4, we listed the types of positions that employment Web pages advertise, and we saw positions ranging from administrative assistants to computer programmers. Most human resources people at companies we contacted post online ads for a variety of jobs, regardless of whether they are technical or non-technical. This includes marketing positions, sales, project management, finance, and more.

Kristine McLaughlin of Symantec Corporation is one of those human resources people. Symantec holds an online cyberfair, and regularly posts jobs at CareerMosaic. "We have noticed a tremendous increase in the amount of resumes we receive; the

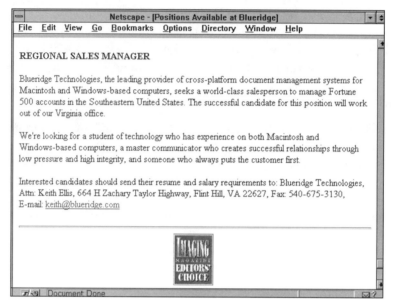

Figure 9.1   A non-technical job posting at Blueridge Technologies.

number of non-technical types of people has actually become larger than the technical. Last year at this time we received 10 to 15 resumes each month. Just this weekend I received 76!"

What Happens Next if a Company Is Interested?

Aaron Privan, editor of ClariNet Communications Corporation (Figure 9.2), is not only responsible for hiring online, but got his job as a result of his online job search. "We tend to treat candidates the same as if they had responded to a job ad in the newspaper: Call them and ask them to come in for a regular interview. The major advantage on the Internet is one of space, which allows us to be much more complete about what the job entails."

We wondered if companies conducted real-time, online interviews with prospective employees. The answer is, for the most part, "no, not yet." While a few companies do this, most still use traditional methods of following up.

Because the Internet tends to connect employers and job hunters in different parts of the country, or even the world, phone interviews tend to be the next step in the hiring process. Then, if the phone interview goes well, the candidate will be scheduled for a face-to-face interview.

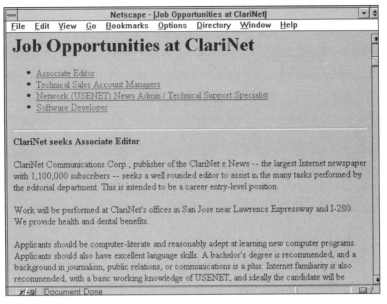

Figure 9.2 Job openings with ClariNet Communications.

Why Do Recruiters Use Online Hiring Methods?

Sheila Marinucci, a Senior Recruiter and Employment Manager for Sun Microsystems (Figure 9.3), knows that online hiring works. "The cost of online advertising is the

Figure 9.3 Sun Microsystems' employment page.

least expensive for the employer, and it's fast. Results allow the employment department to continue justifying the use of the Net. Sun Microsystems has been recruiting online for about ten years."

The Internet is also faster and easier for the job hunter. In some cases, candidates can hear back from the prospective employer in less than an hour.

Caroline Kohout, Human Resources Coordinator for General Magic (Figure 9.4), stresses this point. "The lines of communication on the Internet are much faster and more efficient than those of more traditional methods, such as newspapers or employment agencies. With a bit of training and access to the Web, you can peruse many different companies' Web sites, check out their job listings, and submit all necessary information much more quickly than you could using other traditional methods."

John Jamieson, Blueridge Technologies: "Online job searching gives both job hunters and employers greater exposure to each other, and it benefits job hunters by increasing the likelihood that they will find jobs matching their capabilities and desires."

And from a Microsoft recruiter: "The advantage of the Internet is that you are able to search more quickly and cover more ground. In addition, a job hunter is able to find out much more about the company via a Web site than through a newspaper ad. If I had to choose only one source, and I was looking for a professional job, I would use the Internet."

Microsoft's campus recruiting page is shown in Figure 9.5.

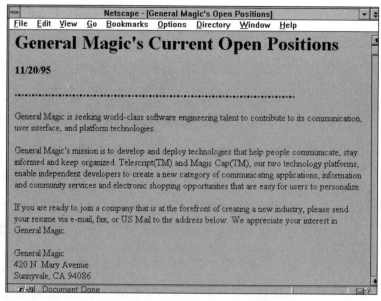

Figure 9.4 The employment area for General Magic.

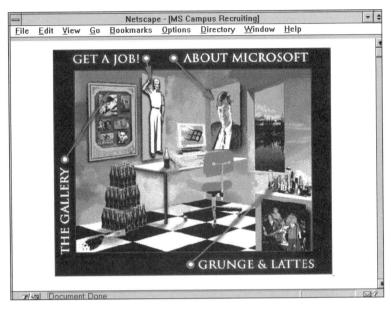

Figure 9.5 *Microsoft campus recruiting page.*

What Keywords Should You Include in Your Resume?

"We look for the same things in electronic resumes that we look for in paper resumes," said a Microsoft recruiter. "Relevant work experience, knowledge of specific technologies, and appropriate educational background." Almost everyone we interviewed agreed about the types of keywords they search for in a resume:

- Skill set
- Experience
- Time in a position
- Education
- Location objectives
- Programming languages
- Education (four-year degree, MBA, etc.)
- A reference to a particular job listing
- Names of positions

- Specific work experience in technologies

- Interests

According to Jamieson (Blueridge Technologies), "Our technical positions have explicit training or experience requirements (Unix, Oracle, Informix, Mac, and so on), and meeting these requirements is the first gate in our search process. Level of experience and how recent the experience is both are qualifying factors."

What Are Recruiters' Pet Peeves?

Recruiters were more than happy to share their online job hunting pet peeves, and many of these recruiters agreed that a lot of prospective employees run into the same problems and make the same mistakes. Take this opportunity to learn from their mistakes.

PROOFREAD AND SPELL-CHECK YOUR RESUMES AND COVER LETTERS

"Responding online doesn't mean you can be sloppy and forego grammar," said Delorme Mapping Human Resources Manager, Elizabeth MacLaren (Figure 9.6). "Make sure you proofread and spell-check your resumes and cover letters just as you would if you were responding in hard copy."

We can't emphasize this enough. In many cases, resumes with typos go directly into the trash or, in the case of online resumes, get deleted. If you use your cover letter as a

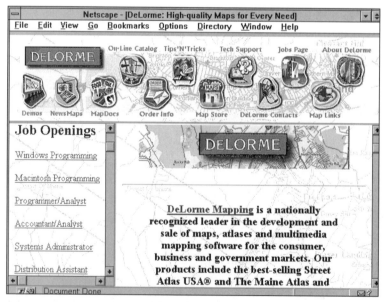

Figure 9.6 The Delorme Mapping job page.

template, making modifications to tailor your letter to the specific expectations of different employers, make sure you proofread each letter carefully. One individual sent a cover letter to The Coriolis Group, seeking employment as an editor. The letter read well and the candidate seemed qualified, until we reached the last line of the letter: "In closing, I would like to stress again that I will be a great asset to Macmillan Publishing."

Huh? Obviously, this particular job candidate forgot to change the closing line of her cover letter template from "Macmillan Publishing" to "The Coriolis Group." This oversight is all the more disastrous when you realize that Macmillan is a direct competitor of Coriolis!

DON'T OVERESTIMATE YOURSELF

When we say not to overestimate yourself, we just mean that you shouldn't waste a recruiter's time by applying for a job that requires ten years experience as a marketing manager when you have only one or even just three or four. If you have nine and a half years of experience in marketing management, that's a different story. Go ahead and express interest.

"Read the posting and reply only if you're qualified," said Tim Franta of Sun Microsystems. "We get way too many underqualified candidates, especially from colleges."

One of the biggest mistakes a recent graduate can make is flooding the employment market with resumes for jobs he or she doesn't have the correct experience for. If you irritate the recruiter by doing this, chances are you won't even be considered for the jobs that you *are* qualified for.

SPECIFY LOCATION

If you're applying for a job with a company that has offices all over the world, but you don't want to leave the country, say so. You should always mention whether you'll be willing to travel, and whether relocation is an option for you. "Definitely indicate if you are open to relocation or if you have a specific geographic preference," said Sheila Carney of Booz, Allen & Hamilton.

DON'T SEND RESUMES AS ATTACHMENTS

All recruiters agreed with this rule. "We may not have a PostScript printer," said Aaron Priven of ClariNet. "We probably don't have your word processing system, and we might run only Macs or only PCs, or only Unix systems. Resumes and cover letters should be plain ASCII email."

Home Page Tips

The staff at the University of Montana's writing center (http://www.montana.edu/~wwwcp/write.html) has some great tips for creating your career-related home page. Take a look at these suggestions:

- Think about the message your page gives: What are you selling yourself as?

- Which employers are you targeting? What jobs?

- Make the page career-search oriented.

- Include an updated resume as one of your links.

- Include phone number, address, and email address.

- Be sure that what you put on your page is information you're willing to have viewed by anybody with Internet access.

- Don't use too much personal information, such as photos, favorite sports teams, and so on.

- Don't use large graphics. They take too long to download.

- Check all links regularly to make sure they work.

- Always be professional.

Cover Letter Help

Rensselear Polytechnic Institute's writing center staff (http://www.rpi.edu/dept/llc/writecenter/web/text/coverltr.html) offers free information on cover letters. This information is good for both online and traditional cover letters. Here's what they have to say:

> The preliminary application for a professional position generally consists of two documents: a cover letter and a resume. While the resume is a somewhat generic advertisement for yourself, which you may send unaltered to scores of different companies, the cover letter allows you to tailor your application to each specific job. Although the thrust of your various letters may remain the same, there is really no reason to have a single, generic cover letter.

> Each of your cover letters should bear the name and address of the company to which you are applying, and should address by name the specific individual who will process your application [if possible]. Each letter should also make specific references to the company and should indicate your knowledge of and interest in the work the company is currently doing.

> In addition to tailoring your application to a specific job, the cover letter also allows you to highlight the most important and relevant accomplishments, skills, and experience listed in your resume. And it is where (if appropriate) you specifically request an interview.

Finally, remember that your cover letter is, in a very real sense, a schematic of yourself. It reflects your personality, your attention to detail, your communication skills, your enthusiasm, and your intellect. Your cover letter and resume are usually all a prospective employer has to decide whether or not you will reach the next phase in the application process: the interview.

In the first paragraph of your letter, you should state what job you are applying for and how you learned about the job opening. If you have any personal contacts in or with the company, you may want to mention them here. You should also state your general qualifications for the job. This paragraph should be brief, perhaps two or three sentences.

The body of your letter should consist of one to three longer paragraphs in which you expand upon your qualifications for the position. Pick out the most relevant qualifications listed in your resume and discuss them in detail, demonstrating how your background and experience qualify you for the job. Be as specific as possible, and refer the reader to the resume for additional details.

In the concluding paragraph of your letter, you should request an interview (or some other response, if appropriate). State where and when you can be reached, and express your willingness to come to an interview or supply further information. Close by thanking your reader for his or her time and consideration.

Where to Start: Experiences of a Real Job Hunter

The following refers to the online job-hunting experiences of Fisseha H. Mariam:

"I found that most of the job-oriented newsgroups, company home pages, and online resume databases are a very important starting point in conducting a job search. In addition to my home page, I posted my resume on some of the online resume directories, applied to jobs advertised over the newsgroups and company home pages, and made a mass distribution of my resume by email to potential employers.

"In the past two months I made a total of four advertisements of my availability on the Net through these methods. As a result, I got a lot of calls directly from employers, consulting firms, and employment agencies, a few interviews, and one job offer. The number of job offers could have easily been higher, if I had continued with the normal follow-ups (going to interviews, etc.)."

Career Talk

Damir Joseph Stimac is the author and developer of *Winning Career Strategies for Today's Competitive Job Market*, designed to give job seekers a comprehensive, interactive video-based tool for launching a successful job search campaign. Stimac is also the Internet's first syndicated career columnist. His column, Career Talk (Figure 9.7), can be found on the Web at http://www.careertalk.com/.

In this section of the book, we've included our favorite "Dear Joe" questions from job hunters, and answers from Stimac himself. Not all of these relate to online job hunting specifically, but to general job hunting, interviewing, negotiations, and so on.

Dear Joe:
I have been told many times that the best way to give yourself a competitive edge in the job market is to tap into the hidden job market. Do you have any suggestions of how I can do that?

—Shut Out in Phoenix

Dear Shut Out:
The "hidden" job market exists because too many people rely solely on help-wanted ads. You can give yourself a significant advantage by learning how to spot opportunities before they are published.

Your local newspapers, magazines, and media continually carry stories about companies. Look for announcements regarding planned expansions, retirement,

Figure 9.7 Career Talk with Damir Joseph Stimac.

new products, new office leases, new contracts, growth announcements, or planned mergers and acquisitions.

Ask yourself: "What employment opportunities does this story represent? How can my background and skills benefit this company?" Then call [or email] the person, mention the article or story, and ask if the company's action will create any new job openings. If the person says yes, give a brief presentation or your background, and offer to meet with him or her.

Dear Joe:
How do I find out what salary the employer is paying for a job if the ad doesn't mention any salary figure? I don't want to waste my or the prospective employer's time applying for a position where the salary may be too low. Any suggestions would be appreciated.

—Money Concerns

Dear Money Concerns:
There are several ways to identify what a prospective employer is paying for a specific position. You can call [or email] a company and ask. You can check out other similar job listings to get an idea, or you can contact an association within the industry to get an idea of what the salary range is. Don't preclude a great job opportunity solely on the basis of money. I invited several of my colleagues to offer their suggestions to your question. Mr. Jack Teems offers this advice:

"I believe most available positions have a range and some latitude. You would also want to know the growth potential once a beginning salary is set, but these questions are best left unasked until the employer has decided that you're the best prospect.

"There are exceptions, of course, particularly in the public sector and more so within pay scales established through collective bargaining. Wage rates tend to be fixed and are public record. You should have no difficulty in determining these.

"Don't neglect the fact that the benefits package and other intangibles may be looked on as parts of the overall compensation. A particularly attractive benefit or an extremely attractive working environment might persuade you to accept a bit lower salary than you had in mind."

—Jack Teems, Personnel Director, City of Rapid City, SD

Dear Joe:
I had a resume professionally developed; however, I am not getting many responses. Is there anything else I can do to get a better response from employers?

—Resume Tips

Dear Resume Tips:

Chances are, your professionally developed resume is generic. You would be better served if you would customize your resume to address the specific requirements for each job opening. Employers won't spend a lot of time reading a generic resume. You can give yourself a distinct advantage by sending only targeted and specific resumes to prospective employers.

Include a cover letter stating the position you are applying for and where you saw the advertised opening. Include a brief paragraph detailing your qualifications and mention the enclosed resume. Conclude the letter with a statement that you will be contacting them next week to follow up.

Dear Joe:

I have an interview coming up and found out it's going to be a group interview. What can I expect in a group interview, and how can I prepare for one?

—Panelist

Dear Panelist:

A panel or group interview usually involves a team of interviewers. The interviewers may include a representative from the department, a representative from personnel, a manager, or any other combinations.

The group interview subscribes to the notion that the more people involved in the hiring decision, the better the chances for hiring the best candidate. The candidates will either meet the entire group at once and answer each member's questions, or the candidate will meet each member individually and the group members will assemble at the end of the interview to compare notes.

The other type of group interview is one where you and several other candidates are interviewed by a panel. Your objective is to rise above the competition. This is no time to be shy *or* to dominate the other candidates. You can get the interviewers to spend more time with you by simply asking them a question after giving your answer. You will notice they will ask you more questions throughout the interview, and that could be a plus for you.

Be sure to look at each member when giving your answer. Practice the group interview with several friends.

Dear Joe:

I have made it to the third round of interviews and I don't know how to negotiate the salary if I get the job offer. What do you suggest?

—Almost There

Dear Almost There:

The salary is only part of the entire compensation package. If you think that your skills are worth more than what is offered, state something like: "I bring _____ years of experience to your organization. In addition, I have personally directed three similar projects with great success. I can do the same for your organization. That's why I'm asking you to consider my counter offer of $___." If they say no, then try to negotiate an extra week of paid vacation or a signing bonus.

Dear Joe:

I just blew an interview with a company that I really wanted to work for. I prepared well, or so I thought, but the interview was completely different from what I expected. First, there were three people conducting the interview. Second, each person asked a series of specific questions. One particular thing about this interview was that a lot of the questions seemed to be negative, like "Give me a specific example of a time when you didn't meet a deadline." Is this type of interview common? Also, how can I prepare for such an interview next time?

—Disappointed in D.C.

Dear Disappointed:

Welcome to the era of Behavioral Interviewing. This interview format is fairly common among major employers and is quickly gaining popularity among smaller firms. The theory behind behavioral interviews centers around the premise that your past performance is the best indicator of future performance, hence the "specific" questions.

The other distinguishing feature of behavioral interviews is that many of the questions ask for a specific event where the outcome was less than positive. Don't dodge the question by telling the interviewer that you really can't think of one. Give an honest answer, but end it with what you learned from the mistake, and what you did to prevent the same mistake from happening again. Prepare for your next interview by identifying several examples for each requirement stated in the job description.

Dear Joe:

I'm about to enter the "real world" and would like to know what mistakes students often make during an interview.

—Anxious in Alexandria

Dear Anxious:

Marc Consentino at Harvard University's Office of Career Services says, "A lot of times, I will ask a question, and students will start to answer before they think about the question. Basically, their answer goes all over the place, and then they go with what they want to get across."

Learn to become comfortable with two seconds of silence to compose your answer. It will impress the interviewer by showing that you are thoughtful and cautious. Marc also adds, "Your answer should be as direct and linear as possible. You want to end an answer within 60 seconds."

Another key area where candidates fail is preparation. "They don't read more than what the company gives them to read. Because they don't prepare, they don't ask good questions," says Marc. If you want to distinguish yourself in an interview, you have to ask questions that show you understand the industry. In addition, ask questions that can help you determine whether you would enjoy working for that company.

Terry's Tips

Terry Devlin is a career counselor at Career Management International. You can find his tips at http://www.cmi-lmi.com/tips/. Here are a couple of his answers to job hunters' questions.

Q. I'm not satisfied in my current position, but I'm not having a lot of luck in finding a new job. People keep giving me contradicting advice, and I don't know what I'm doing wrong. Can you give me some guidelines?

A. We believe that most people don't truly understand their strengths. It is impossible to find an appropriate position without that knowledge. Secondly, job seekers don't seem to know how to effectively involve other people in their search. And most significantly, the average job searcher does not understand or recognize that opportunities are abundant. Successful searchers are able to create the circumstances where opportunities start presenting themselves to the applicant. When these are addressed, finding a new position is very effective and far less stressful.

Q. I recently had a job interview that I think went really well, only I can't seem to find out if I got the job or not. I've already called once to "follow up," but I'm not sure if I should keep calling. Will that make me seem desperate?

A. A second follow-up call may be in order; however, there is one strategy that is almost always certain to result in a yes or no answer. This strategy must be used with caution and skill. You have interviewed with company A. You like everything about the position, and it seems to be a good match for your skills. You have written a thank-you note and expressed interest in the position. Now Company A is dragging their feet. Call the interviewer at Company A and tell him or her that you have received an offer from another company. Go on to explain that Company A is really your first choice, and if there is some interest on their part, you would prefer to see if something could be worked out. You will get an answer. There is the chance, however, that by trying to force the issue, the answer will be no.

t@p Job Tips

t@p Online is an Internet mega-site geared primarily for young people. Its job site (http://www.taponline.com/tap/jobs.html) is shown in Figure 9.8, and is a great resource for all kinds of career information. In an online t@p article, author Al Garner shares some of the main points he discovered through career counseling:

- The right work fills you, the wrong work drains you. You want a job you enjoy because you'll spend a third of your life working.

- Follow your interests, not your abilities.

- Good jobs require judgment—you're paid for decisions.

- Start a job hunt if you haven't been promoted within the first year of the day you stopped growing in your job.

- The best people are continually on the move.

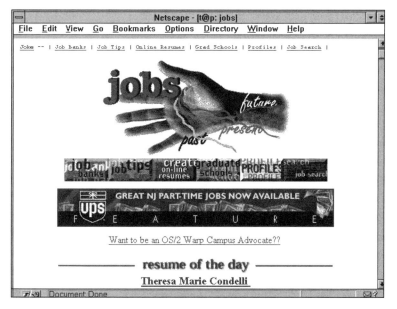

Figure 9.8   t@p's job page.

- Your loyalty is not to the company, but to yourself and your talent. Many careers are handicapped when a person follows the feelings of others. Most people are living for others.

- Job hunting is harder than working, yet it can be one of your best experiences.

t@p also offers some great tips for interviews:

- Temporary work with odd hours gives you free time for interviews.

- One technique is to "interview for information"—asking experts what the trends are and where there might be openings.

- Another is the "proposal." Ask experts in your field their biggest problems. Work out solutions and reapproach them. This can lead to a job. It's not so much who you know as knowing what you know and finding the person who needs it. You're looking for him and he's looking for you. This is part of being in the right place at the right time with more or less the right credentials.

- 80 percent of the good job openings are hidden.

- Interviews are two people sizing up each other; so the more informal, the better. If you feel awkward, you're trying to please him. Treat him as an equal.

- Don't bare your soul. Think before answering. Watch your body language and eye contact. Be brief and to the point. Don't knock your previous employer. Don't bluff; bluffers don't know who they are. Don't assume an employer knows exactly what he wants in a person. Try to figure out his hidden agenda and appeal to it.

- If you can't find the job you want, create it.

Researching the Company

Bradley Richardson is an author, accomplished professional speaker, entrepreneur, consultant, and top sales and marketing executive. He is the author of *JobSmarts for Twentysomethings* (a Vintage book), and speaks to students, recent graduates, and young professionals about creative job searching, what to expect during the first year on the job, how to be effective more quickly, improving communication and organizational skills, and how to be a leader on the job and in the business community.

In this next section, an excerpt from *JobSmarts for Twentysomethings*, Richardson tells you why and how you should learn about a company first.

Nightmare scenario #1: You accept a job offer from your ultimate dream company, only to learn that in three weeks the entire operation is moving to Northern Siberia to save on expenses. Nightmare scenario #2: You're chosen to lead the transition team. How could this have been avoided? Three ways: research, research, research. You wouldn't buy a car first without knowing who it was made by. The same goes for work. Learn about the company before you jump right in. What you find out may just surprise you.

RESEARCH CHECKLIST

Before going into an interview, you should be able to answer the following questions about the prospective company:

- What are the company's major products and services?

- Who are the company's customers?

- How do competitors and customers view the company? (Do they think the company's service is excellent or poor, the products are reasonably priced or a little too expensive?)

- What is the company's standing in the marketplace? Is it a profitable business, or is it teetering on the brink of bankruptcy?

- Who are the company's major competitors?

- What are some of the company's recent success stories?

- What problems is the company trying to solve?

- What is the corporate culture like?

- Is the company privately or publicly owned? Is it an independent organization or part of a larger conglomerate?

- How big is the company? Has it grown or declined over the past five years? Are they hiring or laying people off?

- Is the employee turnover rate high, average, or low? What factors contribute to that turnover rate? (For example, do people leave the company because of low wages?)

- What is the typical interviewing process and hiring process at the company?

Networking

Richardson, in *JobSmarts for Twentysomethings*, also discusses the mysteries of networking:

Networking is rather painless. Often it's merely asking for an introduction. At this stage you are on the receiving end. Networking can also mean introducing business associates to one another, informing them of special helpful knowledge, or giving someone a business lead. Networking does not happen automatically. You must take the initiative in making contacts. If you need an introduction, ask for it. These things rarely fall into your lap unless people know that you are looking. Don't worry whether you will offend someone by asking. If they mind, they will let you know. They will tell you that they don't feel comfortable or that they can't help you. That's OK. No big deal. You never know unless you ask.

For the most part, people will want to help you, especially older people or professionals who are already established. They remember when they first got started and someone gave them a break or opened a door for them. Believe me, what goes around comes around, and they see it as a way to give back. Your peers may feel more important if they are able to help you make contacts.

EVERYONE IS IMPORTANT

It pays to treat everyone with respect, as if they are someone important. You never know when you may need someone's assistance. Look at Bill Clinton. Most of his staff members are either childhood friends, college buddies, or people he met coming up the ladder. Think about it. The guy or girl dribbling next to you in class could be the leader of the free world someday.

- Meredith had just graduated from Iowa State University with a master's degree in costume history. She wanted to work in a museum, but was having difficulty getting in any doors. She was at a friend's house lamenting her situation, when her friend's mother said, "Why don't we call Aunt Jackie?" The mother immediately picked up the phone and called Aunt Jackie, who held a position on the board of a university museum with a large costume collection. Introductions were made, and Meredith was granted interviews and eventually secured a position with the university.

- Michelle worked at J. Crew part-time while she went to school to study graphic design. She was personable and talked to many customers, often asking questions after she had helped them for a while. After asking one customer what he did for a living, she discovered that he owned a graphic design firm. She told him that she was in school and was graduating the next semester. He invited her to show him her work, and ended up offering Michelle a job when she graduated.

YOUR OWN BOARD OF DIRECTORS: MENTORS AND ROLE MODELS

Most corporations have a board of directors. In many cases, they are successful older or established professionals who can use their experiences to advise and guide the direction of a company. For all practical purposes, you are a rookie professional. You need someone to serve as a professional coach or advisor. You have this wisdom at your disposal by forming your own personal board of directors, or board of advisors—a group to serve as mentors, advisors, or coaches for your career.

A mentor is someone you can bounce ideas off of. He or she is who you go to for advice or counsel. Anyone can be a mentor: a parent, boss, professor, family friend, or professional contact—anyone whom you respect and admire for his or her wisdom and success.

Companies pay consultants outrageous fees to dispense advice on managing their company. Think of yourself as a company, with your own personal staff of consultants that you can seek advice from and that will help manage your career (only they're free).

They can save you a lot of heartache. Whenever you have a question, bounce it off one of your personal board members. Use their experience. Ask their advice when faced with a major decision or choice. Ask what they would do in certain situations. Learn from their mistakes and successes.

Never be afraid to ask for advice and help. The intelligent person is the one who can ask for help, and knows his or her limitations. Save yourself some time and aggravation.

10

The Web's Best Job-Hunting Resources

WHAT THE ICONS MEAN

 OFFERS SERVICES AT A COST TO JOB HUNTER

 OFFERS INTERNATIONAL RESOURCES OR JOB LISTINGS

 HIGHLY RECOMMENDED

Throughout this book, we've explained what we think you need to know to get started and get serious about finding your dream job. So far, we've told you about employment newsgroups, BBSes, and company employment pages. You've also read about how to create your own Web pages and how to meet potential employers online.

But job hunting is an evolving process. To help you even more in getting your dream job, we want to point you toward much of the great information you can find on the World Wide Web, including job listings for various professions, networking areas, online employment agencies and resume services, job and resume banks, and other resources that are of direct usefulness to job seekers.

This chapter gives you a sample of some of our favorite job resources on the Web. This list is by no means a comprehensive guide for job seekers, so for more resources, you'll want to conduct your own, more specific Web searches.

3DSite
http://www.lightside.com/~dani/

This site is dedicated to the computer graphics field. It includes a beta release of "the first truly interactive job board," job offers, organizations, newsgroups, and more.

Academic Physician and Scientist
gopher://aps.acad-phy-sci.com/

Academic Physician and Scientist is considered the central resource for positions in academic medicine. Listings at this online publication include academic, ambulatory care, business, chiefs and directors, clinical affairs, communications, dean, education, faculty, health care, information systems, research, and training. Many of these listings are not for entry-level jobs, but if you search carefully, you might find a few gems.

ACM SIGMOD's Database Job Listings
http://bunny.cs.uiuc.edu/jobs/

This site lists tons of open positions in various fields—from teaching to programming—listed in the order in which the job openings were submitted to the database.

Adams JobBank Online
http://www.adamsonline.com

Here you'll be able to search tons of job opportunities in the areas of computer; finance, accounting, and consulting; general; management; medical/healthcare; office/administrative; sales and marketing; teaching and education; and technical. You'll also get access to Adams' Career Services Center, which provides plenty of job-related information, including advice on networking, negotiating, interviewing, and phone techniques. You can also post your resume and cover letter in the Talent Bank.

The Ada Project
http://www.cs.yale.edu/HTML/YALE/CS/HyPlans/tap/tap.html

The Ada Project Web site is designed to serve as a clearinghouse for information and resources relating to women in computing. This site provides links to many other job sites, and gives you general information about events, statistics about women in science, fellowships and grants, and other job information specific to women.

 ### The Airline Employment Assistance Corps.
http://www2.csn.net/AEAC/

For $10, you'll get access to current job openings in the airline industry, current events, links to aviation and aerospace pages, and you'll be able to post your resume.

 ### Airline Information Service
http://www.earthlink.net/~airsvc/

This Web site explains how to receive a current guide listing contact and personnel information for airline jobs. The $9.95 guide also lists current openings for ticket agents, sales, baggage claim, ground personnel, pilots, mechanics, flight attendants, marketing, and customer service.

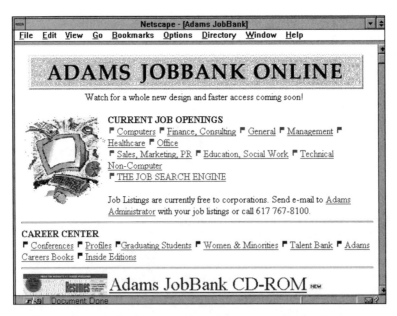

Figure 10.1 Adams JobBank offers a variety of resources for the job seeker.

American Astronomical Society

http://www.aas.org/

This site is for the AAS, the major professional organization in North America for astronomers and other scientists and individuals interested in astronomy. This site lists job openings, mostly in academia.

American Society for Engineering Education (ASEE)

http://www.asee.org/asee/publications/prism/classifieds/pos_open

ASEE's job site has open positions in aerospace, chemical, civil, industrial, mechanical, and electrical engineering; engineering management; and general engineering.

America's Employers

http://www.americasemplo ers.com/

AE includes open jobs, a chat room, a resume bank, networking information, company databases, information on recruiters, job search FAQs, and more.

America's Help Wanted

http://www.jobquest.com/

After you obtain an account, you'll be able to build what AHW calls its "jobQuest Resume," and have access to its job posting search tools to search the postings on this service only. Netscape is the recommended browser for this service.

America's Job Bank

http://www.ajb.dni.us/index.html

This is a great resource for any job hunter. America's Job Bank includes approximately 100,000 job listings for government and private sector positions throughout the country. The listings are searchable by many different criteria. You'll also get links to other job banks, including military and state job banks and a virtual job fair.

Arizona Careers Online

http://amsquare.com/america/arizona.html

This site provides a list of Arizona job hotlines, links to state schools, state associations and jobs, and links to other states.

Asia-Net

http://asia-net.com/

Interested in a job in Japan? Asia-Net publishes Asia-related jobs via email and a Web page. At this site you can search job listings and provide your resume for circulation to companies that subscribe. Most positions are technical in nature.

Atlanta CyberJobs
http://www.atlwin.com/jobs/

This area lists jobs in the Atlanta area for administration, management, data processing, sales, and more.

Atlanta's ComputerJobs Store
http://www.ComputerJobs.com/

This is Atlanta's "premier Web marketplace where computer professionals can advance their careers and companies can fulfill their staffing and consulting needs." You'll find out about high-tech career fairs, computer job openings (contracting, consulting, and permanent), company profiles and contact information, a list of Atlanta's top 100 computer firms, and information on Atlanta employment trends. You can also enter your skills online for recruiters to peruse.

BAMTA (Bay Area Multimedia Technology Alliance)
http://mlds-www.arc.nasa.gov/BAMTA/

This site lists job openings for multimedia and Web technology-related jobs. Job categories include Art design, Business finance, Education, Government, Health care, Media, Product marketing, Programmer, and Telecommunication.

Best Jobs in the *USA Today*
http://www.bestjobsusa.com/

Here you'll be able to search all national, regional, and local employment ads from the *USA Today* newspaper. You'll also be able to search ads from *Employment Review* Magazine, and thousands of individual companies around the world. You'll also be able to read about employment trends, visit the Career Store, and post your resume.

Bio Online
http://www.bio.com/hr/hr_index.html

This site is specifically for biotechnology-related information and services on the Internet. Services include News and Events, Corporate Biotech (an alphabetical index of companies with background and contact information, phone numbers), Marketplace, Career Center, and more. The Career Center is run by Search Masters International, an executive search firm for the pharmaceutical and biotechnology industry.

Boston Job Bank
http://www.bostonjobs.com/

This site lists Boston-area job openings in computers, business, professional, sales, and general.

Broadcast Employment Services
http://www.tvjobs.com/index_a.htm

This site provides a way for employers to quickly locate experienced broadcast talent. You can search the online job bank, post your resume and find out about internships, and more. You'll get links to TV stations, contact information for broadcasting professionals, FAQs and jobline phone numbers.

The California Career & Employment Center
http://www.webcom.com/career

Affiliated with HelpWanted USA, this service offers a job seeker resource center, lists corporate members, and allows you to post your resume online. It also contains the California Job Bulletin Board and Usenet Employment Newsgroups.

Career Connection
http://www.ebi.ac.uk/htbin/biojobs.pl

Career Connection posts jobs related to bioinformatics, biochemistry, and molecular biology. You can search for jobs in government, academia, industry, jobs for post-doctorals, and so on.

Career Magazine
http://www.careermag.com/

Career Magazine offers a variety of job seeker goodies, including searchable job openings, a Resume Bank, employer profiles, and news articles, including the current week's selection from *The Wall Street Journal's National Business Employment Weekly*.

 CareerMosaic
http://www.careermosaic.com/cm/

This opportunities database lets you look for top jobs in a variety of careers from employers throughout North America. In addition to listing openings from major companies, the database also includes the Usenet "jobs.offered" index, with more than 23,000 postings sorted and indexed daily from "jobs.offered" newsgroups around the world. You'll also have access to the international opportunities from the *International Herald Tribune*, "the World's Daily Newspaper," and in-depth profiles of more than 60 of the world's leading companies in high tech, health care, finance, retailing, and more.

 CareerPath.com
http://www.careerpath.com/

CareerPath allows you to search newspaper employment ads from six major cities. You basically get the Sunday classifieds for the *Boston Globe, Chicago Tribune, Los Angeles Times, New York Times, San Jose Mercury News,* and *Washington Post* . At any given time, CareerPath.com can connect you to about 45,000 job listings.

Figure 10.2 CareerPath.com gives you access to help wanted ads from six major newspapers.

 Career Resource Home Page
http://www.rpi.edu/dept/cdc/homepage.html

This site provides links to several valuable job-related pages, including databases of professional organizations, university jobs, newsgroups, career placement centers, sites for listing resumes, and more.

 Career Resumes
http://branch.com/cr/cr.html

This resume-creation service promises that if they don't get you the interview in 30 days, they'll rewrite the resume for free. Cost for resume preparation is anywhere from $150 to $350 depending on length and complexity of the document.

Career Shop
http://www.tenkey.com/cshop

This site has an online databank of resume profiles and job opportunities, and allows you to search job openings. You'll also get information on interviewing and corporate profiles.

CareerSite
http://www.careersite.com/

This site prides itself on matching candidates and employers. Job hunters submit a profile and wait for a "virtual agent" to notify them of opportunities that match their profile.

Careers On-Line at University of Minnesota
http://www.disserv.stu.umn.edu/TC/Grants/COL/

This site provides job search and employment information to people with disabilities. It includes job and internship postings, an adaptive technology products and resources database, the *Job Accommodation Handbook*, resume information, and more.

careerWEB
http://www.cweb.com/

The careerWeb online service offers candidate information to employers, franchisers, and career-related companies. It provides job listings, a resource center, an online bookstore, employer information, and a "career fitness" test. The public area gives you plenty of job searching information, and the paid area gives you the opportunity to use the career advancement service, resume service, and the Job Bank USA Affiliate Program.

Career Web at MecklerWeb
http://www.sgx.com/cw

Career Web lists positions from Account Executive to Trainer for companies like Meckler, Huntington Group, and IMA.

Cell
http://www.cell.com/cell/posi/

Cell is the leading international journal of biological sciences. Its job site lists open jobs for faculty, doctors, and more.

Chicago Tribune Career Finder
http://www.chicago.tribune.com/home.html

This site lists job opportunities, company profiles, and employment-related feature articles. You'll be able to search the latest three *Chicago Tribune* Job Guides.

ComputerWeek Jobs Online
http://www.jobs.co.za/

This site lists computer-related job openings worldwide, and includes a directory of recruitment agencies, a career resource center, and more.

Contract Employment Weekly

http://www.ceweekly.wa.com/

C.E. Weekly is an online resource for people interested in contract work. This site includes a resume center, virtual job fair, human resources center, high-tech career area, links to other contract work information, and C.E. job openings.

crm21.com

http://crm.21.com/

crm21.com provides "Professional Career and Resume Services for Job Seekers, Employers, Recruiters, and Related Personnel." In addition to allowing you to post your resume, you'll be given links to various career centers, recruiting firms, clubs and organizations, publications, job-searching articles, and other resources. A lot of worthy information here is free!

Data Processing Independent Consultant's Exchange (DICE)

http://www.dice.dlinc.com:8181/

DICE is a national electronic job advertising service used by recruiting firms seeking high-tech data processing professionals. This site allows you to search a list of companies on the Web, indexed alphabetically, by geographical location, and by logo. You'll also be able to search current job openings.

The Definitive Internet Career Guide

http://phoenix.placement.oakland.edu/career/internet.htm

This is Oakland University's list of links to hundreds of job resources, including employment opportunities, employment publications, and career centers. Check it out.

e-Math

http://www.ams.org/

This Web page is home to the American Mathematical Society. When you become a member, you'll be able to access AMS publications, apply for academic jobs, be informed about open positions, get great contact information, find out about internships, and you'll be able to network with others in the field.

Employment Edge

http://www.employmentedge.com/employment.edge/

Employment Edge specializes in professional career placement throughout the United States. You'll be able to search open positions by category (Accounting, Auditing, Engineering, Management, Programming/MIS/software engineering, and "everything else").

Employment News
http://www.ftn.net/emplnews/

Employment News is Canada's largest employment publication. This site allows you to preview Employment News' positions online. Positions are updated every Monday and are in the categories of Careers, Office, Skilled and technical, General help, Drivers, Automotive, Hotel/Restaurant, and others.

The Environmental Careers Organization
http://www.eco.org/

ECO is a national, nonprofit organization dedicated to the development of environmental careers. At this site, you'll find ECO's career publications, a placement program, and job listings for anyone interested in environmental jobs—from Anthropology to Toxicology.

Environmental World Careers Online
http://www.infi.net/~ecw/

This is "the clearinghouse" for international environmental and natural resources job opportunities, career news, environmental career seminars, employer profiles, university environmental and natural resources programs, grants, fellowships, professional associations, job search articles and tips for students, entry level employment, and career change opportunities from mid-level through senior executive professionals. Typical job listings are in the categories of Ecology and Biology, Forestry and Natural resources, Environmental Sciences and Engineering, Environmental Education, Policy and Advocacy, Law and Enforcement, and Parks.

E-Span's Interactive Employment Network
http://www.espan.com/

E-Span provides various resources for the job seeker, including current openings, salary guides, resume writing tips, and the *Occupational Outlook Handbook*. This service is employer paid and is free to job hunters. At the time of this writing, there were 1,700 employers on E-Span, with 3,500 job openings, all less than four weeks old. All postings are searchable by keyword, region, industry, date posted, and job title. You can even post your resume to the EIN database.

EuroJobs
http://www.demon.co.uk/EuroJobs/

If you're interested in working in the U.K., Germany, Belgium, Poland, The Netherlands, France, or Switzerland, browse this site or post your resume. Typical positions advertised from this site are in sales, product group management, finance, general management, and logistics. You'll also be able to confidentially post your resume.

Forty Plus of Northern California
http://www.sirius.com/~40plus/40pls.htm

Forty Plus is a not-for-profit organization for highly skilled and experienced executives, managers, and professionals who are in career transition. Membership entitles you to a step-by-step program for a "successful job search." There are several membership requirements.

The Franklin Search Group Online Career Services for the Biotech and Medical Industries
http://www.gate.net/biotech-jobs

This is a staffing resource for the Biotechnology, Pharmaceutical, and Medical industries. It lists salary survey results, information on recruiters and headhunters, jobline phone numbers, and more.

GeoWeb Interactive
http://www.ggrweb.com/

GeoWeb contains online resources for Geographic Information Systems (GIS), Global Positioning Systems (GPS), and Remote Sensing (RS) industries. At GeoWeb, you can search relevant companies and home pages, advertise your home page, search job listings, post your resume, and discuss current issues.

helpwanted.com
http://helpwanted.com/

helpwanted.com lists jobs in the YSS (Your Software Solutions) database, company listings, and more.

HEART/Career Connections
http://www.career.com/

HEART (Human Resources Electronic Advertising and Recruiting Tool) is the "only network that facilitates a direct connection between a candidate and the employer." It includes job classified ads, information on cyberfairs (online job fairs), and information on the featured employers.

InPursuit's Employment Network
http://www.inpursuit.com/e-network/

This site provides links to a variety of job pages on the Web, including The Career Board, Shawn's Internet Resume Center, and Get A Job!

IntelliMatch
http://www.intellimatch.com/
The IntelliMatch Online Job Center lists job openings, gives you information about the employers using IntelliMatch, and lists professional associations, job help organizations, and upcoming job/career fairs.

The Internet Job Locator
http://www.joblocator.com/jobs/

This site lists mostly technical jobs and allows you to post your resume to their database. You can search listings by keyword, job description, category, company, city, state, ZIP code, and so on. Typical listings are for jobs like Database Support Specialists, Programmer, Online Project Manager, Analyst, and Audit Manager.

JobCenter
http://www.jobcenter.com

The JobCenter site allows you to easily post your resume, with the provided resume form, to various newsgroups and to the JobCenter database. You can also get corporate profiles, and link directly to job-related articles by well-known authors and recruiting professionals.

JobHunt
http://rescomp.stanford.edu/jobs/

This "Meta-List" of online job search resources and services includes sites with online job listings, positions in science and engineering, classified advertisements, recruiting agencies, company job resources, resume banks, reference materials, and more.

The Job Hunt
http://www.dsphere.net/jobs.html

This site lets you search job openings in the areas of communication arts, graphic arts, and prepress and printing industries. You'll also get job tips, a glossary of industry terms, and an archive of relevant articles.

Job Search
http://www.adnetsol.com/jsearch/jshome1.html

Job Search aids professionals, managers, and executives in their efforts to find new employment. Job Search maintains information on 40,000 Southern California companies, and more than 100,000 related news stories and editorials.

JOBS Library
ftp://fwux.fedworld.gov/pub/jobs/jobs.htm

This regularly updated site gives you access to federal jobs on the FedWorld Information Network.

JOBTRAK
http://www.jobtrak.com/

JOBTRAK Network is a college job listing service that provides access to company profiles, employment statistics, and job hunting skills information. It posts more than 600 new full- and part-time job listings every day.

JobWeb
http://www.jobweb.com/

JobWeb includes job-search articles and tips, job listings, and company information for college students, recent graduates, and alumni. It also provides resources like career and employment information, training, and services sponsored by the National Association of Colleges and Employers.

JOM
http://www.tms.org/pubs/journals/JOM/classifieds.html

JOM is a technical journal dedicated to exploring the many aspects of materials science and engineering. The JOM Web site lists metallurgical job openings and contact information.

Kansas Careers Mentor Project
http://www.ksu.edu/~dangle/

Located at Kansas State University, this home page features a mentor program specifically for women, especially for non-traditional careers. This site was still under construction at the time of this writing, but it included a women's guide to the Internet and information on professional groups.

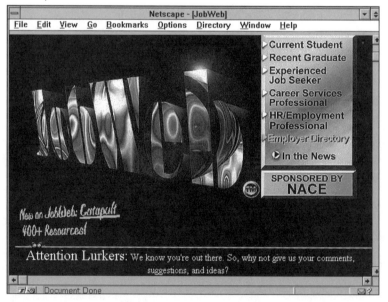

Figure 10.3 JobWeb is great for college students, and alumni.

Landscape Architecture and Architecture Jobs
http://www.clr.toronto.edu/VIRTUALLIB/jobs.html

Here you'll get a free guide to finding a job in architecture, landscape architecture, and planning. You'll also get complete listings (both technical and non-technical) for jobs in private firms, government, and academic—for example, Planning Technician, Network Specialist, Intern Architect, Research Assistant, and Professor.

Law Employment Center
http://www.lawjobs.com/

This site allows you to browse employment listings from the *National Law Journal, New York Law Journal,* and *Law Technology Product News.* You'll also get links to directories, research resources, and classified job ads.

 ### Medical and Scientific Employment
http://www.chemistry.com/biotech-jobs/

This site is "*The* job source for professionals in medicine and science." You'll get salary survey results, find out about recruiters, post your resume, search job listings, find headhunters, and discover telephone joblines.

 ### The Monster Board
http://www.monster.com/home.html

The Monster Board is one of our favorite resources, and includes employer profiles for more than 450 companies, and more than 2,200 job listings. You'll also be able to create your own electronic resume (if you haven't already) with the customized application, and submit it. You can also email your electronic resume, check out career events, and talk to HR people.

 ### National Home Workers Association
http://www.homeworkers.com/homeworkers/

The NHWA is a membership organization dedicated to serving people who work in a home workplace environment. Members are self-employed, skilled and unskilled, full- and part-time professional telecommuters, and those who have established a workplace in their home. The NHWA site includes articles of interest, job-related resources, surveys, sample jobs, news, and FAQs.

National Physician Job Listings Directory
http://www.njnet.com/~embbs/job/jobs.html

This site lists practice opportunities throughout North America for all medical specialties. You can search all job listings here for no fee.

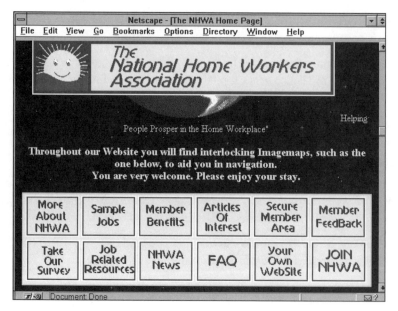

Figure 10.4   If you prefer the home environment to the office, check out the National Home Workers Association site.

NationJob Network
http://www.nationjob.com/

NationJob is an online jobs database that contains thousands of jobs open around the United States (primarily in the Midwest, though). You can search for a job that meets your custom criteria, search for a company, and so on. Listed jobs include those in the categories of: Aviation/Aerospace, Computer Software/Systems, Education, Financial/Accounting/Insurance, Marketing and Sales, Medical/Health Care, Engineering/Manufacturing, and Skilled Technical.

New Jersey Jobs
http://www.njjobs.com/

This site lists weekly job openings for New Jersey businesses. Typical positions are Silicon Graphics Administrator, Client Server Developer, Programmer, Customer Service Representative, and Help Desk Support.

The *News & Observer* Employment Online
http://www.nando.net/classads/employment

This site lists job openings from the *News & Observer* classified advertisements. You'll be able to search jobs by category for the daily classifieds and from the Sunday paper. Listings are in the areas of Financial, Administrative, Data Processing, Educators,

Professional, Sales, Healthcare, Manufacturing, Technical, Trades, Restaurants and Hotels, Retail, Domestic, Marketing, part-time, and full-time.

Omaha CareerLink

http://www.omaha.org/careerlink.html

Lists professional staff opportunities in Nebraska. You can also email your resume to kbragg@omaha.org.

Online Career Center

http://www.occ.com/

The Online Career Center is one of the largest online job search resources, with a database of jobs searchable by type, location, and so on. The site also features a resume posting area, where you can submit an HTML or plain text resume, and career assistance.

PassportAccess Employment Network

http://www.passportaccess.com

PassportAccess matches up employers, human resources departments, recruiters, and job candidates. You can post your resume using the included form, and you can scan job postings.

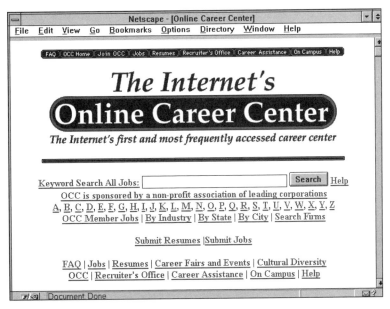

Figure 10.5 The Online Career Center is one of the most popular job sites on the Web.

PeopleBank (The Employment Network)
http://www.peoplebank.com

This site allows you to add your resume—by filling out the provided questionnaire—to a database of other job seekers who are willing to work in Australia or the United Kingdom. This database is searched by employers around the world by downloading special software.

Ray Osborne's Home Page
http://www.america.net/~rayosb/rko.html

This is more than just "some guy's" Web site. Ray offers a networking area called The Grapevine and lists job openings that are both technical and non-technical. You'll also get lists of job hotlines, BBS job resources, and other employment Web pages.

Saludos Web
http://www.hooked.net/saludos/

Saludos Web is a Web site devoted exclusively to promoting Hispanic careers and education, supported by *Saludos Hispanos* Magazine. This site has a resume pool, where you can post your resume for a fee; an education center with information on internships, mentorship, and scholarships; articles from *Saludos Hispanos Magazine*; and a career center with information on current job listings, career fields, trends, and guidance.

The Sensemedia Surfer
http://sensemedia/net/getajob/

This page gives you direct links to hundreds of job-hunting resources, from Career Mosaic to jobs at Duke University's Medical Center. You'll also get direct links to federal jobs, Web jobs, and more. You can post your HTML resume free of charge.

SkillSearch
http://www.internet-is.com/skillsearch/

SkillSearch is a professional membership organization specializing in career networking. More than 700 employers use SkillSearch to look for candidates, and SkillSearch boasts that salaries for positions they have found matches for range from $30,000 to $250,000. Cost for the job hunter includes a one-time fee of $65, and then an additional $15 upon "each anniversary of their enrollment."

Society of Technical Communication (STC)
http://www.clark.net/pub/stc/www/home2.html

This site lists STC job openings, job leads, resume information, and more. Open positions include such titles as Tech Manager, Writers and Documentation Specialists, Info Designer, Web Administrator, Tech Editor, Documentation Manager, and even Sales Manager.

SSC Laboratory Outplacement Center

http://jobs.ssc.gov/

This site lists job opportunities at laboratories around the country. Typical positions are Janitor, Technician, Chief of Operations, Senior Secretary, Battalion Chief, and Environmental Engineer.

Sun-Sentinel Edition

http://www.chicago.tribune.com/career/sentinel_ads.html

This site lists weekly employment classified advertisements, mostly for technical jobs.

t@p Jobs

http://www.taponline.com/tap/jobs.html

t@p is an online magazine geared towards college-aged people. Their job site gives you access to job banks, job tips, graduate schools, online resumes, and more.

Technology Registry

http://www.techreg.com

You can list your resume in this online employment database for about $25. Subscribers to this service range from Fortune 500 companies and international executive search firms to small startups.

WebWATSON

http://www.intellimatch.com/webwatpr.html

WebWATSON is a piece of software that allows job hunters to fill out an online resume at no cost. Then IntelliMatch, an online recruiter, lets employers search the resumes for a substantial fee. At this site you'll also be able to look at tons of job listings for Account Managers, Accountants, Analysts, Artists, Animators, Engineers, Communications Administrators, and Customer Service Specialists.

World Wide Career Network

http://wwbc.com/english/careers/careers.html

Advertise yourself for free by emailing your resume or fill out the Online Resume Form. Employers will conduct a database search and, hopefully, find that you're who they've been looking for. Contains a special section for new college graduates.

WW Jobs Offered/Wanted

http://www.Stars.com/Jobs.html

This Web site lists current Web-related jobs, such as WWW Database Programmer or WWW Presence Engineer, and also allows you to post your resume using the provided form.

Professional Recruiters on the Web

This is a sample of some of the recruiters you can find on the Web. You can find more by conducting a search. Read carefully before making any decisions about using an online recruiter. Some will charge you rather than charge the employer.

Chancellor and Chancellor
http://www.chancellor.com

This is a brokerage firm for computer technology professionals. Offers company profiles and principal information, resources for contractors, and current job listings. If you're a contractor in the technology industry, this site has a lot to offer.

MindSource
http://www.mindsrc.com

MindSource is a Unix contracting and recruiting company owned and operated by Unix software engineers. They provide technical talent in the areas of Unix systems administration, quality assurance, and Web engineering for permanent and contract staffing needs.

Recruiters OnLine Network
http://www.onramp.net/ron/

RON is the largest online association of recruiters, employment agencies, search firms and employment professionals. The company offers a Resource Center, allowing you to search the database for Recruiters OnLine employers, visit the Career Center (where you can post your resume), and view employment listings.

Reed Personnel Recruiting
http://www.reed.co.uk

Reed Personnel Services is the largest independent British employment agency, with more than 200 branches. Reed specializes in providing temporary and permanent secretarial, word processing, clerical, and general office staff.

J. Robert Scott Executive Search
http://j-robert-scott.com/

J. Robert Scott recruits senior-level management for high growth entrepreneurial companies in the areas of financial services, telecommunications, software, retail, biotechnology, and healthcare. You can search the company's opportunities list. All fees are company paid.

Enterprise Client/Server
http://www.enterprise.skill.com/

Enterprise specializes in Client/Server positions, both short and long-term, contract and permanent.

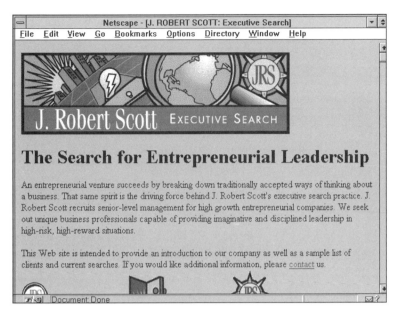

Figure 10.6 The J. Robert Scott Executive Search home page.

National Technical Employment Services (NTES)
http://iquest.com/~ntes/

While you can post your resume at no charge, NTES offers resume services and *HOTFLASH* Magazine (a jobs information publication) for a price.

PC Personnel
http://www.pcpersonnel.com/

PC Personnel is a computer placement service specializing in networking positions in the Northern California area. Take a look at their job openings for Network Technical Support, System Administration, and Network Engineering/Telecom/ Management positions.

Virtual Search's Online Center
http://www.vsearch.com/

Virtual is a company specializing in recruiting highly qualified technical, creative and marketing professionals for companies involved in advanced technologies and next-generation applications and products.

WorkNet
http://www.worknet.co.uk/

This site allows you to post your resume and scan online jobs available throughout the United Kingdom. Job listings are in the categories of accountancy, banking, computer, education, engineering, graduate recruitment, law, management, media, public sector, retail, and secretarial.

Resume Services

There are many resume services on the Web, and they vary wildly in price. We recommend that you create your own resume, using the tips provided in this book. If you use a resume service, your resume is likely to look similar to a host of other job hunters. However, if you really feel that your resume can and should be improved, you'll want to consider the services in this section.

 AAA Resume/Distinctive Documents
http://www.infi.net/~resume/

AAA Resume offers several services, including resume analysis and critique ($15). The company also writes your resume and uploads it to a large database for anywhere from $50 to $80.

 The Resume Center
http://www.msn.fullfeed.com:80/resumecenter/

The Resume Center takes the resume you have written and perfects its layout and design. Choose your resume format and typeface, and send $15 to have the Resume Center do the rest.

 The Resume Publishing Company
http://www.webcom.com/~cha/

This service allows you to post your HTML resume to a URL the company gives you. You must provide the resume. Fees start at $30 and depend on the type of resume, number of graphics, and other variables.

Universities and Government Positions

This section provides university and government position URLs. You can find even more by using the Career Resources Home Page listed above.

The following URLs were found at the FedWorld Information Network:

Alaska
ftp://ftp.fedworld.gov/pub/jobs/ak.txt

Alabama
ftp://ftp.fedworld.gov/pub/jobs/al.txt

Arkansas
ftp://ftp.fedworld.gov/pub/jobs/ar.txt

Arizona
ftp://ftp.fedworld.gov/pub/jobs/az.txt

California
ftp://ftp.fedworld.gov/pub/jobs/ca.txt

Colorado
ftp://ftp.fedworld.gov/pub/jobs/co.txt

Connecticut
ftp://ftp.fedworld.gov/pub/jobs/ct.txt

Delaware
ftp://ftp.fedworld.gov/pub/jobs/de.txt

Florida
ftp://ftp.fedworld.gov/pub/jobs/fl.txt

Georgia
ftp://ftp.fedworld.gov/pub/jobs/ga.txt

Hawaii
ftp://ftp.fedworld.gov/pub/jobs/hi.txt

Iowa
ftp://ftp.fedworld.gov/pub/jobs/ia.txt

Idaho
ftp://ftp.fedworld.gov/pub/jobs/id.txt

Illinois
ftp://ftp.fedworld.gov/pub/jobs/il.txt

Indiana
ftp://ftp.fedworld.gov/pub/jobs/in.txt

Kansas
ftp://ftp.fedworld.gov/pub/jobs/ks.txt

Kentucky
ftp://ftp.fedworld.gov/pub/jobs/ky.txt

Louisiana
ftp://ftp.fedworld.gov/pub/jobs.la.txt

Massachusettes
ftp://ftp.fedworld.gov/pub/jobs/ma.txt

Maryland
ftp://ftp.fedworld.gov/pub/jobs/md.txt

Maine
ftp://ftp.fedworld.gov/pub/jobs/me.txt

Michigan
ftp://ftp.fedworld.gov/pub/jobs/mi.txt

Minnesota
ftp://ftp.fedworld.gov/pub/jobs/mn.txt

Missouri
ftp://ftp.fedworld.gov/pub/jobs/mo.txt

Mississippi
ftp://ftp.fedworld.gov/pub/jobs/ms.txt

Montana
ftp://ftp.fedworld.gov/pub/jobs/mt.txt

North Carolina
ftp://ftp.fedworld.gov/pub/jobs/nc.txt

North Dakota
ftp://ftp.fedworld.gov/pub/jobs/nd.txt

Nebraska
ftp://ftp.fedworld.gov/pub/jobs/ne.txt

New Hampshire
ftp://ftp.fedworld.gov/pub/jobs/nh.txt

New Jersey
ftp://ftp.fedworld.gov/pub/jobs/nj.txt

New Mexico
ftp://ftp.fedworld.gov/pub/jobs/nm.txt

Nevada
ftp://ftp.fedworld.gov/pub/jobs/nv.txt

New York
ftp://ftp.fedworld.gov/pub/jobs/ny.txt

Ohio
ftp://ftp.fedworld.gov/pub/jobs/oh.txt

Oklahoma
ftp://ftp.fedworld.gov/pub/jobs/ok.txt

Oregon
ftp://ftp.fedworld.gov/pub/jobs/or.txt

Pennsylvania
ftp://ftp.fedworld.gov/pub/jobs/pa.txt

Puerto Rico
ftp://ftp.fedworld.gov/pub/jobs/pr.txt

Rhode Island
ftp://ftp.fedworld.gov/pub/jobs/ri.txt

South Carolina
ftp://ftp.fedworld.gov/pub/jobs/sc.txt

South Dakota
ftp://ftp.fedworld.gov/pub/jobs/sd.txt

Tennessee
ftp://ftp.fedworld.gov/pub/jobs/tn.txt

Texas
ftp://ftp.fedworld.gov/pub/jobs/tx.txt

Utah
ftp://ftp.fedworld.gov/pub/jobs/ut.txt

Virginia
ftp://ftp.fedworld.gov/pub/jobs/va.txt

Vermont
ftp://ftp.fedworld.gov/pub/jobs/vt.txt

Washington State
ftp://ftp.fedworld.gov/pub/jobs/wa.txt

Wisconsin
ftp://ftp.fedworld.gov/pub/jobs/wi.txt

Wyoming
ftp://ftp.fedworld.gov/pub/jobs/wy.txt

 The Academic Position Network
gopher://rodent.cis.umn.edu:11111/

This network provides notice of academic position announcements around the world, including faculty, staff, and administrative positions; post-doctoral positions; graduate fellowships and assistantships; and more.

 Chronicle of Higher Education
http://chronicle.merit.edu/.ads/.links.html

Use this site to discover academic positions around the world for faculty and research positions (humanities, social sciences, science and technology, and professional fields), administrative positions, and executive positions. You can search job listings by keywords or by region.

Department of the Interior Automated Vacancy Announcement Distribution System (AVADS)
http://info.er.usgs.gov/doi/avads/index.html

This site gives you access to government jobs nationwide in the Bureau of Indian Affairs, Bureau of Land Management, Bureau of Mines, Bureau of Reclamation, Fish and Wildlife Services, Minerals Management Service, National Biological Service, National Park Service, Office of the Secretary, Office of Surface Mining, and U.S. Geological Survey.

Federal Aviation Administration (FAA)
http://web.fie.com/web/fed/faa/faamnfn.htm

This site gives information on the FAA and lists position announcements, like transportation specialist and teaching positions for aviation schools.

Federal Information Exchange, Inc.
http://fedix.fie.com/

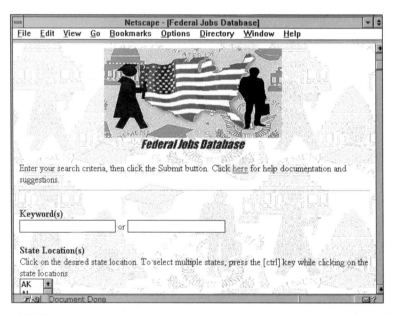

Figure 10.7 There are tons of government job resources available online.

This comprehensive site lists available opportunities and activities information for the Department of Energy (DOE), Air Force Office of Scientific Research (AFOSR), Department of Agriculture (USDA), Federal Aviation Administration (FAA), National Aeronautics and Space Administration (NASA), National Institute of Allergy and Infectious Diseases (NIAID), National Institute of Environmental Health Sciences (NIEHS), and the Office of Naval Research (ONR).

Federal Jobs Database

http://www.jobweb.org/fedjobsr.htm

Part of JobWeb, this site allows you to search government job openings by keyword or state.

Indiana State Department of Personnel

http://www.ai.org

This site includes the ISDP job bank and allows you to download all job listings. It lists rules for application and gives you access to the locations of Statewide Workforce Development Offices (for typing tests).

Purdue Gopher

gopher://gopher.adpc.Purdue.edu/11/personnel/

The Purdue Gopher lists current job openings at Purdue University.

Texas Parks and Wildlife

http://www.tpwd.state.tx.us/involved/jobvac/job.htm

This site lists jobs with the Texas Parks and Wildlife Department in areas like Human Resources, Wildlife, Coastal Fisheries, Inland Fisheries, Public Lands, Law Enforcement, Conservation Communications, Resource Protection, and more. It also has an online Texas State job application.

APPENDIX

A

The U.S. Internet Service Providers List

everal lists of ISPs can be found online, but if you were able to get online, you probably wouldn't need an ISP in the first place. The following information and listings are maintained on the World Wide Web at http://www.primus.com/providers/ and at its mirror site at http://www.cerf.net/staff/peggy/provider.html. It's one of the most comprehensive and up-to-date listings we've found.

This list of providers is indexed by area code, and then alphabetically by name of service provider. All providers offer at least interactive TCP connections (such as telnet and ftp). Providers who offer only email or other limited access (such as small BBS systems) are not listed here.

To find an Internet access provider for your area, simply look up your area code in the index and find the names of providers who service your area code. Then look them up in the main list and contact them via the information found there. Please note that not all providers have furnished information by area code, so while they are in this list, they may not be in the index of area codes.

If your area code is not listed in the index, there are providers who have nationwide access whom you can contact. These providers are listed at the beginning of the index. If you can't find any local dial-in numbers, your only option is to choose providers who are closest to you or choose providers who have 800 dial-in access. These providers are also listed at the beginning of the index.

How to Get Connected

All you need to do is contact your provider either by phone, fax, or electronic mail. While a lot of information is listed here, we highly recommend calling the providers to find out about other services they may provide (technical support, network consulting, etc.) and/or their latest information.

The modem numbers listed for the providers are a method for people to register online. Just dial up the number listed and leave the necessary information. This type of service generally allows users to get started with an Internet account much faster than handling it via the phone. Generally, registration of this type requires a credit card.

What the Services Are

Shell: Offers a basic connection running in a Unix environment. Services include electronic mail, Usenet news, FTP, telnet, gopher, IRC (Internet Relay Chat—which allows you to carry on discussions online, in real time), and so on, but you will not be able to access the World Wide Web.

UUCP: Stands for Unix-to-Unix Copy Protocol, and offers a method for Unix-based computers to transfer files from machine to machine. It's not useful for PC or Mac users.

SLIP: Allows computers to be temporarily connected to the Internet. You can run services such as FTP and telnet directly from a PC or Mac. This also allows you to run some of the popular graphical user interface software (such as Mosaic and other World Wide Web clients).

PPP: Similar to SLIP but considered to be a more efficient protocol. Either a SLIP or PPP account will support Web access.

LAN: This is for connecting an organization's local area network to the Internet—not something you're likely to need as an individual subscriber.

ISDN: Stands for Integrated Services Digital Network, and refers to high-speed (from 56 K baud to 128 K baud) network connections that are offered as dial-up access via digital connections (because it's all digital, no modem is required and faster access speeds can be supported). ISDN is only available in certain areas that are set up with the required digital switching equipment. Your system also needs special hardware to connect to an ISDN line, so ISDN is not very practical for a beginning Internet user. However, ISDN costs are becoming lower almost monthly, so ISDN access is something to keep in mind for the future. Many mid- to large-size ISPs support ISDN connections.

Leased lines: Any of a number of approaches in which the user directly leases access to high-speed, long distance phone lines (such as from MCI, Sprint, AT&T, and others), rather than connecting to the Internet via an ISP. Leased line connections are currently as fast as 45 mega*bits* per second, but cost thousands of dollars per year to lease. For this reason, leased-line connections are typically purchased by medium- to large-size companies that need to make sure their users have extremely fast access.

Index of Providers by Area Code

Nationwide   ACM, AlterNet, ANS, BIX, CIX, CRIS, Delphi, Exec-PC, free.i.net, Gateway, Global Connect, HoloNet, IGC Networks, Internetworks, Moran Communications Group, Network 99, NovaLink, Pipeline, Portal, PSI, Vnet

800   ACM, Centurion, CERFnet, Colorado SuperNet, denver.net, Futuris, FXnet, INS, Internet Express, Internet Online, Internet Services, Interpath, Msen, National Internet, NeoSoft, New Mexico Technet, OARnet, Pacific Rim, Ping,
Rabbit Network, Sacramento Network, South Coast, VoiceNet, WLN, Zone

201   Digital, Dorsai, Echo, Interactive, Internet Online, National Internet, Mordor, Neighborhood, Netcom, New York Net, Panix, Planet, Zone

202   CAIS, CAPCON, Charm Net, ClarkNet, Digital, LaserNet, NCM, NovaNet, US Net

203 Connix, Dorsai, Futuris, I-2000, MiraCom, New York Net, PCNet, Internet Access Company

205 interQuest, Nuance, Planet, Traveller

206 Cyberlink, Eskimo North, Netcom, Network Access, NorthWest CommLink, Northwest Nexus, NorthwestNet, Pacifier, Pacific Rim, RAINet, SeaNet, SenseMedia, Skagit, Teleport, Townsend, WLN

207 maine.net

208 Evergreen, Primenet, WLN

209 Sacramento Network, West Coast Online

210 CRL, Freeside

212 Blythe, Creative Data, CRL, Escape, Dorsai, I-2000, Ingress, Interport,Maestro, Mordor, Netcom, New York Net, NYSERNet, Panix, Phantom Pipeline, Internet Access Company, Walrus, Zone

213 CRL, CSUnet, DHM, DigiLink, Earthlink, KAIWAN, Network Intensive, Primenet,ViaNet

214 CRL, Dallas Vietnamese, DFW, Metronet, National Knowledge, NeoSoft, Netcom, On-Ramp

215 FishNet, VoiceNet, You Tools

216 APK, Exchange, OARnet

217 FGInet, Sol Tec

218 Minnesota Regional Network, Red River

301 CAIS, CAPCON, Charm Net, ClarkNet, Digital, FredNet, LaserNet, NCM, NovaNet, SURAnet, US Net

302 SSNet

303 Colorado Internet Cooperative, Colorado SuperNet, DASH, denver.net, Ever green, Internet Express, Netcom, New Mexico Technet, Nyx, Rocky Mountain

304 WVnet

305 Acquired Knowledge, CyberGate, Florida Online, IDS, SatelNET

310 CERFnet, CRL, CSUnet, DHM, DigiLink, Earthlink, KAIWAN, Leonardo Internet, Lightside, Los Nettos, Network Intensive, ViaNet

312 AIS, InterAccess, MCSNet, Netcom, Ripco, Tezcat, WorldWide

313 Innovative Data, Msen, MichNet, CICnet, ICNet

314 NeoSoft, ThoughtPort

315 NYSERNet

316 SouthWind, Tyrell

317 IQuest, Network Link, Sol Tec

319 INS, Planet

360 Telebyte

401 IDS, Internet Access Company

402 INS, MIDnet, Internet Nebraska, Synergy

404	CRL, Intergate, Internet Atlanta, Internet Services, Lyceum, Netcom, MindSpring, Ping
405	GSS, Internet Oklahoma, Questart Network Services
406	WLN
407	CyberGate, Florida Online, IDS, InternetU
408	Aimnet, BEST, CCnet, CSUnet, Darex, Duck Pond, ElectriCiti, Internet Connection, InterNex, Netcom, Web Professionals, Inc., Scruz-Net, SenseMedia, South Valley, ViaNet, West Coast Online, zNET
409	Brazos, Info-Highway, Internet Connect Services, Inc, NeoSoft
410	CAIS, CAPCON, Charm Net, ClarkNet, Digital jaguNET
412	PREPnet, PSCNET, Telerama
414	BINCnet, FullFeed, Internet Connect, MIX, WorldWide
415	Aimnet, APlatform, BARRnet, BEST, Catch22, CCnet, CERFnet, CRL, CSUnet, Darex, ElectriCiti, InterNex, Internet Service, LineX, Little Garden, Netcom, North Bay Network, QuakeNet, Scruz-Net, Sirius, ViaNet, Well, West Coast Online, Zocalo
419	OARnet
501	Sibylline
502	IgLou
503	Hevanet, Internetworks, Netcom, RainDrop, RAINet, Teleport, WLN
504	NeoSoft, Tyrell
505	Evergreen, Internet Express, Network Intensive, New Mexico Technet, Road runner, Southwest
507	Millennium, Minnesota Regional Network
508	Destek, DMC, Internet Access, intuitive, North Shore, Schunix, Internet Access Company, UltraNet World
509	Internet On-Ramp, WLN
510	Aimnet, Access InfoSystems, BDT, BEST, Catch22, CCnet, CERFnet, Community ConneXion, CRL, CSUnet, ElectriCiti, IACNet, InterNex, Netcom, Sacramento Network, West Coast Online, Zocalo
512	CRL, Eden Matrix, Freeside, Illuminati, Internet Connect Services, Inc., Moontower, Netcom, Onramp, Real/Time, THEnet, The Turning Point, Zilker
513	EriNet, Freelance, IgLou, Internet Access Online, OARnet, IACNet
515	Des Moines Internet, eCity Internet, Freese-Weather, INS
516	Cosmic, Creative Data, Dorsai, Echo, I-2000, LI Net, Long Island Info, Maestro, Network Internet, New York Net, NYSERNet, Panix, Phantom, Savvy, Zone
517	ICNet, Msen, MichNet
518	AlbanyNet, Internet Online, NYSERNet, Wizvax
602	ACES, CRL, Crossroads, Evergreen, GetNet, Internet Direct, Internet Ex press, Netcom, New Mexico Technet, Primenet
603	Destek, MV Communications, NETIS, Internet Access Company

606	IgLou
607	NYSERNet
608	BINCnet, FullFeed, WiscNet
609	Digital, New Jersey Computer, New York Net
610	FishNet, SSNet, YouTools
612	Cloudnet, InterNetwork, MicroNet, Millennium, Minnesota Regional Network, Sound Communications, Skypoint, StarNet
614	InfiNet, OARnet
615	Edge, Telalink
616	ICNet, Msen, MichNet
617	Channel 1, CRL, Delphi, Internet Access Company, Netcom, NEARNET, NorthShore, Pioneer, Wilder, World, Xensei
619	CERFnet, CSUnet, CTS, Data Transfer, ElectriCiti, ESNET, Netcom, Network Intensive, Network Link
701	Red River
702	Evergreen, Great Basin, Netcom, NevadaNet, Sacramento Network, Sierra, @wizard
703	CAIS, CAPCON, Charm Net, ClarkNet, Digital, LaserNet, Netcom, NCM, PSI, NovaNet, US Net
704	FXnet, Vnet
706	Internet Atlanta, InteliNet, MindSpring
707	Access InfoSystems, CRL, CSUnet, Northcoast Pacific Internet, West Coast Online
708	AIS, InterAccess, MCSNet, netILLINOIS, Ripco Tezcat, WorldWide
712	INS
713	The Black Box, CRL, Info-Highway, Internet Connect Services, Inc., NeoSoft, On-Ramp, Sesquinet, South Coast
714	CERFnet, CRL, CSUnet, DHM, DigiLink, KAIWAN, Lightside, Netcom, Network Intensive
715	BINCnet, FullFeed,
716	NYSERNet
717	SuperNet, You Tools
718	Blythe, Creative Data, Escape, Digital, Dorsai, I-2000, Ingress, Interport, Maestro, Mordor, New York Net, NYSERNet, Panix, Phantom, Walrus, Zone
719	Colorado SuperNet, denver.net, Internet Express, Old Colorado, Rocky Mountain
801	Evergreen, Internet Direct, XMission
802	Destek
803	FXnet, GlobalVision, InteliNet, SIMS, South Carolina SuperNet, A World of Difference
804	Widomaker, VERnet

805	The Central Connection, Datawave KAIWAN, Network Intensive, SmartDOCS Data Services,
808	Hawaii OnLine, PACCOM, Pacific Information Exchange, SenseMedia
810	ICNet, Innovative Data, Rabbit Network, MichNet, Msen
812	IgLou, The Point
813	Centurion, CyberGate, Florida Online, Intelligence, PacketWorks
814	Telerama
815	InterAccess, MCSNet, Sol Tec, WorldWide
816	Primenet, Q-Networks, SkyNET, Tyrell
817	ACM, DFW Metronet, National Knowledge, ONRAMP
818	The Central Connection, CERFnet, CRL, CSUnet, DHM, DigiLink, Earthlink, KAIWAN, Lightside, Netcom, Network Intensive, Primenet, ViaNet
904	CyberGate, Florida Online, Jax, SymNet
906	ICNet, MichNet, Msen
907	Internet Alaska
908	Digital, I-2000, New York Net, Planet, Zone
909	KAIWAN, Lightside
910	Vnet
912	Internet Atlanta
913	SkyNET, Tyrell
914	Cloud 9, Dorsai, Futuris, I-2000, IDS, MHVNet, New York Net, NYSERNet, Panix, Phantom, TZ-Link, WestNet, Zone
915	New Mexico Technet
916	CSUnet, Netcom, Sacramento Network, Sierra, West Coast Online
917	I-2000, New York Net, Zone
918	South Coast
919	Atlantic Internet, Interpath, Netcom, CONCERT, Vnet

Alphabetical Listing of Providers

Access InfoSystems
Contact: Sales
Phone: (707) 422-1034
Fax: (707) 422-0331
Email: info@community.net
Services: Shell, SLIP, PPP
Area Codes: 708, 510
Fees:
Shell: $17.50/month (flat rate)
SLIP, PPP: $25-$44.50/month (flat rate)

ACES Research
Contact: Sales
Phone: (602) 322-6500
Fax: (602) 322-9755
Email: sales@aces.com
URL: http://www.aces.com/
Services: SLIP, 56-T1
Area Codes: 602
Fees:
SLIP: $1200/month (flat rate)

56K: $400/month

T1: $1200/month

Acquired Knowledge Systems, Inc.

Contact: Wieslaw Samek

Phone: (305) 525-2574

Fax: (305) 462-2329

Email: samek@aksi.net

Modem: (305) 462-2638 (login "new")

URL: http://www.aksi.net/

Services: Shell, SLIP, PPP, UUCP, BBS, WWW

Area Codes: 305

Fees:

Shell: $17/month, $169/year

SLIP, PPP: $20/month, $199/year

UUCP: $20/month (20 hrs, $1/hr add'l)

Other: Call

ACM Network Services

Contact: Angela Abbott

Phone: (817) 776-6876

Fax: (817) 751-7785

Email: account-info@acm.org

URL: http://www.acm.org/

Services: Shell, SLIP, PPP, WWW, T1

Area Codes: 800, 817, nationwide

Fees: Call or write

Aimnet Information Services

Contact: Sales

Phone: (408) 257-0900

Fax: (408) 257-5452

Email: info@aimnet.com

Modem: (408) 366-9000 (login "guest")

URL: http://www.aimnet.com/

Services: Shell, SLIP, PPP, UUCP, DNS, WWW, ISDN, 56-T1

Area Codes: 408, 415, 510

Fees:

Shell: $19.95/setup, $18-$35/month

SLIP, PPP: $45-$450/setup, $20-$145/month

UUCP: $49.95/setup, $25/month

DNS: $49.95/setup, $35/month

Other: Call

AlbanyNet

Contact: Sales

Phone: (518) 465-0873

Email: sales@albany.net

Modem: (518) 432-1751 (login "new")

URL: http://www.albany.net/

Services: Shell, SLIP, PPP, UUCP, LAN, WWW, FTP, 56-T3

Area Codes: 518

Fees:

Shell, SLIP, PPP: $15-$60/month

AlterNet (UUNET Technologies)

Contact: Sales

Phone: (800) 4UUNET4

Fax: (703) 204-8007

Email: info@uunet.uu.net

URL: http://www.uu.net/

Services: Telnet only, UUCP, SLIP, PPP, 56, 128 T1, 10Mps

Area Codes: All

Fees: Call

American Information Systems, Inc. (AIS)

Contact: Mike Hakimi, Josh Schneider

Phone: (708) 413-8400

Fax: (708) 413-8401

Email: schneid@ais.net

Services: Shell, SLIP, PPP, UUCP, WWW, LAN, FTP, leased lines

Area Codes: 708, 312

Fees:

Shell: $16.95/month (flat rate)

SLIP, PPP: $22.50/month (flat rate)

Other: Call

APK Public Access UNI*

Contact: Zbigniew Tyrlik

Phone: (216) 481-9428

Email: support@wariat.org

URL: http://www.wariat.org/
Services: Shell, SLIP, PPP, www/gopher service, ISDN, 56, 128
Area Codes: 216
Fees:
Shell: $15/month (20 hours), $35/month (flat rate)
SLIP, PPP: $95/setup, $2/hour
Other: Call or write

APlatform
Contact: Michael Teicher
Phone: (415) 941-2641
Fax: (415) 941-2647
Email: support@aplatform.com
URL: http://usa.net/
Services: Shell, SLIP, PPP
Area Codes: 415
Fees:
Shell: $13/month
SLIP, PPP: $30/month

ANS
Contact: Sales
Phone: (800) 456-8267, (703) 758-7700
Fax: (703) 758-7717
Email: info@ans.net
URL: gopher://gopher.ans.net/
Services: 56, T1, T3
Area Codes: Nationwide

Atlantic Internet
Contact: Customer Service
Phone: (919) 833-1252
Fax: (919) 833-1208
E-mail: info@ainet.net (automated), sales@ainet.net (human)
URL: http://www.ainet.net/
Area codes: 919
Services: Shell, C/SLIP, PPP, WWW, ISDN, 56-T1.
Fees:
Shell: $10+/month
C/SLIP, PPP: $10+/month
ISDN: $20+/month

BARRNet
Contact: Sales
Phone: (415) 725-1790
Fax: (415) 725-3119
Email:info@barrnet.net URL: http:www.barrnet.net/

Beckemeyer Development (BDT)
Contact: Sales
Phone: (510) 530-9637
Fax: (510) 530-0451
Email: info@bdt.com
URL: http://www.bdt.com/
Services: UUCP, SLIP, PPP, ISDN, 56-T1
Fees: Email/News: $3/month
UUCP: $20/setup, $10/month
SLIP, PPP: $20-$250/setup, $1/hr - $100/month
56: $1100/setup, $350/month
T1: $2200/setup, $950/month
Other: Call

Best Internet Communications, Inc. (BEST)
Contact: Rich White
Phone: (415) 964-2378
Fax: (415) 691-4195
Email: info@best.com
URL: http://www.best.com
Services: Shell, SLIP, PPP, FTP, LAN, WWW, Leased lines
Area Codes: 408, 415, 510
Fees:
Shell: included with SLIP/PPP
SLIP,PPP: $30 setup, $30/month (flat rate V.34)
LAN: $450 setup, $85/month (dedicated line)
WWW: 25MB on server free with SLIP/PPP
FTP: 25MB on server free with SLIP/PPP

BINCnet
Contact: Dave Ward
Phone: (608) 233-5222
Fax: (608) 233-9795
Email: ward@binc.net
Services: SLIP, PPP, 56-T1, WWW, LAN
Area codes: 608 414, 715

Fees:

SLIP, PPP: $20-$150/month

56: $500/month

T1: $1500/month

BIX (Delphi Internet Services)

Contact: BIX Member Services

Phone: (800) 695-4775, (617) 354-4137

Fax: (617) 441-4903

Email: info@bix.com

Modem: (800) 695-4882, (617) 491-5410 (login "bix")

Services: Shell

Area Codes: Nationwide

Fees:

$13/month + connect fees ($1-$9/hr)

Des Moines Internet

Contact: Brent Finer

Phone: (515) 270-9191

Fax: (515) 270-8648

Email: brentf@dsmnet.com

URL: http://www.dsmnet.com/

Services: Shell, SLIP

Area Codes: 515

Fees: Shell: $20/month (flat rate)

SLIP: $30/month (flat rate)

The Black Box

Contact: Marc Newman

Phone: (713) 480-2684

Email: info@blkbox.com

Services: Shell, SLIP, PPP, ISDN, Other

Area Codes: 713

Fees:

Shell: $21.65/month (flat rate)

SLIP,PPP: $43.30/month

ISDN: $270.63/month

Blarg! Online Services

Contact: Marc Lewis

Phone: (206) 783-8981

Fax: (206) 706-0618

Email: marc@blarg.com

URL: http://www.blarg.com/

Modem: (206) 784-9681 (login as "new")

Services: Shell, UUCP, SLIP, PPP, FTP, LAN, WWW, 56-T1, consult

Fees:

Shell: $10/setup, $15/month (flat rate)

SLIP,PPP: $20-$200/setup, $20-$125/month

UUCP: $20/setup, $5/month + $1/hour

Blythe Systems

Contact: Max Hudson

Phone: (212) 348-2875

Fax: (212) 633-2889

Email: accounts@blythe.org

Modem: (212) 675-9690 (login "blythe info")

Services: Shell

Area Codes: 212, 718

Fees:

Email/News: $8/month

Shell: $20/month

Brazos Information Highways Services

Contact: Butch Kemper

Phone: (409) 693-9336

Email: info@bihs.net

Services: PPP, 56-128, WWW, FTP, UUCP

URL: http://www.bihs.net/

Area Codes: 409

Fees:

PPP: $20/month (40 hours)

CAPCON Library Network

Contact: Jeanne Otten

Phone: (202) 331-5771

Fax: (202) 797-7719

Email: info@capcon.net

Services: Shell, SLIP, PPP, FTP, training

Area Codes: 202, 301, 410, 703

Fees:

Shell: $35/setup + $150/year + $25/month

Other: Call or write

Capitol Area Internet Service (CAIS)
Contact: Debbie Alston
Phone: (703) 448-4470
Fax: (703) 790-8805
Email: dalston@cais.com
Services: Shell, UUCP, SLIP, PPP, ISDN, FTP, WWW, 56-T1
Area Codes: 202, 301, 410, 703
Fees:
Shell: $20/month (flat rate)
SLIP, PPP: $20/month (4 hrs/day)
Other: Call

Catch22
Contact: Sales
Phone:(415) 431-9903
Email: info@catch22.com
Modem: (415) 865-2550 (login as "new")
Services: Shell, PPP, FTP, ISDN, WWW, 56-T3
Area Codes: 415, 510
Fees:
Shell, PPP: $0.50/hr

CCnet Communications
Contact: Information
Phone: (510) 988-0680
Fax: (510) 988-0689
Email: info@ccnet.com
Modem: (510) 988-0680, 419-3600, 355-3030 (login "guest")
URL: http://www.ccnet.com/
Services: Shell, SLIP, PPP, ISDN, 56-T1
Area Codes: 510, 415, 408
Fees:
Shell: $16-$18/month (flat rate)
SLIP, PPP: $25-$99/month
Other: Call

The Central Connection
Contact: Sales
Phone: (818) 735-3000
Fax: (818) 879-9997
Email: info@centcon.com

URL: http://www.ccnet.com/
Services: Shell, SLIP, PPP, UUCP, ISDN, DNS, 56-T1
Area Codes: 510, 415, 408
Fees:
Shell, SLIP, PPP, ISDN: $25/month (100 hours)
DNS: $50/domain

Centurion Technology, Inc.
Contact: Jeffrey Jablow
Phone: (813) 572-5556
Fax: (813) 572-1452
Email: jablow@cent.com
Services: Shell, PPP, 56, 128, T1
Area Codes: 800, 813
Fees:
Shell: $25/month (flat rate)
800: $15/first two hours, .10/min add'l
Other: Call

CERFnet
Contact: Sales
Phone: (800) 876-2373, (619) 455-3900
Fax: (619) 455-3990
Email: info@cerf.net, sales@cerf.net
Modem: (800) 723-7363 (login "newuser")
URL: http://www.cerf.net/
Services: Shell, SLIP, PPP, ISDN, 56-T3
Area Codes: 800, 310, 415, 510, 619, 714, 818
Fees: Call or write

Channel 1
Contact: Jamie Walsh
Phone: (617) 864-0100
Email: (617) 354-3100
Email: info@channel1.com
Modem: (617) 354-3230
URL: http://www.channel1.com
Services: Shell, SLIP, PPP, WWW
Area codes: 617
Fees:
$8/month and up

Charm Net

Contact: Erik Monti

Phone: (410) 558-3900

Fax: (410) 558-3901

Email: emonti@charm.net

Modem: (410) 558-3300 (login "guest")

URL: http://www.charm.net

Services: Shell, PPP, WWW

Area codes: 410, 301, 202, 703

Fees:

$25/month

CICnet

Contact: Sales

Phone: (800) 947-4754, (313) 998-6703

Fax: (313) 998-6105

Email: info@cic.net

URL: http://www.cic.net/

Clark Internet Services (ClarkNet)

Contact: ClarkNet Office

Phone: Call (800)735-2258 (MD Relay Service) then give (410)730-9764 to the answering operator. This is a deaf owned/operated company so you will be using a voice service to communicate with the sales staff.

Fax: (410) 730-9765

Email: info@clark.net

URL: http://www.clark.net/

Services: Email/News, Shell, SLIP, PPP, ISDN, 56, T1

Area Codes: 410, 301, 202, 703

Fees:

Email/News: $14/month

Shell: $23/month

UUCP: $33/month

SLIP/PPP: $33-$150/month

IDSN: $300/month

Other: Call

Cloud 9 Internet

Contact: Scott Drassinower

Phone: (914) 682-0626

Fax: (914) 682-0506

Email: scottd@cloud9.net

URL: http://www.cloud9.net

Services: Shell, SLIP, PPP, ISDN, 56 and higher

Area Codes: 914

Fees:

Shell: $45/quarter

SLIP, PPP: $90/quarter (personal)

Other: Call

Cloudnet

Phone: (612) 240-8243

Email: info@cloudnet.com

URL: http://magellan.cloudnet.net

Services: Shell

Area Codes: 612

Fees: $25/month (100 hrs, $0.25/hr add'l)

Colorado Internet Cooperative Association

Phone: (303) 443-3786

Fax: (303) 443-9718

Email: contact@coop.net

URL: http://www.coop.net/coop

Services: SLIP, PPP, 56, T1, ISDN

Area Codes: 303

Fees:

SLIP, PPP: $1500/setup, $100/month

56K: $1300-$1900/setup, $200-$250/month

ISDN: $1900-$2600/setup, $250-$350/month

T1: $2400-$3100/setup, $400-$500/month

Colorado SuperNet, Inc

Contact: Sales/Help Desk

Phone: (303) 296-8202

Fax: (303) 296-8224

Email: info@csn.org

URL: http://www.csn.org/

Services: Shell, UUCP, SLIP, 56, T1

Area Codes: 303, 719, 800

Fees:

Shell: $20/setup, $1-$3/hour ($15 min/$250 max)

UUCP: $60/setup, $1-$3/hour ($15 min/$250 max)

SLIP: $40/setup, $1-$3/hour ($15 min/$250 max)

800: $8/hr

Commercial Internet Exchange (CIX)
Contact: Lou Scanlan
Phone: (703) 8-CIX-CIX
Email: info@cix.org
URL: http://www.cix.org

Community ConneXion
Contact: Sameer Parekh
Phone: (510) 841-2014
Email: info@c2.org
URL: http://www.c2.org/
Services: Shell, FTP, WWW, SLIP/PPP(soon)
Area Codes:510
Fees: $10/month, $27/3 months, $45/6 months

CRIS
Phone: (517) 895-0500
Fax: (517) 895-0529
Email: sysop@cris.com
Modem: (517) 895-0510
Serivces: Shell, SLIP
Area codes: Nationwide
Fees:
Shell, SLIP: $30/month (flat rate)
800: $5/hour

CONCERT
Contact: Naomi Courter
Phone: (919) 248-1999
Fax: (919) 248-1405
Email: info@concert.net
URL: http://www.concert.net/

The Connection
Contact: Sales
Phone: (201) 435-4414
Fax: (201) 435-4414
Email: info@cnct.com
Modem: (201) 435-4000 (login "guest")
Services: Shell, SLIP
Fees:
Shell: $20/setup, $10/month (3 month minimum)
SLIP: $25/month

Connix: The Connecticut Internet Exchange
Contact: Jim Hogue
Phone: (203) 349-7059
Email: office@connix.com
Modem: (203) 349-1176
URL: http://www.connix.com/
Services: Shell, SLIP, PPP, leased lines
Area Codes: 203
Fees:
Shell: $20/month (20 hours, $1/hr add'l)
SLIP, PPP: $25/month (20 hours, $1/hr add'l)
Other: Call or write

Cosmic Internet Services
Phone: (516) 342-7597
Modem: (516) 342-7270 (login "guest")

Creative Data Consultants (silly.com)
Contact: Matt Preston
Phone: (718) 229-0489 x23
Email: info@silly.com
Modem: (718) 229-7096 (login "guest")
Services: Shell, FTP, WWW, BBS
Area Codes: 718, 212, 516
Fees:
Shell: $6/month (1 hr/day)
Other: Call

CRL Network Services
Contact: Sales
Phone: (415) 837-5300
Email: sales@crl.com
Services: Shell, SLIP, PPP, ISDN, 56, 128, T1
Area Codes: 210, 212, 213, 214, 310, 404, 415, 510, 512, 602, 617, 707, 713, 714, 818
Fees:
Shell: $17.50/month

Crossroads Communications
Phone: (602) 813-9040
Fax: (602) 545-7470
Email: info@xroads.com
Modem: (602) 813-9041 (login "guest")

URL: http://xroads.xroads.com/home.html
Services: Shell, C/SLIP, PPP, UUCP, WWW, 56-T1
Area codes: 602
Fees:
Shell: $18-$31/month
SLIP, PPP: $19.95-$32.95/month

CSUnet (California State Unversity)
Contact: Mary Jane Whitson
Phone: (310) 985-9445
Fax: (310) 985-9093
Email: maryjane@csu.net
URL: http://www.calstate.edu/
Services: 56, 128, 384, T1. Services are only available to educational and non-profit organizations.
Area Codes: All in California
Fees: Call

CTS Network Services
Contact: Sales
Phone: (619) 637-3637
Fax: (619) 637-3630
Email: support@cts.com
URL: http://www.cts.com/
Services: Shell, SLIP, PPP, UUCP, LAN, ISDN, WWW, 56, T1
Area Codes: 619
Fees:
Shell: $18/month
SLIP, PPP: $23/month
Other: Call

CyberGate, Inc
Contact: Dan Sullivan, Tom Benham
Phone: (305) 428-4283
Fax: (305) 428-7977
Email: sales@gate.net, sullivan@gate.net
URL: http://www.gate.net/
Services: Shell, SLIP, PPP, UUCP, 56, T1
Area Codes: 305, 407, 813, 904
Fees:

Shell: $17.50/month
SLIP, PPP: $29.50
Other: Call

Cyberlink Communications
Contact: Jack Valko
Phone: (206) 281-5397, (515) 945-7000
Fax: (206) 281-0421
Email: sales@cyberspace.com
URL: http://www.cyberspace.com/
Services: Shell, SLIP, PPP
Area Codes: 206
Fees:
Shell: $15/month, $40/quarter (flat rate)
SLIP, PPP: additional $40/

Dallas Vietnamese Network
Contact: Stephen Jones
Phone: (214)248-8701
Fax: (214)317-2574
Email: support@sdf.lonestar.org
Modem: (214)248-9811 (login "visitor")
Services: Shell, UUCP
Area Codes: 214

Darex Associates
Contact: Alex
Phone: (415) 903-4720
Email: info@darex.com
URL: http://www.darex.com/
Services: Dedicated SLIP, PPP, WWW, FTP
Area Codes: 415, 408
Fees:
$75/month (flat rate)

DASH - Denver Area Super Highway
Contact: Angel Prouty
Phone: (800) 624-8597, (303) 674-9784
Email: info@dash.com, custserv@dash.com
URL: http://www.dash.com
Services: Shell, SLIP, PPP, WWW, Leased lines
Area Codes: 303

Datawave Network Services
Contact: Michael Fredkin
Phone: (805) 730-7775
Fax: (805) 730-7779
Email: sales@datawave.net
URL: http://www.datawave.net/inet-service
Services: 56
Area codes: 805
Fees: $450/mo

Data Transfer Group
Phone: (619) 220-8601
Email: help@access.thegroup.net
URL: http://www.thegroup.net/
Area Codes: 619

Delphi Internet Services Corp
Contact: Walt Howe
Phone: (800) 695-4005
Fax: (617) 491-6642
Email: walthowe@dephi.com
URL: http://www.delphi.com/
Services: Shell
Area Codes: All - 617 direct, others through Sprintnet
& Tymnet
Fees: $13/month for 4 hours + $4/hr additional $24/
month for 20 hours + $1.80/hr additional

denver.net
Contact: Andy Cook
Phone: (303) 973-7757
Fax: (303) 973-7504
Email: info@denver.net
URL: http://www.denver.net
Services: PPP
Area Codes: 303, 719, 800
Fees:
PPP: $25/month for 100 hrs + $1/hr additional 800:
$8/hr

The Destek Group, Inc.
Contact: New Accounts
Phone: (603) 635-3857 or (508) 363-2413
Fax: (508) 363-2155

Email: info@destek.net
URL: http://www.destek.net/Destek
Services: SLIP, PPP, WWW, wireless, 56, T1 ISDN,
DNS, FTP, gopher, POP, SMTP, NNTP/NNRP
Area Codes: 508, 603, 802
Fees:
SLIP/PPP: $75-$250/setup, $25-$140/month
ISDN: $125-$175/setup, $40-$400/month
Leased: Call
WWW: $25/setup, $5/month + $1/Meg
FTP: $25/setup, $5/month + $1/Meg

DFW Internet Services, Inc.
Contact: Jack Beech
Phone: (817) 332-5116
Fax: (817) 870-1501
Email: sales@dfw.net
Modem: (817) 429-3520 (login "info")
URL: http://www.dfw.net/
Services: Shell, SLIP, PPP, UUCP, WWW, FTP,
56 through T1
Area Codes: 214, 817
Fees:
Shell: $17.50/month
PPP: $25/month
Other: Call

DHM Information Management, Inc.
Contact: Dirk Harms-Merbitz
Phone: (310) 214-3349
Fax: (310) 214-3090
Email: dharms@dhm.com
URL: http://www.dhm.com/
Services: LAN, PPP, SLIP, WWW, FTP, T1-56,
Shell
Area codes: 213, 310, 714, 818
Fees: Call or write

DigiLink Network Services
Contact: Sales (Bob Atkins)
Phone: (310) 542-7421
Email: info@digilink.net, bob@digilink.net
Services: ISDN, PPP

Area codes: 213, 310, 714, 818

Fees:

$150-$595/setup, $105-$495/month

Digital Express Group

Contact: Sales Department

Phone: (301) 220-2020, (410) 813-2724, (800) 969-9090

Fax: (301) 220-0477

Email: sales@digex.net

URL: http://www.digex.net

Services: Shell, SLIP, PPP, 56, T1

Area Codes: 201, 202, 301, 410, 609, 703, 718, 908

Fees:

Shell: $25/month

SLIP, PPP: $35/month

Other: Call

The Dorsai Embassy

Contact: Charles Rawls, Jack Brooks

Phone: (718) 392-3667

Email: info@dorsai.org

Modem: (718) 392-4060 (login "new")

URL: http://www.dorsai.org/

Services: Shell, SLIP, PPP

Area Codes: 718, 212, 201, 203, 914, 516

Fees:

Shell: $125/year (suggested donation)

SLIP, PPP: $75/year (extra)

DMConnection

Contact: Sales

Phone: (508) 568-1618

Fax: (508) 562-1133

Email: postmaster@dmc.com

Services: Shell, SLIP, PPP, UUCP

Area Codes: 508

Fees:

Shell: $5-$40/month

Other: Call

The Duck Pond Public Unix

Contact: Nick Sayer

Fax: (408) 249-9630

Email: postmaster@kfu.com

Modem: (408) 249-9640 (login "guest")

URL: http://www.kfu.com/

Services: Shell

Area Codes: 408

Fees: $10/month

Earthlink Network, Inc.

Contact: Sales

Phone: (213) 644-9500

Fax: (213) 644-9510

Email: info@earthlink.net

URL: http://www.earthlink.net/

Services: Shell, SLIP, PPP, ISDN, 56, T1, WWW, FTP, DNS

Area Codes: 213, 310, 818

Fees:

SLIP, PPP: $50-$500/setup, $10-$150/month

ISDN: $50-$2955/setup, $45-$575/month

56: $500/setup, $400/month

T1: $1250/setup, $500-$1000/month

WWW: $200/setup, $100-$300/month

FTP: $100/setup, $50-$150/month

Echo Communications Group

Contact: Stacy Horn

Phone: (212) 255-3839

Fax: (212) 255-9440

Email: horn@echonyc.com

Modem: (212) 989-8411, (212) 989-3386 (login "newuser")

Services: Shell, SLIP, PPP

Area Codes: 201, 516

Fees: $40/setup, $19.95/month (30 hours)

eCity Internet

Contact: JTM MultiMedia, Inc.

Phone: (515) 277-1990

BBS: (515) 277-1038

Fax: (515) 397-9717

Email: jtm@ecity.net

URL: http://www.ecity.net/

Services: PPP, WWW, FTP, email, telnet

Area Codes: 515

Fees:

PPP: $30/month, $165/6 month, $300/12 month

The Eden Matrix

Contact: John Herzer

Phone: (512) 478-9900

Fax: (512) 478-9936

Email: jch@eden.com

URL: http://www.eden.com/

Services: Shell, SLIP, PPP, T1

Area Codes: 512

Fees:

Shell: $12/month, $70/year (flat rate)

SLIP: $15/month, $120/year (flat rate)

Other: Call or write

The Edge

Contact: Tim Choate, Jon Lusky, Bob Neal

Phone: (615) 455-9915 (Tullahoma), (615) 726-8700 (Nashville)

Fax: (615) 454-2042

Email: info@edge.net

Modem: (615) 256-0050 (login "newuser")

URL: http://www.edge.net/

Services: Shell, SLIP, PPP, BBS, LAN, FTP, ISDN, WWW, 56

Area Codes: 615

Fees:

Shell: $9.95/month

SLIP: $9.95/month + $2/hour

Other: Call

ElectriCiti Incorporated

Contact: Sales

Phone: (619) 338-9000

Email: info@electriciti.com

Modem: (619) 687-3930 (login "guest")

URL: http://www.electriciti.com, gopher. electriciti.com

Services: SLIP, CSLIP, PPP

Area Codes: 619,408,415,510

Fees: $295/year

EriNet Online Communications

Contact: Luke Gain

Phone: (513) 436-1700

Fax: (513) 436-1466

Email: info@erinet.com

Modem: (513) 436-9915

URL: http://www.mall2000.com/eri/eri.html

Services: Shell, SLIP, PPP, UUCP

Area Codes: 513

Fees:

Shell: $29.99/month

SLIP, PPP: $69.99/month

Other: Call

Escape (Kazan Corp)

Contact: Sales

Phone: (212) 888-8780

Fax: (212) 832-0344

Email: info@escape.com

Modem: (212) 888-8212 (login "new")

URL: http://www.escape.com/

Services: Shell, SLIP, PPP, UUCP, WWW, FTP, 56

Area Codes: 212, 718

Fees:

Shell: $16.50/month

SLIP, PPP: $16.50-$200/month

UUCP: $16.50/month

Other: Call

Eskimo North

Contact: Sales

Phone: (206) 367-7457

Email: nanook@eskimo.com

URL: http://www.eskimo.com/

Modem: (206) 367-3837 (login "new")

Services: Shell

Area Codes: 206

Fees:

$20/month, $45/quarter

ESNET Communications

Contact: Steve Froeschke

Phone: (619) 287-5943

Email: steve@cg57.esnet.com

Services: Shell, UUCP

Area Codes: 619

Fees:

Shell: $15/month (flat rate)

UUCP: $10/month (flat rate)

Evergreen Internet

Contact: Jody Coombs

Phone: (602) 230-9330

Fax: (602) 230-9773

Email: sales@enet.net

Services: Shell, SLIP, PPP, WWW, WAN, LAN, 56-T1

Area Codes: 702, 801, 602, 208, 303, 505

Fees:

Shell: $25/setup, $20/month

SLIP, PPP: $60/setup, $29/month (150 hours)

Other: Call

Exchange Network Services, Inc

Contact: Michael Krause

Phone: (216) 261-4593

Email: info@en.com

URL: http://www.en.com

Services: Shell, UUCP

Area Codes: 216

Fees:

Shell: $30/setup, $20/month (flat rate)

Other: Call or write

Exec-PC BBS

Contact: Internet Dept

Phone: (800) EXECPC-1, (414) 789-4200

Fax: (414) 789-1946

Email: info@execpc.com

URL: http://www.execpc.com/

Services: Shell, SLIP, PPP, FTP, WWW, ISDN

Area codes: Nationwide

Fees:

Shell: $25/quarter, $75/year (5 hrs/wk)

Shell: $12/month (15 hrs/wk)

SLIP, PPP: $4/hr-$20/month

ISDN: no additional charge

FGInet, Inc.

Contact: Tom Woodward

Phone: (217) 544-2775

Fax: (217) 522-8716

Email: newuser@mail.fgi.net

URL: http://www.fgi.net

Services: Shell, SLIP, PPP

Area codes: 217

Fees:

Shell: $20/month (flat rate)

SLIP, PPP: $30/month (flat rate)

FishNet (Prometheus Information Corp)

Contact: Peter Sardella

Phone: (610) 337-9994

Fax: (610) 337-9918

Email: info@pond.com

URL: http://www.pond.com/

Services: Shell, SLIP, PPP, FTP, WWW

Area Codes: 215, 610

Fees:

Shell: $20/month (60 hours), $200/year

SLIP, PPP: $35/month (60 hours) $350/year

Other: Call

Florida Online

Contact: Jerry Russell

Phone: (407) 635-8888

Fax: (407) 635-9050

Email: jerry@digital.net

Modem: (407) 633-4710 (login "new", password "newuser")

URL: http://digital.net/

Services: Shell, SLIP, PPP, UUCP, ISDN, BBS, WWW, 56-T1

Area Codes: 407, 305, 904, 813

Fees:
Shell: $17-$20/month (flat rate)
SLIP, PPP: $17-$20/month (flat rate)
UUCP: $15/month
Other: Call

FredNet
Phone: (301) 69802386
Email: info@fred.net
Modem: (301) 698-5006, (301) 293-0207 (login "guest")
URL: http://www.fred.net
Services: Shell, SLIP
Area codes: 301
Fees:
Shell: $15/setup, $23/month
SLIP: $30/setup, $33/month
UUCP: $10/month

Freese-Weather.Net
Contact: Freese-Notis
Phone: (515) 282-9310
Fax: (515) 282-6832
Email: hfreese@weather.net
URL: http://www.weather.net/html/internet.html
Services: PPP, WWW, 56K-T3
Area Codes: 515
Fees:
PPP: $200/month (flat rate)

Freelance Systems Programming
Contact: Tom
Phone: (513) 254-7246
Email: fsp@dayton.fsp.com
Services: Shell, SLIP
Area Codes: 513
Fees: $1/hour (2 hour minimum)

free.i.net
Contact: Sales
Phone: (503) 233-4774
Fax: (503) 233-0344
Email: info@i.net

Modem: (801) 471-2266 (login "PPP")
Services: SLIP, PPP
Fees: None

Freeside Communications
Contact: Sales
Phone: (800) 968-8750
Fax: (512) 837-0343
Email: sales@fc.net
URL: http://www.fc.net/
Services: Shell, SLIP, PPP, ISDN, FTP, UUCP, WWW, UUCP, 56-T1
Area codes: 210, 512
Fees:
Shell: $15/month (45 hours)
SLIP, PPP: $25/month
UUCP: $10/month

FullFeed Communications
Contact: Katie Stachoviak
Phone: (608) 246-4239
Email: info@fullfeed.com
Modem: (608) 246-2701 (login "guest")
URL: http://www.fullfeed.com/
Services: Shell, UUCP, PPP, 28.8, 56, 384, T1
Area Codes: 608, 414, 715
Fees:
Shell, PPP, UUCP: $24-$54/month

Futuris Networks Inc
Contact: Hugh Brower
Phone: (203) 359-8868
Email: sales@futuris.net
URL: http://www.futuris.net/
Services: SLIP, PPP, 56-T1, consulting
Area Codes: 203, 914, 800
Fees:
SLIP, PPP: $9-$15/month + $1 hour (28.8 kb)
56K: $350-$500/month

FXnet
Contact: Sales
Phone: (704) 338-4670

Fax: (704) 338-4679
Email: info@fx.net
URL: http://www.fx.net
Services: Shell, UUCP, SLIP, PPP, ISDN, 56, T1
Area Codes: 800, 704, 803
Fees:
Shell: $25/month (flat rate)
UUCP: $30/month + $0.50/hr
SLIP, PPP: $30-$200/month
Other: Call

Gateway to the World, Inc.

Contact: Michael Jansen
Phone: (305) 670-2930
Email: mjansen@gate.com
URL: http://www.gate.com/
Services: Shell
Area codes: Nationwide (also Latin America)
Fees:
South Florida: $15/month
DC area: $7.50/month + $2/hour
Elsewhere: $7.50/month + $5/hour
Latin America: Call

Genuine Computing Resources

Email: info@gcr.com
URL: http://www.gcr.com/
Services: Shell
Fees:
$15/month

GetNet International, Inc.

Contact: Support
Phone: (602) 468-7455
Fax: (602) 468-7838
Email: info@getnet.com
URL: http://www.getnet.com
Services: Shell, SLIP, WWW, UUCP, 56-T1, training, consulting
Area Code: 602
Fees:
Shell, SLIP: $9.99/setup; $9.99/month

Global Connect Inc

Contact: Sales
Phone: (804) 229-4484
Fax: (804) 229-6557
Email: info@gc.net
URL: http://www.gc.net/
Services: Shell, CSLIP, SLIP, PPP, UUCP, DNS, WWW, consulting
Area Codes: Nationwide (including Canada)
Fees:
SLIP, PPP: $30/month + dial-up charges : $200/month (flat rate)
UUCP: $15-$30/month + dial-up charges
Other: Call

Global Enterprise Services, Inc.

Contact: Cheryl Ferrell
Phone: (609) 897-7324, (800) 35-TIGER
Fax: (609) 897-7310
Email: market@jvnc.net
Services: Shell, SLIP, ISDN, LAN
Fees:
Shell: $29/month + $4.95/hr

Global Vision, Inc

Contact: George Derdziak
Phone: (803) 241-0901
Fax: (803) 297-5649
Email: derdziak@globalvision.net
URL: http://globalnews.globalvision.net:8001/index.html
Services: Shell, SLIP, PPP, UUCP, LAN, WWW, FTP, ISDN, 56-T1
Area codes: 803
Fees:
SLIP, PPP: $35/month (flat rate)
Other: Call

Great Basin Internet Services

Contact: Customer Service
Phone: (702) 829-2244
Fax: (702) 829-9926
Email: info@greatbasin.com

Modem: (702) 348-4844 (login "new")

URL: http://www.greatbasin.com/

Services: UUCP, SLIP, PPP, FTP, LAN, WWW, gopher, mailing lists, Leased lines

Area Codes: 702

Fees:

UUCP: $35 setup; $20/month (flat rate)

SLIP, PPP: $20 setup; $20/month (dialup flat rate)

Others: call, write, or check the URL

GSS Internet

Contact: Mike Lester, Jeff Jones

Phone: (918) 835-3655

Fax: (918) 835-9996

Email: info@galstar.com

Services: Shell, SLIP, PPP

Area Codes: 405, 918

Hawaii OnLine

Contact: Lynn Taylor, Larry Cross

Phone: (808) 246-1880, (808) 533-6981

Fax: (808) 246-4734

Email: info@aloha.net

Modem: (808) 533-7113 (login "guest")

URL: http://www.aloha.net/

Services: Shell, SLIP, PPP, WWW, 56-T1, DNS, UUCP, ISDN

Area Codes: 808

Fees:

Shell: $20/month (40 hours, $0.50/hr add'l)

SLIP, PPP: $30/month (40 hours, $0.75/hr add'l)

Other: Call

Hevanet Communications

Contact: Craig Swift

Phone: (503) 228-3520

Fax: (503) 274-4144

Email: info@hevanet.com

URL: http://www.hevanet.com/

Services: Shell, SLIP, PPP, telnet, WWW, FTP

Area Codes: 503

Fees:

Shell: $96/year (flat rate)

SLIP, PPP: $96/year (flat rate)

Telnet: $50/year (flat rate)

Other: Call

HoloNet/Information Access Technologies, Inc.

Contact: Sales

Phone: (510) 704-0160

Fax: (510) 704-8019

Email: support@holonet.net

URL: http://www.holonet.net/

Services: Shell, SLIP, CSLIP, PPP, UUCP, DNS, WWW

Area Codes: Nationwide

Fees:

Shell: $2/hour - $8.50/hour ($6/month minimum)

UUCP: $75/setup + dial-up charges

SLIP, PPP: $75/setup + dial-up charges $75/setup + $150-$200/month

Other: Call

I-2000

Contact: Mike Farina

Phone: (516) 867-6379

Email: mikef@i-2000.com

Modem: (516) 249-5488 (login "info" password "new user")

Services: SLIP, PPP

Area Codes: 203, 212, 516, 718, 908, 914, 917

IACNet

Contact: Devon Sean McCullough

Phone: (513) 887-8877

Email: Info@iac.net

URL: http://www.iac.net/

ICNet/Innovative Concepts

Contact: Sales

Phone: (313) 998-0090

Fax: (313) 998-0816

Email: info@ic.net

URL: http://www.ic.net, gopher://gopher.ic.net

Services: Shell, SLIP, PPP, UUCP, DNS, WWW, FTP, ISDN, 56K, T1

Area Codes: 313, 810, 616, 517, 906

Fees: SLIP $30/month

IDS World Network
Contact: Info
Phone: (800) IDS-1680
Email: info@ids.net
URL: http://www.ids.net/
Services: Shell, SLIP, PPP, ISDN, 56, 128, 256, T1
Area Codes: 401, 305, 407, 914
Fees:
Shell: $15/month (flat rate)
SLIP, PPP: $20/month for 20 hrs + $2/each additional
Other: Call

IgLou Internet Services
Contact: Sales
Phone: (800) 436-IGLOU
Fax: (502) 968-0449
Email: info@iglou.com
Modem: (502) 964-5390, (606) 431-0081 (login "new")
URL: http://iglou.com/
Services: Shell, SLIP, PPP, UUCP, ISDN
Area Codes: 502, 812, 606, 513
Fees:
Shell: $6.95-$19.95/month
SLIP, PPP: $11.95-$29.95/month
Other: Call

Illuminati Online
Contact: Sales
Phone: (512) 462-0999, (512) 447-7866
Email: admin@io.com
URL: http://io.com/
Services: Shell, SLIP, PPP, ISDN, WWW, mailing list
Area Codes: 512
Fees:
Telnet only: $10/month (flat rate)
Shell, SLIP, PPP: $15-$28/month
Dedicated: $395/setup, $250/month

InfiNet (Infinite Systems)
Contact: Sales

Phone: (614) 268-9941
Fax: (614) 268-3668
Email: sales@infinet.com
URL: http://www.infinet.com/
Modem: (614) 224-3410 (login "new" or "guest")
Services: Shell through T1, UUCP, WWW
Area Codes: 614
Fees:
Shell: $15/month (flat rate)
SLIP, PPP: $25/month (flat rate)

Info-Highway International, Inc
Contact: Steve McNeely
Phone: (713) 447-7025, (800) 256-1370
Fax: (713) 351-0956
Email: smcneely@infohwy.com
URL: ftp://ftp.infohwy.com/
Services: Shell, SLIP, PPP
Area Codes: 409, 713
Fees:
Email only: $10/month
Shell: $25/month
SLIP, PPP: $35/month

Ingress Communications, Inc
Phone: (212) 679-8592
Fax: (212) 213-0736
Email: info@ingress.com
URL: http://www.ingress.com/
Modem: (212) 679-0179 (login "guest")
Services: Shell, SLIP, PPP, UUCP, LAN, WWW, FTP, 56-T1
Area Codes: 212, 718

Innovative Data Services
Contact: Sales
Phone: (810) 478-3554
Fax: (810) 478-2950
Email: info@id.net
URL: http://www.id.net/
Services: Shell, UUCP, [C]SLIP, PPP, FTP, LAN, WWW, 56-T1, consult
Area Codes: 313, 810

INS Info Services
Contact: Customer Service
Phone: (800) 546-6587
Fax: (515) 830-0345
Email: service@ins.infonet.net
URL: http://www.infonet.net/
Services: Shell, SLIP, UUCP, WWW, FTP, 56-T1
Area Codes: 800, 319, 402, 515, 712
Fees:
800: $0.15/minute
Shell: $30/month (flat rate)
SLIP: $40/month (flat rate)
UUCP: $20/month (flat rate) + $0.15/min for 800
Other:
Call

Institute for Global Communications (IGC)
Contact: Sarah Hutchison
Phone: (415) 442-0220
Fax: (415) 546-1794
Email: support@igc.apc.org
Modem: (415) 322-0162 (login "new")
URL: http://www.igc.apc.org/
Services: Shell, SLIP, PPP
Fees:
$10/month + connection fees

INTAC Access Corporation
Contact: Sales
Phone: (201) 944-1417
Fax: (201) 944-1434
Email: info@intac.com
Modem: (201) 944-3990 (login "newuser")
URL: http://www.intac.com
Services: Shell, SLIP, PPP, UUCP,ISDN, 56, T1
Fees:
Shell: $30/setup, $20/month (flat rate)
SLIP, PPP: $50/setup, $30/month (100 hrs, $2/hr add'l)
UUCP: $50/setup, $30/month (100 hrs, $2/hr add'l)
ISDN: $75/setup, $40/month (100 hrs, $2/hr add'l)
56: $2000/setup, $450/month
T1: $4000/setup, $750/month

Intelligence Network Online, Inc.
Contact: Sales
Phone: (813) 442-0114
Email: sales@intnet.net
URL: http://www.intnet.com, ftp://ftp.intnet.net
Services: Shell, SLIP, PPP, WWW, FTP, 56-T1
Fees:
Shell: $29/month (flat rate)
SLIP, PPP: $29/month (20 hrs, $1/hr add'l)

InterAccess Company
Contact: Lev Kaye
Phone: (800) 967-1580
Fax: (708) 498-3289
Email: info@interaccess.com
URL: http://www.interaccess.net/
Services: Shell, SLIP, PPP, ISDN, 56, 384, T1
Area Codes: 708, 312, 815
Fees:
Shell: $23/month (flat rate)
SLIP/PPP: $26/month - $190/month
Other: Call

Interactive Networks, Inc.
Contact: Frank Altieri
Phone: (201) 881-1878, (800) 561-1878
Fax: (201) 881-1788
Email: frank@interactive.net
URL: http://www.interactive.net/
Modem: (201) 881-0794 (login "newuser")
Services: Shell, SLIP, PPP, FTP, LAN, WWW, leased lines
Area Codes: 201
Fees:
Shell:$15.95/Month
SLIP, PPP: $34.95/Month
Other: Call

InterCom, Inc.
Email: info@intercom.com

Intergate, Inc.
Phone: (404) 429-9599
Modem: (404) 423-1122

Services: Shell, UUCP, SLIP, PPP, FTP, WWW
Area codes: 404

International Internet Association
Email: info@iia.org
URL: http://www.iia.org/

The Internet Access Company
Contact: Sales
Phone: (617) 276-7200
Fax: (617) 275-2224
Email: info@tiac.net (auto), sales@tiac.net (reader)
URL: http://www.tiac.net/
Modem: (617) 275-0331, (508) 452-4040
Services: ISDN, PPP, Shell, ISDN, WWW, 56K-T1
Area Codes: 203, 212, 401, 508, 603, 617
Fees:
Shell: $20/setup, $19.50/month (flat rate)
SLIP, PPP: $29-$79/setup, $20-$300/month
ISDN: $40/setup, $40-$60/month
56K: $1200-$2900/setup, $495-$595/month

Internet Access Online Communications Service
Contact: Sales
Phone: (513) 887-8877
Email: sales@iac.com
Modem: (513) 887-8855
Services: Shell, SLIP, PPP, LAN, 56, T1
Area Codes: 513
Fees:
Email/News: $15/month
Shell: $25/month
LAN: $35-$45/month
Other: Call

Internet Alaska
Contact: Lance Ahern
Phone: (907) 562-4638
Fax: (907) 562-1677
Email: info@alaska.net
URL: http://www.alaska.net
Services: Shell, 56-T1

Area codes: 907
Fees:
Shell: $35/month, $225/6 months (flat rate)

Internet Atlanta
Contact: Dorn Hetzel
Phone: (404) 410-9000
Fax: (404) 410-9005
Email: info@atlanta.com
URL: http://www.com/atlanta/
Services: UUCP, SLIP, PPP, ISDN, 56, T1, WWW
Area Codes: 404, 706, 912 (dialup) - frame relay and T1 (nationwide)
Fees:
UUCP: $0.25-$1/hour
SLIP, PPP: $0.25/hour-$150/month
ISDN: $400-$600/month

Internet Connect, Inc.
Contact: Sales
Phone: (414) 476-ICON (4266)
Email: info@inc.net
Modem: (414) 47-MODEM
Services: Shell, SLIP, PPP, FTP, LAN, WWW, ISDN, 56-T1
Area Codes: 414
Fees:
PPP: $1.20/hr-$75/month
56K: $275/month
T1: $750/month

Internet Connect Services, Inc
Contact: Tom Sterne, Bill Fashbaugh
Phone: (512) 572-9987, (713) 439-0949
Fax: (512) 572-8193
Email: staff@icsi.net
Services: Shell, SLIP, PPP, FTP, LAN, WWW, ISDN, 56-T1
Area Codes: 409, 512, 713
Fees:
Shell: $20/setup, $4.95-$17.95/month
SLIP: $20/setup, $9.95-$28.95/month

The Internet Connection

Contact: Martin Levy

Phone: (408) 461-INET

Fax: (408) 438-8390

Email: sales@ico.net

URL: http://www.ico.net

Services: SLIP, PPP, WWW, ISDN, 56-T1, FTP

Area Codes: 408

Fees:

SLIP, PPP: $26/month (flat rate)

Internet Direct, Inc.

Contact: Sales

Phone: (602) 274-0100, (602) 324-0100

Fax: (602) 274-8518

Email: sales@indirect.com

URL: http://www.indirect.com/

Services: Shell, SLIP, PPP

Area Codes: 602

Fees:

Shell: $16.50/month (150 hours)

SLIP, PPP: $24.50/month (150 hours)

Internet Direct of Utah

Contact: John Hardy

Phone: (801) 578-0300

Fax: (801) 578-0330

Email: johnh@indirect.com

URL: http://www.cyber-street.com/

Services: Shell, SLIP, PPP, UUCP, 56-T1

Area Codes: 801

Fees:

Shell: $16.50-$19.50/month

SLIP, PPP: $21.50-$24.50/month (flat rate)

UUCP: $28.75-$99.75/month

56K: $275/month, $2400/year

T1: $750/month, $7800/year

Internet Express

Contact: Customer Service

Phone: (800) 592-1240

Fax: (719) 592-1201

Email: service@usa.net

Modem: n/a

USA.NET

URL: http://usa.net/

Services: Shell, SLIP, PPP, dedicated lines

Area Codes: 719, 303, 505, 602, 800 Fees:

Shell, SLIP, PPP: $29.95-$59.95/setup, $11.95-$250/month

Internet Services of Atlanta

Contact: Allan Chong

Phone: (404) 454-4638

Fax: (404) 919-9527

Email: allan@is.net

URL: http://www.is.net

Services: Shell, SLIP, PPP, WWW< ISDN, T1, DNS, FTP, gopher

Area Codes: 404, 800

Fees:

Shell: $17.95

SLIP: $20.95/month (30 hours)

ISDN: $32.95/month (30 hours)

Internet Nebraska

Contact: Steve Reichenbach

Phone: (402) 434-8680

Email: info@inetnebr.com

URL: http://www.inetnebr.com/

Services: Shell, SLIP, PPP

Area codes: 402

Fees:

Flat-rate dialup: $29/mo, $69/3mo

Metered: $19/3mo, $.01-$.02/min

Internet Online Services

Contact: Suzie Park

Phone: (800) 221-3756

Fax: (800) 928-1057

Email: accounts@ios.com

URL: http://www.ios.com/

Services: Shell, SLIP, PPP, leased lines, DNS

Area Codes: 201, 212, 518

Fees:

Shell: $15/month (flat rate)

SLIP, PPP: $35/month (flat rate)

Internet On-Ramp, Inc.
Contact: Sales
Phone: (509) 927-RAMP (7267), (509) 927-7267
Fax: (509) 927-0273
Email: info@on-ramp.ior.com
URL: http://www.ior.com/
Services: Shell, SLIP, CSLIP, PPP, UUCP, leased line
Area Codes: 509
Fees:
Shell: $14.95-$19.95/setup, $7.95-$14.95/month,
SLIP, PPP: $39.95/setup, $24.95/month
UUCP: $49.95/setup, $34.95/month
Other: Call or write

InternetU
Contact: Jim Wells
Phone: (407) 952-8487
Fax: (407) 722-2863
Email: info@iu.net
URL: http://iu.net/
Services: Shell, WWW, leased, training, consulting
Area Codes: 407
Fees:
Shell: $10-$20/month
PPP: $50-$200/setup, $20-$140/month
Other: Call

InterNetwork Services
Contact: Sales
Phone: (612) 391-7300
Email: info@inet-serv.com
URL: gopher://proteon.inet-serv.com
Services: Shell, SLIP, PPP, UUCP, 56-T1
Fees:
Email only: $4.95/month
Email/News: $9.95/month
Shell: $19.95/month
SLIP, PPP: $34.95/month

Internetworks
Contact: Sales
Phone: (503) 233-4774
Fax: (503) 233-0344

Email: info@i.net
Services: SLIP, PPP, FTP, WWW, FTP, LAN, ISDN, leased lines
Area Codes: Nationwide
Fees:
Dialup, ISDN: hourly & monthly rates
56: From $100/month
T1: From $500/month
T3: Call

InterNex Information Services, Inc
Contact: Sales
Phone: (415) 473-3060
Fax: (415) 473-3062
Email: sales@internex.net
URL: http://www.internex.net
Services: ISDN, WWW, FTP
Area Codes: 415, 408, 510
Fees:
ISDN: starting at $29/month
Frame relay: starting at $349/month
WWW/FTP space: starting at $50/month

Interpath
Contact: Sales
Phone: (919) 890-6305, (800) 849-6305
Fax: (919) 890-6319
Email: info@interpath.net
URL: http://www.interpath.net/
Services: Shell, SLIP, PPP
Area Codes: 919, 800

Interport Communications Corp
Contact: Sales and Information
Phone: (212) 989-1128
Email: sales@interport.net, info@interport.net (autoreply)
Modem: (212) 989-1258 (login "newuser")
URL: http://www.interport.net/
Services: Shell, SLIP, PPP, dedicated lines, WWW
Area Codes: 212, 718
Fees:
Shell, SLIP, PPP: $25/month
Other: Call

interQuest inc.
Contact: Paul Stephanouk
Phone: (205) 464-8280
Fax: (205) 464-8281
Email: paul@iquest.com
Modem: (205) 464-8244
URL: http://www.iquest.com/
Services: Shell, SLIP, PPP, UUCP, WWW, FTP, LAN
Area codes: 205
Fees:
Shell: $30/month (flat rate)
SLIP, PPP: $30-$225/month
UUCP: $60/month

intuitive information, inc.
Contact: Jim Winkleman
Phone: (508) 342-1100
Fax: (508) 342-2075
Email: info@iii.net
Modem: (508) 342-1174, (508) 370-3934, (508) 854-8152
URL: http://www.iii.net/
Services: Shell, [C]SLIP, PPP, LAN, 56
Area Codes: 508
Fees:
Shell: $20/month (30 hrs, $.50/hr add'l, max $50)
SLIP/PPP: $30/month (40 hrs, $.50/hr add'l, max $65)
LAN: $250/month
Other: Call or email

IQuest Network Services
Phone: (317) 259-5050, (800) 844-UNIX
Fax: (317) 259-7289
Email: info@iquest.net
URL: http://www.iquest.net
Services: Shell, SLIP, PPP, UUCP, WWW, FTP, ISDN, 56, T1
Area Codes: 317
Fees:
Shell: $10/month (menu driven)

SLIP, PPP: $20/month
ISDN: $30/month + $2.50/hour
UUCP: $25/month
56: $375/month
T1: Call

jaguNET
Contact: Sales
Phone: (410) 931-7060
Fax: (410) 931-3157
Email: info@jagunet.com
URL: http://www.jagunet.com/
Services: Shell, PPP, ISDN, WWW, 56K

Jax Gateway to the World
Contact: Sales
Phone: (904) 730-7692
Fax: (904) 730-8045
Email: sales@jax.gttw.com
Modem: (904) 448-0444 (login "demo")
URL: http://jax.gttw.com/
Services: Shell, PPP, UUCP, ISDN, DNS, WWW

KAIWAN Corporation
Contact: Rachel Hwang
Phone: (714) 638-2139
Fax: (714) 638-0455
Email: sales@kaiwan.com
Services: Shell, SLIP, PPP, 56, 256, 512, 768, T1
Area Codes: 714, 213, 310, 818, 909, 805
Fees:
Shell: $14/month (flat rate)
SLIP, PPP: $20/month + $2/hour

LaserNet
Contact: Rick Bill, Keith Choate, John Hervey, Terry Milard
Phone: (703) 591-4232
Fax: (703) 591-7164
Email: info@laser.net
Modem: (703) 934-9020
URL: http://www.laser.net/
Services: Shell, SLIP, PPP, 56-T1

Area Codes: 202, 301, 703
Fees:
Shell: $20/month (flat rate)
SLIP, PPP: $20/month (4 hrs/day)

Leonardo Internet
Contact: Jim Pickrell
Phone: (310) 395-5500
Fax: (310) 395-9924
Email: jimp@leonardo.net
URL: http://www.laser.net/
Services: Shell, PPP, WWW, DNS, 56-T1, consult
Area Codes: 310

LI Net, Inc.
Contact: Michael Reilly
Phone: (516) 476-1168
Email: questions@li.net
Modem: (516) 265-1065 (login "newuser")
URL: http://www.li.net/
Services: Shell, SLIP, 56, T1
Area Codes: 516
Fees:
Shell: $22/month (flat rate)
SLIP: $22/month + $3/hour

Lightside, Inc.
Contact: Fred Condo, Dennis Hescox
Phone: (818) 858-9261
Fax: (818) 858-8982
Email: lightside@lightside.com
URL: http://www.lightside.com/
Services: Shell, SLIP, PPP, WWW, 56-T1
Area Codes: 818, 310, 714, 909
Fees:
Shell, SLIP, PPP: $29.95-$160/month
56: $1999/setup, $499/month
T1: $1999/setup, $999/month
WWW: $250/month

LineX Communcations
Contact: Sales
Phone: (415) 455-1650
Email: info@linex.com

Modem: (415) 455-1655 (login "guest")
URL: http://linex.com/
Services: Shell
Area Codes: 415
Fees: $16/month (flat rate)

The Little Garden
Phone: (415) 487-1902
Email: info@tlg.org
URL: http://www.tlg.org/
Services: 56-T1

Los Nettos
Contact: Joe Kemp
Phone: (310) 822-1551
Fax: (310) 823-6714
Email: los-nettos-info@isi.edu

Long Island Information, Inc.
Contact: Sales
Phone: (516) 248-5381
Email: info@liii.com
URL: http://www.liii.com/
Modem: (516) 294-0124
Services: Shell, SLIP
Area Codes: 516
Fees:
Shell: $15/month
SLIP: $30-$225/month

Lyceum
Contact: Sales
Phone: (404) 377-7575
Fax: (404) 377-7878
Email: info@lyceum.com
URL: gopher://infoserver.lyceum.com/

Maestro Technologies, Inc.
Contact: Raj Lekhi, Sue Bathla
Phone: (212) 240-9600
Email: staff@maestro.com, rlekhi@maestro.com
Services: Shell, SLIP, PPP
Area Codes: 212, 718, 516
Fees:

Shell: $25/setup + $12/month (flat rate)
SLIP, PPP: $25/setup + $30/month (flat rate)
Others: Call

maine.net, Inc.
Contact: Andy Robinson
Phone: (207) 780-6381
Fax: (207) 780-6301
Email: atr@maine.net
URL: ftp://ftp.maine.net/public/service.txt
Services: SLIP, PPP, 56, T1
Area Codes: 207
Fees:
SLIP, PPP: $30-$500/setup, $30-$225/month
56: $1000/setup, $550/month
T1: $3000/setup, $1375/month

MCSNet
Contact: Sales or Customer Service
Phone: (312) 248-8649
Fax: (312) 248-8649
Email: info@mcs.net
URL: http://www.mcs.net/
Services: Shell, SLIP, PPP, dedicated, UUCP, ISDN, WWW
Area Codes: 312, 708, 815
Fees:
Email/News: $20/3 months, $30/6 months
Shell: $10/first 15 hours, $25/month
Other: Call or write

Metronet, Inc.
Phone: (214) 705-2900, (817) 543-8756
Fax: (214) 401-2802
Email: info@metronet.com
Modem: (214) 705-2901, (817) 261-1127 (login "info")
URL: http://www.metronet.com:70/0h/metronet info/About.html
Services: Shell, SLIP, PPP, UUCP
Area codes: 214, 817
Fees:
Shell: $20/setup, $19/month

SLIP, PPP: $30-$100/setup, $19-$150/month
UUCP: $30-$50/setup, $20-$50/month

MHVNet
Contact: Chris Hawkinson
Phone: (914) 229-9853, (800) 998-7131
Email: info@mhv.net
Modem: (914) 473-0191
URL: http://www.mhv.net/
Services: BBS, Shell, SLIP, PPP, UUCP, FTP, WWW, mailing lists, gopher
Area Codes: 914
Fees:
BBS: $55-$204/month
Shell: $180-$240/month
SLIP, PPP: $180-$300/month
Other: Call

MichNet
Contact: MichNet Recruiting Staff
Phone: (313) 764-9430
Fax: (313) 747-3185
Email: recruiting@merit.edu
Services: SLIP, PPP, host services, 56, T1
Area Codes: 313, 616, 517, 810, 906
Fees: Call or write

MIDnet

Contact: Network Information Center
Phone:(402) 472-7600
Fax: (402) 472-5640
Email: nic@westie.mid.net

Millennium Communications
Phone: (507) 282-8943, (612) 338-5509
Fax: (507) 282-8943
Email: info@millcom.com
URL: http://www.millcomm.com
Services: Shell, SLIP, PPP, mailing lists
Area codes: 507, 612
Fees:
Email only: $5/month

Shell: $20/month
SLIP, PPP: $30-$100/month

MindSpring Enterprises, Inc.
Contact: Sales
Phone: (404) 888-0725
Fax: (404) 870-0220
Email: sales@mindspring.com
URL: http://www.mindspring.com/
Services: Shell, SLIP, PPP, WWW, consulting
Area Codes: 404, 706
Fees:
SLIP, PPP: $15-$175/month

Minnesota MicroNet
Phone: 681-8018
Fax: (612) 452-6360
Email: info@mm.com
Modem: (612) 681-9265 (login "guest")
Services: SLIP, SLIP, PPP
Area Codes: 612
Fees:
Shell: $5-$10/month ($2/hour add'l)
SLIP, PPP: $20-$30/month ($2/hr add'l)

Minnesota Regional Network (MRNet)
Contact: Sales
Phone: (612) 342-2570
Email: sales@mr.net
URL: http://www.mr.net/Services/dialup.html
Services: SLIP, UUCP, 56, T1
Area Codes: 612, 507, 218
Fees:
SLIP: $135-$175/setup, $49-$229/month
Other: Call

MiraCom
Contact: Sales
Phone: (203) 523-5677
Fax: (203) 523-5805
Email: info@miracle.net
Modem: (203) 586-7450
URL: http://www.miracle.net

Services: SLIP, PPP, ISAD, WWW, 56-T3
Area Codes: 203

MIX Communications
Contact: Dean Roth
Phone: (414) 228-0739
Email: sales@mixcom.com
Modem: (414) 241-5469 (login "newuser")
URL: http://www.mixcom.com/mixcom/
Services: BBS, SLIP, PPP
Area Codes: 414
Fees:
BBS: $12-$40/month
SLIP, PPP: $12-$40/month
Other: info@mixcom.com

MoonTower, Inc.
Contact: Luther Keeler
Phone: (512) 837-8670
Email: help@moontower.com
URL: gopher://moontower.com/
Services: Shell, UUCP, WWW
Area codes: 512
Fees:
Shell: $16.20/month, (flat rate)

Moran Communications Group
Contact: Joe Moran
Phone: (716) 639-1254
Email: info@moontower.com
URL: http://www.moran.com/
Services: PPP, 56-T1
Area codes: Nationwide

Mordor International
Phone: (201) 433-7343, (212) 843-3451
Fax: (201) 433-4222
Email: info@ritz.mordor.com
Services: Shell, TIA-SLIP, UUCP
Area Codes: 201, 212, 718
Fees:
Shell, TIA-SLIP: $20/setup, $30/quarter
UUCP: $30/setup, $90/quarter

Msen Inc

Contact: Owen Scott Medd

Phone: (313) 998-4562

Fax: (313) 998-4563

Email: info@msen.com

URL: http://www.msen.com/

Services: Shell, SLIP, PPP, ISDN, FTP, WWW, 56 to T1

Area Codes: 800, 313, 517, 616, 906

Fees:

Shell: $20/month (flat rate includes Web home page)

SLIP, PPP: $20/month $2/hour

Other: Call or write

MV Communications

Contact: Sales

Phone: (603) 429-2223

Fax: (603) 424-0386

Email: info@mv.mv.com

URL: http://www.mv.com/

Services: Shell, SLIP, PPP, UUCP, 56

Area Codes: 603

Fees:

Shell: $5/month (minimum)

SLIP, PPP: $25-$150/month

Other: Call

National Internet Source, Inc. (NIS, Inc)

Contact: Sales

Phone: (201) 825-4600

Fax: (201) 825-0650

Email: info@maple.nis.net

Modem: (201) 236-0558 (login "newuser")

Services: Shell, SLIP, PPP, 56, T1

Area Codes: 201, 800

National Knowledge Networks, Inc.

Phone: (214) 880-0700

Fax: (214) 880-0704

Email: info@nkn.net

URL: http://www.nkn.net

Services: SLIP, PPP, ISDN, 56-T3

Area Codes: 214, 817

Fees: SLIP, PPP: $19.95-$150/setup, $19.95-$150/month

ISDN: $39-$78/month, $39-$78/month

NCM, Inc.

Contact: Morgie or Robert

Email: morgie@tpe.ncm.com

URL: http://www.ncm.com/

Modem: (703) 749-9150 (login "bbs")

Services: Shell

Area Codes: 301, 202, 703

Fees: $10/setup, $12.50/month or $5/month + $0.50/hour

NEARNET

Contact: NEARNET Information Hotline

Phone: (617) 873-8730

Fax: (617) 873-5620

Email: nearnet-join@near.net

URL: http://www.near.net

Neighborhood Internet Connection

Contact: Richard Combes

Phone: (201) 934-1445

Fax: (201) 934-1445

Email: info@nic.com, combes@nic.com

Modem: (201) 236-8360 (login "new")

Services: Shell

Area Codes: 201

Fees:

Shell: $10-$20/month

Other: Call or write

NeoSoft, Inc.

Contact: Jay M. Williams

Phone: (713) 684-5969

Fax: (713) 684-5922

Email: jmw3@neosoft.com

URL: http://www.neosoft.com/

Services: Shell, SLIP, PPP, ISDN, 56, T1, UUCP

Area Codes: 800, 713, 409, 214, 504, 314

Fees:

Shell: $19.95/month

SLIP: $39.95/month

Other: Call

NetAxis
Contact: Luis Hernandez
Phone: (203) 969-0618
Fax: (203) 921-1544
Email: luis@netaxis.com
URL: http://www.netaxis.com
Services: Shell to T1

Netcom On-Line Communication Services
Contact: Sales
Phone: (408) 554-8649, (800) 501-8649
Fax: (408) 241-9145
Email: info@netcom.com
URL: http://www.netcom.com/
Modem: (408) 554-8649 (login "guest")
Services: Shell, SLIP, PPP, UUCP, 56, T1
Area Codes: 201, 206, 212, 214, 303, 310, 312, 404, 408, 415, 503, 510, 512, 602, 617, 619, 702, 703, 714, 818, 916, 919
Fees:
Shell: $17.50-19.50/month
SLIP, PPP: $19.50-$200/month
UUCP: $50-$90/month
56: $200/month
T1: $1000/month

netILLINOIS
Contact: Peter Roll
Phone: (708) 866-1825
Fax: (708) 866-1857
Email: proll@illinois.net

NETIS Public Access Internet, Londonderry, New Hampshire
Contact: Eric Poole
Phone: (603) 437-1811
Fax: (603) 437-1811
Modem: (603) 432-2517, (login "GUEST CALLER" password "VISITOR")
Email: epoole@scoot.netis.com
Services: Shell, UUCP, SLIP
Area Codes: 603
Fees:

E-Mail only: $5/month (flat rate)
UUCP: $10-$20/month (flat rate)
Shell: $10-$30/month (flat rate)
SLIP, PPP: $30/month (flat rate)

The Netside Network
Contact: Greg Ferrante
Phone: (803) 732-7757
Modem: (803) 732-7340
Email: info@netside.com
URL: http://www.netside.com/
Services: SLIP, PPP, WWW, LAN, WAN, 56-T1
Area Codes: 803
SLIP, PPP: $25/setup, $15-$35/month
Corportate: $35/setup, $45-$65/month (flat rate)

Network 23, Inc.
Contact: Nick Jarecki
Phone: (212) 786-4810
Email: info@net23.com
Services: Shell, FTP, WWW
Area codes: 212, 917
Fees:
$10/setup, $10-$16/month

Network 99, Inc.
Contact: Sales
Phone: (702) 442-7353, (602) 780-7533, (800) NET-99IP
Email: net99@cluster.mcs.net
Services: 56K-T3
Area codes: Nationwide
Fees:
T1: $1999.99/month

Network Access Services
Contact: Sales
Email: info@nas.com
URL: http://www.nas.com
Modem: (206) 733-9279
Services: Shell
Fees:
Personal: $30/setup, $20/month (20 hours)

Business: $150/setup, $20/month (20 hours)
Dedicated: $600/setup, $200/month

Network Intensive
Contact: Michelle Bilder
Phone: (800) 273-5600
Fax: (714) 450-8410
Email: info@ni.net
Modem: (714) 450-8400 (login "guest")
URL: http://www.ni.net/
Services: Shell, SLIP, PPP, UUCP, 56, ISDN, T1, WWW, FTP
Area Codes: 213, 310, 505, 619, 714, 805, 818
Fees:
Shell, UUCP: starting at $25/month
SLIP, PPP: starting at $20/month
56: starting at $500/month
Other: Call

Network Internet Services
Contact: Sales
Phone: (516) 543-0234
Fax: (516) 543-0274
Email: info@netusa.net
URL: http://www.netusa.net/
Services: Shell, SLIP, PPP, UUCP
Area Codes: 516
Fees:
Shell: $10/setup, $23/month
SLIP, PPP: $15/setup, $33-$120/month
UUCP: $15/setup, $16-$38/month

The Network Link, Inc.
Contact: Steve Froeschke
Phone: (619) 278-5943
Email: stevef@tnl1.tnwl.com
Services: Shell, NNTP, UUCP, IDSN, 56, FT1, T1
Area Codes: 619, 317

NevadaNet
Contact: Braddlee, Ph.D.
Phone: (702) 784-6861
Fax: (702) 784-1108
Email: braddlee@nevada.edu

URL: http://www.scs.unr.edu
Services: Dedicated connections for non-profit organizations in the state of Nevada. No personal accounts. Inquire about commercial sites.
Area Codes: 702
Fees: On request

New Jersey Computer Connection
Contact: Brian Kramer
Phone: (609) 896-2799
Fax: (609) 896-2994
Email: info@pluto.njcc.com
URL: http://www.njcc.com
Services: Shell, SLIP, PPP, UUCP, WWW, FTP, mailing lists
Area Codes: 609
Fees:
Shell: $9.95/setup, $14.95/month
SLIP, PPP: $9.95/setup, $34.95/month
Other: Call or write

New Mexico Technet, Inc.
Contact: Marianne Granoff
Phone: (505) 345-6555
Fax: (505) 435-6559
Email: granoff@technet.nm.org
Services: Shell, SLIP, PPP, leased line
Area Codes: 505, 602, 303, 915, 800
Fees: Call or write

New York Net
Contact: Bob Tinkelman
Phone: (718) 776-6811
FAX: (718) 217-9407
Email: sales@new-york.nct
Services: SLIP, PPP, 56, 64, 128 to T1
Area Codes: 201, 203, 212, 516, 609, 718, 908, 914, 917
Fees:
SLIP, PPP: $75-200/mo (unmetered 28.8K)
56K: $700/month
Others: Call or write

North American Internet Company
Phone: (800) 952-INET
Fax: (203) 953-5635
Email: info@nai.net
URL: http://www.nai.net/

North Bay Network
Phone: (415) 472-1600
Email: support@nbn.com
URL: http://www.nbn.com/
Services: UUCP, 56-T1

North Shore Access
Contact: Adam Gray
Phone: (617) 593-3110
Fax: (617) 593-6858
Email: info@shore.net
Modem: (617) 593-4557 (8N1, login "new")
URL: http://www.shore.net/
Services: Shell, SLIP, PPP, UUCP, WWW, FTP
Area Codes: 617, 508
Fees:
Shell: $10/setup, $10-$27/month
SLIP, PPP: $50/setup, $30/month (60 hrs, $0.50/hr add'l)
UUCP: $35/setup, $10/month + $1/hour
FTP, WWW: 25MB/month included, ($1/MB/month add'l)
DNS: $25/year

Northcoast Internet
Contact: Sales
Phone: (707) 443-8696
Email: info@northcoast.com
URL: http://www.northcoast.com/
Services: Shell, SLIP, PPP
Area Codes: 707
Fees:
Shell, SLIP, PPP: $20/month (20 hours, $1/hr additional)
28.8kbps: $40/month
Other: Call

NorthWest CommLink
Contact: Garlend Tyacke
Phone: (206) 336-0103
Email: gtyacke@nwcl.net
Services: Shell, SLIP, PPP, FTP, 56 - T1
Area Codes: 206
Fees:
Email/News: $15/month (flat rate)
Shell: $30/setup, $25/month (flat rate)
SLIP, PPP: $50/month (flat rate)
Other: Call

Northwest Nexus, Inc.
Contact: Information
Phone: (206) 455-3505
Fax: (206) 455-4672
Email: info@nwnexus.wa.com
Modem: (206) 382-6245 (login "new")
URL: http://www.halcyon.com/nwnexus
Services: Shell, SLIP, PPP, UUCP, 56, T1
Area Codes: 206
Fees:
Shell: $30/setup, $20/month
UUCP: $50/setup, $10/month (10 hours, $3/hr add'l)
SLIP, PPP: $30/month (flat rate)
56: $150-$750/setup, $150-$500/month
Other: Call or write

NorthwestNet
Contact: Member Relations
Phone: (206) 562-3000
Fax: (206) 562-4822
Email: info@nwnet.net

NovaLink
URL: gopher://gopher.novalink.com/
Services: Shell
Area codes: Nationwide and international
Fees:
$9.96/month (5 hours, $1.80-$30.20/hr add'l)

NovaNet, Inc.
Contact: Sales
Phone: (703) 524-4800
Fax: (703) 524-4801
Email: sales@novanet.com
Modem: (703) 524-4802 (login "guest")
URL: http://www.novanet.com
Services: Shell, SLIP, PPP, UUCP, LAN, WWW, FTP, 56-T1
Area codes: 703, 202, 301
Fees:
Shell: $24/setup, $18/month
SLIP, PPP: $28/month
56K: $1000/setup, $800/month
Frac T1: $1500/setup, $1000/month
Other: Call

Nuance Network Services
Contact: Sales
Phone: (205) 533-4296
Fax: (205) 533-4296
Email: info@nuance.com
URL: http://www.nuance.com/
Services: Shell, SLIP, PPP, ISDN
Area Codes: 205
Fees:
Shell: $35/setup, $25/month (flat rate)
SLIP, PPP: $35/setup, $25-$30/month
Other: Call

NYSERNet
Contact: Information
Phone: (315) 453-2912
Fax: (315) 453-3052
Email: info@nysernet.org
URL: http://nysernet.org/
Services: Shell, WWW, FTP, gopher, training, 56-T3
Area codes: 212, 315, 516, 518, 607, 716, 718, 914

Nyx
Contact: Andrew Burt
Phone: (303) 871-3308

Email: info@nyx.cs.du.edu
Services: Shell, semi-anonymous accounts
Area Codes: 303
Fees: Donations

OARnet
Contact: Sales
Phone: (800) 627-8101, (614) 728-8100
Fax: (614) 728-8110
Email: info@oar.net
URL: http://www.oar.net/
Services: SLIP, PPP, ISDN, 57, 64, 128, LVT1, T1, Frame Relay
Area Codes: 614, 419, 513, 216, 800
Fees:
SLIP, PPP: $40-$295/month

Old Colorado City Communications
Contact: Sales
Phone: (719) 528-5849
Fax: (719) 528-5869
Email: thefox@oldcolo.com
Services: Shell, 56
Area Codes: 719 Fees:
Email: $10/month
Shell: $25/month

Onramp Access, Inc.
Contact: Chad Kissinger
Phone: (512) 322-9200
Email: info@onr.com
URL: http://www.onr.com
Services: SLIP, PPP, WWW Advertising
Area Codes: 512
Fees: $14.95-$30.00 per month depending on the number of hours

On-Ramp Technologies, Inc.
Contact: Andrew Komochank
Phone: (214) 746-4710
Fax: (214) 746-4856
Email: sales@onramp.net
URL: http://www.onramp.com
Services: SLIP, PPP, UUCP, WWW, LAN, FTP,

ISDN, 56-T1, MAE
Area Codes: 214, 817, 713
Fees:
SLIP,PPP: $39-$250/setup, $39-$250/month
UUCP: $49.95/setup, $49.95/month
ISDN: $95-$995/setup, $95-$995/month
56K: $354/setup, $345/month
T1: $1295/setup, $1295/month
MAE: $1495/setup, $1495/month

PACCOM

Contact: Torben Nielsen
Phone: (808) 956-3499
Email: torben@hawaii.edu

Pacific Information Exchange, Inc.

Contact: Sales
Phone: (808) 596-7494
Fax: (808) 593-1403
Email: info@pixi.com
URL: http://www.pixi.com
Services: Shell, SLIP, PPP, UUCP, WWW, FTP, 56-T1
Area code: 808
Fees:
Shell: $25/setup, $20/month (flat rate)
SLIP, PPP: $100/setup, $45/month (flat rate)

Pacific Internet

Contact: James Persky
Phone: (707) 468-1005
Fax: (707) 468-8266
Email: info@pacific.net
URL: http://www.pacific.net/
Services: Shell, SLIP, PPP, UUCP, WWW, 56K-T1
Area Codes: 707
Fees:
Shell, SLIP, PPP: $25/setup, $25/month (25 hours)
56K: $1300/setup, $425/month
Other: Call

Pacific Rim Network, Inc.

Contact: Richard Huff
Phone: (206) 650-0442
Fax: (206) 738-8315
Email: sales@pacificrim.com
URL: http://www.pacificrim.com/
Services: Shell, SLIP, PPP, ISDN, 56K-T1
Area Codes: 800, 206

Pacifier Computers

Contact: Sales
Phone: (206) 693-2116
Fax: (206) 254-3898
Email: sales@pacifier.com
Modem: (206) 693-0325
URL: http://www.pacifier.com/
Services: Shell, SLIP, PPP Area Codes: 206
Fees:
Shell: $50-$270/year
SLIP, PPP: $125-1000/year
Other: Call or write

PacketWorks, Inc.

Contact: Chip Short
Phone: (813) 446-8826
Fax: (813) 447-1585
Email: info@packet.net
URL: http://www.packet.net
Services: PPP, ISDN, WWW
Area Codes: 813

Panix/Public Access Networks

Contact: New User Staff
Phone: (212) 741-4400
Fax: (212) 741-5311
Email: info-person@panix.com
Modem: (212) 741-4545 (login "newuser")
URL: http://www.panix.com/
Area codes: 212, 718, 516, 201, 914
Services: Shell, SLIP, PPP, 56 - T1
Fees:
Shell: $40/setup, $19/month

SLIP, PPP: $35/month
Other: Call

pcnet
Contact: Sales
Phone: (800) 66-4INET
Fax: (203) 250-2250
Email: sales@pcnet.com
Modem: (203) 250-1205, (203) 666-6100 (login "info")
Services: Shell, SLIP, PPP, UUCP, LAN, WWW, FTP, ISDN, 56, T1
Area codes: 203
Fees:
Shell: $35-$50/month
UUCP: $40/month
SLIP, PPP: $1/hour-$325/month
Other: Call

Phantom Access Technologies, Inc.
Contact: Bruce Fancher
Phone: (212) 989-2418
Fax: (212) 989-8648
Email: info@phantom.com
URL: http://www.phantom.com
Services: Shell, SLIP, PPP, 56-T1, WWW, consult, training
Area Codes: 212, 718, 516, 914

Ping
Contact: Brett Koller
Phone: (800) 746-4635, (404) 399-1670
Email: bdk@ping.com
Services: Shell, SLIP, PPP, FTP, UUCP, 56
Area Codes: 404, 800 (includes Hawaii and Alaska)
Fees:
Shell: $30/setup, $1-$40/month
FTP: $2/meg
56: $1000/setup, $200/month

Pioneer Global
Contact: Craig Komins
Phone: (617) 375-0200

Fax: (617) 375-0201
Email: sales@pn.com
URL: http://www.pn.com
Services: Shell, UUCP, 28.8, 56, T1, LAN, BBS, WWW
Area Codes: 617
Fees: Call or write

The Pipeline Network
Contact: Sales
Phone: (212) 267-3636
Fax: (212) 267-4380
Email: staff@pipeline.com
Services: Shell
Area codes: Nationwide
Fees: $20/month (20 hours)

Planet Access Networks
Contact: Fred Laparo
Phone: (201) 691-4704
Fax: (201) 691-7588
Email: fred@planet.net
URL: http://www.planet.net/
Services: Shell, SLIP, PPP, dedicated lines, WWW
Area Codes: 201, 908, 319, 205
Fees: Call

The Point
Phone: (812) 246-8032
Email: arlie@thepoint.com
URL: http://www.thepoint.com/
Services: Shell, SLIP, PPP, UUCP, FTP, WWW, T1
Fees:
Shell: $20/month
SLIP, PPP: $30/month
Other: Call

Portal Information Network
Contact: Customer Service
Phone: (800) 433-6444, (408) 973-9111
Fax: (408) 725-1580
Email: cs@portal.com

URL: http://www.portal.com
Services: Shell, SLIP, PPP, UUCP
Area Codes: Nationwide
Fees: $19.95/setup, $19.95/month, $2.95/hour

PREPnet
Contact: Thomas Bajzek
Phone: (412) 268-7870
Fax: (412) 268-7875
Email: twb+@andrew.cmu.edu

Primenet
Contact: Sales
Phone: (602) 870-1010, (800) 4 NET FUN
Fax: (602) 870-1010
Email: info@primenet.com
Modem: (602) 395-1111 (login "guest")
URL: http://www.primenet.com/
Services: Shell, SLIP, PPP, 56, 128, T1, WWW
Area Codes: 602, 213, 818
Fees:
Shell: $15.95/month (flat rate)
SLIP, PPP: $20.95/month (150 hours)
Other: Call

PSCNET
Contact: Eugene Hastings
Phone: (412) 268-4960
Fax: (412) 268-5832
Email: psscnet-admin@psc.edu

PSINet
Contact: Sales
Phone: (800) 82PSI82, (703) 620-6651
Fax: (703) 620-2430
Email: info@psi.com
URL: http://www.psi.net/

Q-Networks, Inc
Contact: Sales
Phone: (816) 795-1000
Fax: (816) 795-8500
Email: webhost@qni.com

URL: http://www.qni.com/
Area Codes: 816

QuakeNet
Contact: Mike Park
Phone: (415) 655-6607
Email: info@quake.net (autoreply), admin@
quake.net (human)
URL: http://www.quake.net/
Services: SLIP, PPP, DNS, WWW, 56-T1
Area Codes: 415
Fees:
SLIP, PPP: $25-$500/setup, $25-$160/month
56: $1800/setup, $325/month
T1: $2800/setup, $800/month

The Rabbit Network, Inc
Contact: Customer Liaison Services
Phone: (800) 456-0094
Fax: (810) 790-0156
Email: info@rabbit.net
Services: Shell, SLIP, PPP, UUCP, leased lines
Area Codes: 810, 800 (entire U.S. and Canada)

RAINet, Inc.
Contact: Robert Chew
Phone: (503) 227-5665
Fax: (503) 297-9078
Email: robert@rain.net
URL: http://www.rain.net
Services: SLIP, PPP, 56-T1
Area codes: 206, 503
Fees:
SLIP, PPP: $20-$350/month
56K: $350
T1: $1000

RainDrop Laboratories
Contact: Alan Batie
Email: info@agora.rdrop.com
Modem: (503) 293-1772 (login "apply")
URL: http://www.rdrop.com/
Services: Shell, SLIP

Area Codes: 503

Fees: See online information

Real/Time Communications
Contact: Sales
Phone: (512) 451-0046
Fax: (512) 459-3858
Email: info@realtime.net
URL: http://www.realtime.net/
Services: Shell, SLIP, PPP, IDSN, Custom services
Area Codes: 512
Fees: Call

Red River Net
Contact: Craig Lien
Phone: (701) 232-2227
Email: lien@rrnet.com
URL: http://www.rrnet.com
Services: Shell
Area Codes: 701, 218
Fees: $20/month (20 hrs during peak, unlimited off-peak)

Ripco Communcations, Inc.
Contact: Bruce Esquibel
Phone: (312) 665-0065
Email: info@ripco.com
URL: http://www.ripco.com
Services: Shell, WWW, UUCP, FTP
Area Codes: 312, 708
Fees:
Shell: $15/month, $35/3 months (flat rate)

Roadrunner Computer Systems
URL: http://www.roadrunner.com/
Area Codes: 505

Rocky Mountain Internet, Inc
Contact: Rick Mount, Jim Welch
Phone: (800) 900-RMII
Fax: (719) 576-0301
Email: mountr@rmii.com, jimw@rmii.com
Services: Shell, SLIP, PPP, 56, T1

Area Codes: 303, 719
Fees:
Shell: $25/month (100 hours)
SLIP: $15-$200/month
56: $300/month
Other: Call

Sacramento Network Access, Inc.
Contact: George Hall
Phone: (916) 565-4500
Fax: (916) 565-4501
Email: sales@sna.com
URL: http://www.sna.com
Services: Shell, SLIP, PPP
Area Codes: 800, 916, 209, 510, 702
Fees:
Shell: $35/Month (flat rate)
SLIP, PPP: $35/Month (flat rate)

SatelNET Communications
Contact: Yanek Martinson
Phone: (305) 434-8738
Fax: (305) 680-9848
Email: martinson@satelnet.org
Modem: (305) 587-1930, (305) 461-2190
URL: http://www.satelnet.org/
Services: Shell, SLIP, PPP, UUCP, WWW
Area Codes: 305
Fees:
Shell: $17/month, $60/4 months
SLIP, PPP: $25/month, $90/4 months
UUCP: $35/month

Savvy
Contact: Sales
Phone: (516) 626-2090
Email: info@savvy.com
Modem: (516) 626-2109
Services: Shell
Fees: $249/year

Schunix
Contact: Robert Schultz

Phone: (508) 853-0258
Fax: (508) 757-1645
Email: info@schunix.com
Modem: (508) 853-0340 (login "guest")
URL: http://schunix.com
Services: Shell, UUCP, SLIP, PPP, ISDN, 56, 128, T1
Area Codes: 508
Fees:
Shell: $1/hour ($5 minimum)
UUCP: $1/hour ($5 minimum)
SLIP, PPP: $1/hour ($5 minimum)

Scruz-Net
Contact: Matthew Kaufman
Phone: (800) 319-5555, (408) 457-5050
Fax: (408) 457-1020
Email: info@scruz.net
URL: http://www.scruz.net/
Services: SLIP, PPP, ISDN, 56, T1
Area Codes: 408, 415
Fees:
SLIP: $12.50-$400/setup, $25-$86/month
ISDN: $25/setup, $50/month (100 hours)
Other: Call

SeaNet
Contact: Igor Klimenko
Phone: (206) 343-7828
Fax: (206) 626-0722
Email: igor@seanet.com
URL: http://www.seanet.com/

The SenseMedia Network
Contact: Sales
Email: info@sensemedia.com
URL: http://sensemedia.com/
Services: SLIP, PPP, DNS
Area Codes: 206, 408, 808
Fees:
SLIP, PPP: $34-$50/month

Sesquinet
Contact: Farrell Gerbode
Phone: (713) 527-4988
Fax: (713) 527-6099
Email: farrell@rice.edu

Sibylline, Inc
Contact: Dan Faules
Phone: (501) 521-4660
Fax: (501) 521-4659
Email: info@sibylline.com
URL: http://www.sibylline.com/
Services: Shell, SLIP, PPP, 56, 128, T1, DNS, Advertising
Area Codes: 501
Fees:
Telnet: $10/month (flat rate)
Shell: $24.95/month (45 hours, $1/hr add'l)
SLIP, PPP: $34.95/month (45 hours, $1/hr add'l)
Other: Call

Sierra-Net
Contact: Giles Rider, Bruce Komito
Phone: (702) 832-6911
Fax: (702) 831-3970
Email: info@sierra.net
Services: Shell, SLIP, PPP, UUCP, 56-T1 , Gopher, WWW, mail lists
Modem: (702) 832-8441 (login "guest")
URL: http://www.sierra.net/home.html
Area Codes: 702, 916
Fees:
SLIP, PPP: $30/setup, $30/month (flat rate)
Other: Call

SIMS, Inc.
Contact: Jim Sims
Phone: (803) 762-4956
Fax: (803) 762-4956
Email: info@sims.net
URL: http://www.sims.net
Services: Shell, SLIP, PPP, ISDN, 56, 128, 256
Area Codes: 803

Fees:

Shell: $25/month, $250/year

SLIP, PPP: $30/month, $300/year (flat rate up to 20hr/wk)

Other: Call

Sirius Connections

Phone: (415) 284-4700

Email: info@sirius.com

URL: http://www.sirius.com/

Services: SLIP

Skagit On-Line Services

Contact: Patrick Garrett

Phone: (206) 755-0190

Email: info@sos.net

URL: http://www.sos.net/

Services: Shell, UUCP, SLIP, PPP

Area Codes: 206

Fees:

Shell: $15/setup, $20/month

UUCP: $15/setup, $15/month

SLIP: $20/setup, $23/month

SkyNET Corp

Contact: Mike Johnson

Phone: (816) 483-0002

Fax: (816) 483-8852

Email: info@sky.net

Services: Shell, UUCP, SLIP, PPP, 56-T1

Area Codes: 816, 913

Fees:

Shell: $13.95/month (flat rate)

SLIP, PPP: $17.95-$79.95/month

Skypoint Communications, Inc.

Contact: Sales

Phone: (612) 475-2959

Fax: (612) 449-0488

Email: info@skypoint.com

Modem: (612) 473-5646 (login "guest")

URL: http://www.skypoint.com/

Services: Shell, UUCP, SLIP, PPP, DNS, WWW, FTP

SmartDOCS Data Services

Contact: Sales

Phone: (805) 294-1273

Email: admin@smartdocs.com

Modem: (805) 295-3972

URL: http://www.smartdocs.com/

Sol Tec, Inc.

Contact: Christina Heal

Phone: (317) 920-1765

Fax: (317) 925-7260

Email: xheal@soltec.com

URL: http://www.soltec.com

Services: Shell, UUCP, SLIP, PPP, DNS, WWW, FTP

Area code: 317, 217, 815

Sound Communications Internet

Phone: (612) 772-8470, (612) 381-6794

Email: root@scc.net

Modem: (612) 722-2221

URL: http://www.scc.net/

Services: SLIP, PPP, WWW, 56-T3

Area Codes: 612

South Carolina SuperNet, Inc.

Contact: Brian Connelly

Phone: (803) 748-1207

Fax: (803) 771-2300

Email: info@scsn.net

Modem: (803) 779-0055 (login "info")

URL: http://www.scsn.net/

Services: SLIP, PPP, WWW, 56-T1

Area Codes: 803

Fees:

SLIP, PPP: $25-$35/setup, $25-$65/month

South Coast Computing Services, Inc.

Contact: Sales

Phone: (800) 221-6478

Fax: (713) 917-5005

Email: sales@sccsi.com

URL: http://www.sccsi.com/

Services: Shell, UUCP, SLIP, PPP, 56, T1

Area Codes: 800, 713, 918

Fees:

Shell, SLIP, PPP: $30/month for 40 hours

Other: Call

South Valley Internet

Contact: Sales

Phone: (408) 683-4533

Fax: (408) 683-4533

Email: info@garlic.com

URL: http://www.garlic.com

Services: Shell, SLIP, PPP, UUCP, Dedicated, Leased

Area Codes: 408

Fees:

Shell: $15/setup, $25/month, $70/quarter

SLIP, PPP: $20/setup, $40/month, $110/quarter

UUCP: $20/setup, $28/month, $82/quarter

Southwest Cyberport

Contact: Mark Costlow

Phone: (505) 271-0009

Email: costlow@swcp.com

Modem: (505) 294-2816 (login "guest", password "guest")

URL: http://www.swcp.com

Services: Shell, SLIP, PPP, UUCP, DNS, 56-T1

Area Codes: 505

SouthWind Internet Access, Inc.

Contact: Jeff Stehman

Phone: (316) 263-7963

Fax: (316) 267-3943

Email: staff@southwind.net

Services: Shell, TIA-SLIP, UUCP

Area codes: 316

Fees:

Shell, TIA-SLIP: $22/month, $225/year (flat rate)

UUCP: $20-$40/month (30-75 hours)

SprintLink

Contact: Marti Kiser

Phone: (703) 904-2156

Email: info@sprintlink.net

URL: http://www.sprintlink.net/

Services: 9.6 (ditigal), 56, 64, 128, 256, 384, 512, 640, T1

Fees: $660-$1000/setup, $550-$600/month

SSNet, Inc.

Contact: Scott Harris

Phone: (302) 378-1386

Fax: (302) 378-3871

Email: info@ssnet.com, sharris@ssnet.com

Services: Shell, SLIP, PPP UUCP

Area Codes: 610, 302

Fees:

Email/News: $20/setup, $15/month

Shell: $20/setup, $25/month

UUCP: $45/setup, $25-$45/month

SLIP, PPP: $45-$450/setup, $25-$150/month

StarNet Communications, Inc. (Winternet)

Contact: Mike Horwath

Phone: (612) 941-9177

Fax: (612) 942-9871

Email: info@winternet.com

URL: http://www.winternet.com

Services: Shell, SLIP, PPP Area Codes: 612

Fees:

Shell: $19.95/month   SLIP, PPP: $34.95-$105/month

SuperNet Internet Services

Contact: John Banghart

Phone: (800) HOOKED-UP

Fax: (717) 390-8944

Email: john@success.net, info@success.net

URL: http://www.success.net/

Services: Shell, SLIP, UUCP, FTP, LAN, WWW, ISDN, 56-T1

Area codes: 717

Fees:

Email/News: $8.95/month

Shell, SLIP: $15-$39/month

Other: Call

SURAnet
Contact: Kimberly Donaldson
Phone: (301) 982-4600
Fax: (301) 982-4605
Email: kdonalds@sura.net
URL: http://www.sura.net/

Synergy Communications
Contact: Jamie Saker
Phone: (402) 346-4638
Fax: (402) 346-0208
Email: jsaker@synergy.net
URL: http://www.synergy.net/

SymNet
Contact: Sales
Phone: (904) 385-1061
Email: info@symnet.net
URL: http://www.symnet.net/
Services: Shell, SLIP, PPP
Area Codes: 904
Fees:
Shell: $15/month (flat rate)
SLIP, PPP: $30/month - $200/month

Telalink Corporation
Contact: Sales
Phone: (615) 321-9100
Fax: (615) 321-9129
Email: sales@nashville.net
URL: http://www.nashville.net/
Services: SLIP, CDS-64, CDS-T1
Area Codes: 615
Fees:
SLIP: $35/month (flat rate)
64K: $300/month
T1: $900/month

Telebyte
Contact: Sales
Phone: (800) 936-5220, (360) 613-5220
Fax: (360) 613-5235
Email: info@kendaco.telebyte.com
Area Codes: 360

Teleport, Inc.
Contact: Sales
Phone: (503) 223-0076
Fax: (503) 223-4372
Email: sales@teleport.com
URL: http://www.teleport.com/
Services: Shell, SLIP, PPP, ISDN
Area Codes: 503, 206
Fees:
Shell: $10/month (flat rate)
SLIP/PPP: $15/month (flat rate)
Other: Call or email to info@teleport.com

Telerama Public Access Internet
Contact: Peter Berger
Phone: (412) 481-3505
Fax: (412) 481-8568
Email: sysop@telerama.lm.com
URL: http://www.lm.com
Services: Shell, SLIP, PPP, ISDN, 56, 128, T1
Area Codes: 412, 814
Fees:
Shell: $20/month (flat rate)
SLIP, PPP: $20/month (3 hrs free, $2/hr add'l)

Tezcatlipoca, Inc.
Contact: Charles Ewen MacMillan
Phone: (312) 850-0181
Fax: (312) 829-1627
Email: ilixi@tezcat.com
Modem: (312) 850-0112 (8N1, login "new") or 198.6.68.2
URL: http://tezcat.com/
Services: Shell, TIA, FTP, WWW
Area Codes: 312, 708
Fees: $24/month (flat rate), $50/quarterly (TIA included)

THEnet
Contact: Frank Sayre
Phone: (512) 471-2444
Fax: (512) 471-2449
Email: f.sayre@utexas.edu

ThoughtPort Inc.
Contact: David Bartlett
Phone: (314) 474-6870
Fax: (314) 474-4122
Email: info@thoughtport.com
URL: http://www.thoughtport.com

Townsend Communcations, Inc.
Contact: Ned Schumann
Phone: (206) 385-0464
Email: inquiries@olympus.net
URL: http://www.olympus.net/
Services: PPP, 56
Area Codes: 206
Fees: $75/3 months

Traveller Information Services
Contact: Jay Davis
Phone: (800) 840-TNET, (204) 883-2686
Fax: (205) 883-4293
Email: info@traveller.com
URL: http://www.traveller.com/tis
Services: Shell, CSLIP, PPP, ISDN, FTP, WWW, LAN, UUCP
Area codes: 205
Fees:
UUCP: $15/month (10 hours, $2/hr add'l)
SLIP, PPP: $30/month (10 hours, $2/hr add'l)
ISDN: $480-$580/month

The Turning Point
Contact: Mike Byrnes
Phone: (512) 499-8400, (512) 703-4401
Email: help@tpoint.net
Services: SLIP, PPP, ISDN, LAN, 56-T1
Area Codes: 816, 913, 504, 316
Fees:
SLIP, PPP: $20-$200/setup $15-$65/month
LAN: $200-$475/setup, $125/month
ISDN: $50/setup, $50-$150/month

Tyrell Corp
Contact: Kerri McCoy
Phone: (800) TYRELL-1

Fax: (816) 741-5315
Email: support@tyrell.net
Modem: (816) 454-6788 (login "info")
Services: Shell, [C]SLIP, PPP, DS0/DS1, UUCP
Area Codes: 816, 913, 504, 316
Fees:
Shell, SLIP, PPP: $10/month, $90/year (30 hrs/month)
UUCP: $5-$40/month

TZ-Link
Contact: Drew Monroe
Phone: (914) 353-5443
Email: drew@j51.com
Modem: (914) 353-4618 (login "guest", password "guest")
URL: http://www.j51.com/
Services: Shell
Area Codes: 914
Fees: $12/month (60 hours)

UltraNet Communications, Inc.
Contact: Sales
Phone: (508) 229-8400, (800) 763-8111
Fax: (508) 229-2375
Email: info@ultranet.com
Modem: (508) 229-8111
URL: http://www.ultranet.com/
Services: SLIP, PPP, FTP, WWW, LAN, ISDN, 56, 128, 384
Area Codes: 508
Fees:
SLIP, PPP: $5-$100/month
Other: Email or call

US Net, Inc.
Contact: Service
Phone: (301) 572-5926
Fax: (301) 572-5201
Email: info@us.net
URL: http://www.us.net/
Services: Shell, SLIP, PPP, UUCP, LAN, DNS, 56-T1

Area Codes: 301, 202, 703
Fees:
Shell: $9.95/setup, $6.95-$24.95/month
SLIP, PPP: $6.95-$24.95/month
UUCP: $34.95/month (10 hours, $3/hr add'l)
LAN: $170/month (flat rate)
56: $350/setup, $750/month
T1: $2000/setup, $1995/month

UUnet Technologies
Please see AlterNet

VERnet
Contact: James Jokl
Phone: (804) 924-0616
Fax: (804) 982-4715
Email: net-info@ver.net

ViaNet Communications
Contact: Joe McGuckin
Phone: (415) 903-2242
Fax: (415) 903-2241
Email: joe@via.net
Modem: (415) 969-1387 (login "guest")
URL: http://www.via.net/
Services: Shell, SLIP, PPP, UUCP
Area Codes: 408, 415, 213, 818, 310
Fees:
Shell: $17.50/month
SLIP, PPP: $60/month (flat rate)
UUCP: $20/month

Vnet Internet Access, Inc
Contact: Sales
Phone: (800) 377-3282
Fax: (704) 334-6880
Email: info@vnet.net
URL: http://www.vnet.net/
Services: Shell, SLIP, PPP, UUCP, ISDN, 56, 128, T1
Area Codes: 704, 910, 919
Fees:
Email/News only: $14.95/month

Shell: $24.95/month (80 hours)
SLIP, PPP: $15/setup, $29.95-$49.95/month
UUCP: $15/setup, $25/month

VoiceNet/DCS
Contact: Sales
Phone: (215) 674-9290
Fax: (215) 674-9662
Email: info@voicenet.com
Services: Shell, SLIP, PPP, UUCP, ISDN, FTP, mailing lists
Area codes: 800, 215
Fees:
Shell: $14-$20/month
SLIP, PPP: $10-$500/setup, $5-$150/month
UUCP: $50/setup, $20-$150/month
ISDN: $800/setup, $400/month
Other: Call

Walrus
Contact: Jodie Kahn
Phone: (212) 406-5000
Email: info@walrus.com
URL: http://www.walrus.com/
Services: Shell, SLIP, PPP, ISDN, 56-T3
Area Codes: 212, 718
Fees:
Email only: $10/month
Shell: $15/month (flat rate)
SLIP, PPP: $35/month (flat rate)
ISDN: $55-$85/month (flat rate)

Web Professionals, Inc.
Phone: (408) 865-0899
Fax: (408) 865-1618
Email: info@professionals.com
URL: http://professionals.com/
Services: Shell, PPP, ISDN, WWW, DNS
Fees:
Shell: $20/month, $160/year
PPP: $30-$50/month $240-$400/year,
ISDN: $195-$275/month
DNS: $50/setup + 1year

WestNet

Contact: Sales

Phone: (805) 289-1000

Fax: (805) 289-1001

Email: info@west.net

URL: http://www.well.com/

Services: Shell, ISDN, 56-T3

Area Codes: 805

Fees:

Shell: $22/month (flat rate)

ISDN: $60-$90/month

The Well

Contact: Sales

Phone: (415) 332-4335

Fax: (415) 332-WELL

Email: info@well.com

URL: http://www.well.com/

Services: Shell

Area Codes: 415

Fees: $15/month + $2/hour

West Coast Online!

Contact: Christopher Ward

Phone: (800) WCO INTERNET

Fax: (707) 586-5254

Email: info@calon.com

Services: Shell, SLIP, PPP, ISDN, 56-T1

Area Codes: 415, 510, 707, 408, 916, 209

Fees:

Shell: $15/month (flat rate)

PPP: $25-$45/month

56K: $250/month

WestNet

Contact: Lillian or Chris

Phone: (914) 967-7816

Email: staff@westnet.com

Modem: (914) 967-7802 (login "new")

URL: http://www.westnet.com

Services: Shell

Area Codes: 914

Fees:

Shell: $15/month, $150/year

Widomaker Communications

Contact: Ben Loyall

Phone: (804) 253-7621

Email: bloyall@widomaker.com

URL: http://www.widomaker.com/

Services: Shell, BBS, SLIP, PPP, UUCP

Area Codes: 804

Fees:

Shell: $20/month (60 hours, $0.50 each add'l)

SLIP, PPP: $30/month (60 hours, $0.50 each add'l)

Wilder Systems, Inc.

Contact: Webster Mudge

Phone: (617) 933-8810

Fax: (617) 933-8648

Email: info@id.wing.net

URL: http://www.wilder.com/wing.html

Services: Shell, pipeline, PPP, SLIP, ISDN, WWW, LAN, 56-T1

Area Codes: 617

Fees:

Shell: $5/month + $2/hour

Pipeline: $20-$35/month

SLIP, PPP: $25/startup, $20-$35/month

WiscNet

Contact: Tad Pinkerton

Phone: (608) 262-8874

Fax: (608) 262-4679

Email: tad@cs.wisc.edu

@wizard.com

Contact: George Jacobs

Phone: (702) 871-4461

Fax: (702) 871-4249

Email: info@wizard.com

Modem: (702) 871-3102

Services: Shell, TIA-SLIP

Area Codes: 702

Fees:

Email/News only: $10/month (flat rate)
Shell, TIA-SLIP: $14.95/setup, $25/month
(150 hours)

Wizvax Communications
Contact: Sales
Phone: (518) 271-6005
Email: root@wizvax.com
Modem: (518) 271-0049 (login "new")
Services: Shell, SLIP, CSLIP, PPP
Area Codes: 518

WLN
Contact: Rushton Brandis
Phone: (800) DIAL-WLN, (800) 342-5956,
(206) 923-4000
Fax: (206) 923-4009
Email: info@wln.com
URL: http://www.wln.com
Services: Shell, SLIP, PPP, LAN, 56-T1, listserv,
training
Area Codes: 800, 206, 509, 503, 208, 406, 360
Fees:
Shell: $19.95/month (20 hours, $1/hr add'l)
SLIP, PPP: Included with shell account
800: $8.50/hour
Other: Call

The World
Contact: Staff
Phone: (617) 739-0202
Fax: (617) 739-0914
Email: staff@world.std.com
URL: http://www.std.com/
Modem: (617) 739-9753, (508) 366-4422
Services: Shell, DNS
Area Codes: 617, 508
Fees:
Shell: $5/mo + $2/hr or $20/mo (20hrs, $1/hr add'l)
DNS: $25/setup, $75/year

A World of Difference, Inc.
Phone: (803) 769-4488
Email: info@awod.com

Services: Shell, PPP
Area Codes: 803
Fees:
Shell, PPP: $25/month–$432/year

WorldWide Access
Contact: Kathleen Vrona
Phone: (708) 367-1870
Fax: (708) 367-1872
Email: support@wwa.com
URL: http://www.wwa.com
Services: Shell, SLIP, PPP, ISDN, WWW, Leased
lines
Area Codes: 312, 708, 815, 414
Fees:
Shell: $5/month and up
SLIP, PPP: $25/month, $65/quarter
UUCP: $5/month
Other: Please contact

WVnet
Contact: Harper Grimm
Phone: (304) 293-5192
Fax: (304) 293-5540
Email: cc011041@wvnvms.wvnet.edu

The Xensei Corporation
Contact: Theresa Antrim
Phone: (617) 773-4785
Email: sales@xensei.com, terri@xensei.com
URL: http://www.xensei.com/
Services: SLIP, PPP, LAN, WWW, FTP, GOPHER,
ISDN, 56K
Area Codes: 617
Fees:
SLIP, PPP: $10-$65/month
Other: Call

XMission
Contact: Support
Phone: (801) 539-0852
Fax: (801) 539-0853
Email: support@xmission.com

URL: http://www.xmission.com/
Services: Shell, SLIP, PPP, leased line
Area Codes: 801
Fees:
Shell, SLIP, PPP: $19/month (flat rate), $102/6 months
Other: Call

You Tools Corporation (FAST.NET)
Contact: Internet Sales
Phone: (610) 954-5910
Fax: (610) 954-5925
Email: internet@youtools.com
URL: http://www.youtools.com/fastnet
Services: SLIP, PPP, ISDN, 56K-T1, UUCP, WWW
Area Codes: 610, 215, 717
Fees:
SLIP, PPP: $19.95/month
UUCP: $29/month (30 hrs, $1.50/hr add'l)
56K: $399/month FASTFRAME (tm)

Zilker Internet Park
Contact: Support
Phone: (512) 206-3850
Fax: (512) 206-3852
Email: info@zilker.net
URL: http://www.zilker.net/
Services: Shell, SLIP, PPP, ISDN
Area Codes: 512
Fees: Call or write

zNET
Contact: Sales
Phone: (408) 477-9638
Fax: (619) 755-8149
Email: info@znet.com
URL: http://www.znet.com/
Services: SLIP, PPP, ISDN, WWW, DNS
Area Codes: 408
Fees:
SLIP, PPP: $19-$500/setup, $19.95-$150/month
ISDN: $50-$2955/setup, $45-$575/month
WWW: $200-$2000/setup, $100-$400/month

Zocalo Engineering
Contact: Bill Woodcock
Phone: (510) 540-8000
Fax: (510) 548-1891
Email: info@zocalo.net
Services: Shell, news, POP3, SLIP, PPP, ATCP, IPXCP, ARA, AALAP
Area Codes: 510, 415
Fees:
SLIP, PPP: $100/month (flat rate)
Others: Call

Zone One Network Exchange (ZONE)
Contact: Lee Chen
Phone: (718) 549-8078
Fax: (718) 884-3889
Email: info@zone.net
Modem: (718) 884-5405 (login "newuser")
URL: http://www.zone.net/
Services: UUCP, SLIP, PPP, 56-T1

APPENDIX B

What's on the CD-ROM ?

The companion CD-ROM to this book is filled with applications and clip art that will help you design and build great Web pages.

Keep in mind that most of the software on this disk is either shareware or freeware. Shareware means that the author or authors of the software are allowing you to try out the software with the expectation that if you like it, you will pay them for it or upgrade to a commercial version. Freeware means that you can use the software as much as you want with no charge, but there is usually a more advanced version available for a price. Check for a README or LICENSE file with each of the applications you use to see what restrictions the author has placed on the software and its distribution and use.

Here's a description of the four main directories on the CD:

\BOOKSTUF Chapters 4 and 10, complete with direct Internet links and helpful job-hunting software.

\CLIPART   Thousands of images, videos, and sound files you can use.

\INTERNET Shareware and freeware programs to help you navigate the Web and create your own pages.

\TOOLS   Great selection of sound and video tools, and helpful tools for image editing.

Now, let's go through and take a look at some of the more useful applications on the CD. Don't be afraid to experiment a little and play with all the different types of software. Most of the software is described below, but for those applications that aren't, just check in the applications directory for more information.

Application: Clipart
Where on CD: \CLIPART
Where Online: http://www.lycos.com (Lycos search for "CLIPART ARCHIVES")

http://sunsite.nus.sg/ftpmultimedia.html
http://seidel.ncsa.uiuc.edu/ClipArt/funet.html

Description: This collection of clipart was gathered from many different places. You can find images here that can really spice up your Web pages. Check out the collections in \CLIPART\ART\COHEN and \CLIPART\ART\FUNET to see some really impressive line art pieces.

Some of the more useful images are in the \BARS, \DOTS, and \SYMBOLS directories. These simple images don't take up much space, but they can really liven up a Web page and give it that custom look. There are also many images that can be used as separator bars and custom list bullets. Why stick to what Netscape has to offer you? Use custom images to give your page a unique style. But, be careful. Too many images can really slow things down! In the \CLIPART\AUDIO directory, there are many sound effects and samples that you can use to give feedback to the people visiting your pages. Once again, though, you need to be careful that you don't use too many. Sound and video are also not supported on everyone's systems, so you may want to consider the people who will visit your site before you load up your pages with multimedia files.

Application: Paint Shop Pro
Where on CD: \TOOLS\PSP3
Where Online: http://www.jasc.com/

Description: The complete Windows graphics program for image creation, viewing, and manipulation. Features include painting, photo retouching, image enhancement and editing, color enhancement, an image browser, batch conversion, and TWAIN scanner support. Also included are 20 standard image processing filters and 12 deformations. The program supports Adobe-style image processing plug-in filters. Over 30 file formats are supported, including JPEG, Kodak Photo-CD, PBM, and GIF. This is one graphics package you won't want to be without. It has many of the features of much more expensive graphics programs at a fraction of the cost. If you have never bought a shareware package, this may be the first!

Application: Kenn Nesbitt's WebEdit
Where on CD: \INTERNET\HTML\WEBEDIT
Where Online: http://www.nesbitt.com/

Description: WebEdit is a very intuitive and feature-packed HTML editor. Some of its features include HTML 3.0 tags (math functions, icon entities, tables, and more), a Home Page Wizard, server side include tags, improved Web browser support, and much more.

WebEdit also saves every URL you enter, letting you choose from a list rather than having to retype the same URLs repeatedly. Also included are a tool for removing

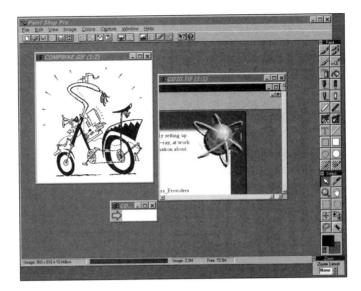

HTML tags from a document and one for quickly producing a template of tags commonly used in your HTML documents. WebEdit also features MDI —multiple-document interface—which allows you to work on up to ten different HTML documents simultaneously.

WebEdit does have some very interesting new features, like floating customizable toolbars, a Table Builder, and a multilingual spelling checker; unfortunately, all of these features are crippled in the evaluation package, so you will have to register the product to get the full benefit of its features.

WebEdit also lets you call your favorite Web browser so that you can view the page you are currently working on. Additional features include word wrap, time/date stamping, search and replace, and almost every HTML command imaginable (including many HTML3 tags). A new version of this product is also about to be released and will include WYSYWIG page viewing and many other cool features, so you may want to consider jumping online and getting the new version.

Application: MPEG movie players
Where on CD: \TOOLS\VIDEO\MPEGWIN
Where Online: http://www-plateau.cs.berkeley.edu/mpeg/mpegptr.html

Description: MPEG (Moving Pictures Experts Group) is a group of people who meet under ISO (the International Standards Organization) to generate standards for digital video (sequences of images in time) and audio compression. In particular, this group defines a compressed bit stream, which implicitly defines a decompressor.

However, the compression algorithms are up to the individual manufacturers, and that is where proprietary advantage is obtained within the scope of a publicly available international standard. MPEG itself is a nickname. The official name is: ISO/IEC JTC1 SC29 WG11. MPEG is quickly becoming the standard for video playback for games because it is one of the few protocols that supports full-screen playback at 30 frames per second. The applications on the CD are easy to use and offer many options for playback.

Application: QuickTime Player from Apple
Where on CD: \TOOLS\VIDEO\QUIKTIME
Where Online: http://quicktime.apple.com/

Description: Although QuickTime has been a Macintosh standard for years, it is just beginning to catch on with Windows users. QuickTime offers a few features that Video for Windows does not have yet and some of the new technology being developed for QuickTime is amazing. Check out the QuickTime Web page for the latest and greatest versions and look for the QuickTime VR players and editors that are beginning to appear. Note: There is a QuickTime VR player now available for Windows. Head to the QuickTime Web site to download it; very cool!

Application: Video for Windows 1.1e
Where on CD: \TOOLS\VIDEO\VFW11E

Description: Video for Windows (VfW) was originally an add-on product for Windows 3.1. It has since been upgraded continuously and is now in its fifth generation, which includes support for 32-bit compression and decompression. With the release of Windows 95, Microsoft has finally integrated VfW into the operating system itself. For people still using Windows 3.11 or older, here is the latest version of VfW.

Application: WinJammer
Where on CD: \TOOLS\SOUND\WINJAMR
Where Online: http://www.netscape.com/MCOM/tricks_docs/helper_docs/

Description: WinJammer is a fully featured MIDI sequencer. It uses standard MIDI files and gives you access to a huge number of songs. WinJammer also contains a companion program called WinJammer Player, which is used to play MIDI song files in the background.

Major features of WinJammer include:

- imports Adlib ROL files

- up to 64 tracks

- runs in *all* Windows modes (including enhanced mode)
- powerful editing commands
- unique piano roll style notation for editing
- full online help
- supports standard MIDI files
- supports MIDI system exclusive bulk dumps
- supports Windows Multimedia Extensions

Major features of WinJammer Player include:
- support for standard MIDI files
- up to 64 tracks
- runs in *all* Windows modes (including enhanced mode)
- in enhanced mode, will even play while in DOS
- full online help
- builds albums of songs to play (forever if desired)
- supports Windows Multimedia Extensions

Application: WPlayAny
Where on CD: \TOOLS\SOUND\WPLANY
Where Online: http://burgoyne.com/vaudio/netsound.html

Description: WPlayAny is a compact utility that will detect and play almost any sound file you will encounter on the Web. Use WPlayAny to create and edit audio and use this as a helper program for your Web browser. The proper drivers for your sound card (or PC speaker) must be loaded prior to using WPlayAny. This program does not have an interface; it simply plays files that are sent to it by your browser.

Currently supported sound types:
- SoundBlaster .VOC
- Sun/NeXT/DEC .AU
- Windows .WAV
- Sounder/Soundtools .SND
- Amiga .8SVX .IFF

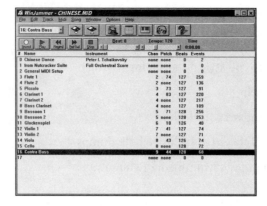

Application: McAfee Virus Scanner
Where on CD: \TOOLS\ANTIVRUS
Where Online: http://www.mcafee.com/

Description: McAfee makes some of the best anti-virus software available. Check their Web site frequently for updates—there are new viruses being found every day.

Application: Color Manipulation Device
Where on CD: \TOOLS\GRAPHICS\CMD
Where Online: http://www.meat.com/software/cmd.html

Description: This simple little application takes the guesswork out of selecting colors and graphics for your Web page backgrounds. If you have ever become confused by all the hexadecimal mumbo jumbo, then this tool will make Web-page creation easier for you. Simply pick colors for backgrounds and text then click on COPY. Then, paste the text into your Web page editor and you're done! Very handy and easy to use.

Application: WebImage
Where on CD: \TOOLS\GRAPHICS\WEBIMAGE
Where Online: http://www.group42.com/webimage.htm

Description: WebImage is the next generation of Internet media tools created by Group 42. It all came about when their users told the company to create an easy-to-use product that consolidated all the special requirements needed for Web/Internet images. WebImage includes features like:

- Visually define and view transparent GIF regions

- Easily create and edit NCSA and CERN compliant Image Map files.

- Create interlaced GIF and PNG files

- Optimize images based on color content, improving compression

- High quality color reduction methods to preset or user-defined number of colors

- Buttonize images, add text, or create new images

WebImage can even encode or decode files for easy Internet use. This is another fine program that makes life easy for Webmasters.

Application: Eudora
Where on CD: \INTERNET\EMAIL\EUDORA
Where Online: http://www.qualcomm.com/ProdTech/quest/

Description: Eudora is one of the most popular email programs in use, as we discussed in the book. It is very easy to set up and use, and there are plenty of options you can customize. This is the freeware version of Eudora for Windows. There is also a commercial version of Eudora called "Eudora by QUALCOMM" (Version 2.0 and above). If you would like information about the commercial version, a brief description is provided in the Help menu of this freeware. Select About Commercial Eudora to display this dialog.

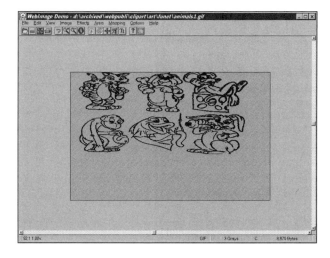

Application: Pegasus Mail
Where on CD: \INTERNET\EMAIL\EUDORA
Where Online: http://www.cuslm.ca/pegasus/

Description: Pegasus Mail is another Internet email system with a ton of options. Actually, Pegasus Mail has more features than Eudora, including automatic distribution, NetWare compatibility, and automatic abbreviations. Try both programs and see which one suits you better.

Application: WS-FTP
Where on CD: \INTERNET\FTP\WS_FTP16\INTERNET\FTP\WS_FTP32
Where Online: http://cwsapps.texas.net/ftp.html

Description: FTP remains one of the most widely used Internet applications, and WS-FTP makes this oft-used tool quick and painless. Configurability options include several alternative screen layouts, the ability to associate remote files with local programs, automatic logging, and quick screen sizing. WS-FTP also comes pre-configured with an extensive array of FTP sites to check out. Multiple copies of the program can be launched to download multiple files at the same time. WS-FTP comes in two varieties: a 16-bit and a 32-bit version. The only features missing are drag 'n' drop capabilities between local and remote file listings. WS-FTP is another of the must-have Internet applications.

Application: CuteFTP
Where on CD: \INTERNET\FTP\CUTEFTP
Where Online: http://papa.indstate.edu:8888/CuteFTP/

Description: CuteFTP is another standalone FTP program that expands on some of the features of WS-FTP. One of the best features of CuteFTP is its robust STOP command, similar in nature to the stop button found on many Web browsers. This command allows a user to stop any operation in progress while still maintaining the connection.

Beyond the STOP command, CuteFTP also integrates the file listing process with file descriptions obtained from the index files found at many anonymous FTP sites (extremely helpful for deciphering cryptic file names). Caching of recently visited directories is another distinctive feature found in CuteFTP. In addition to fixing many bugs, the newer releases of CuteFTP have implemented WS-FTP's File Manageresque approach to listing both remote and local directories side-by-side, comprehensive login listings, selectable file viewers, selectable colors, the ability to recursively download directory trees, and the ability to easily send multiple files at once.

Application: HomePage Creator
Where on CD: \INTERNET\HTML\HPC

Description: HomePage Creator is a new tool designed to help you automatically create your own Web pages and resume Web pages. It's not just another HTML editor, though. It allows you to insert a picture, text, and links to your favorite sites on the Web and then does the dirty work of generating HTML tags for you.

The installation procedure for HomePage Creator is easy: Just run the SETUP.EXE program in the directory \TOOLS\HPC. You'll need to specify the directory where you want to install the HomePage Creator program. The developer of this program, Demetris Kafas, is currently developing a more feature-rich version of HomePage Creator that you'll be able to purchase in the future.

Application: HTMLed
Where on CD: \INTERNET\HTML\HTMLED
Where Online: http://www.ist.ca/

Description: HTMLed incorporates many advanced features into a program that is extremely easy to use. Intelligent tag insertion, tag removal, automatic saving with or without HTML tags, word wrap, and configurable floating toolbars are just a few of HTMLed's advanced features. In addition, the task of creating background images and identifying colors for your Web pages is made easy with HTMLed. HTMLed also makes good use of right mouse button functionality.

Application: WinVN News Reader
Where on CD: \INTERNET\NEWS\WINVN
Where Online: http://www.ksc.nasa.gov/software/winvn/winvn.html

Description: WinVN is a Microsoft Windows, Microsoft 95, and Microsoft/NT based news reader. Its name stands for "Windows Visual Newsreader." Like other news readers, it can be used to select, view, write, sort, and print Usenet News articles. Articles can be saved locally, cut into the Windows Clipboard, or forwarded to other individuals via email.

WinVN offers a more visual approach to Usenet News than earlier news readers. WinVN also allows the user to easily navigate between newsgroups and articles via its point-and-click interface. It allows the viewing of multiple articles simultaneously and for multitasking operating systems like Microsoft Windows/NT, it even allows multiple simultaneous news server connections.

Application: VocalTec Internet Phone
Where on CD: \INTERNET\PHONE
Where Online: http://www.vocaltec.com/

Description: With Internet Phone, you can use the Internet to speak with any other user, from any point in the world! Realtime voice conversations over the Internet, at the price of a local phone call or even less! All you need is Internet Phone, a TCP\IP Internet connection and a Windows-compatible audio device. Plug in a microphone and speaker, run Internet Phone, and, by clicking a button, get in touch with Internet users all over the world who are using the same software.

A friendly graphic user interface and a Voice-Activation feature make conversation easy. VocalTec's sophisticated voice compression and voice transfer technology ensures that your voice gets across in a flash, using only a fraction of the available bandwidth. Internet Phone now also supports Full Duplex audio: it lets you speak and listen at the same time. This software is getting better all the time. Look for some hot stuff from VocalTec and other companies in the near future.

Application: Trumpet Winsock
Where on CD: \INTERNET\TRUMPET
Where Online: Http://www.webcom.com/~llarrow/trouble.html

Description: Trumpet Winsock is probably one of the most widely-used shareware programs ever written. Why? Because it's simple and reliable. Trumpet can be used as a TCP/IP stack for internal or external use. It other words, it works over a LAN or a phone line. Trumpet is usually used over a phone line to connect to a service provider.

The documentation that comes with Trumpet tells you everything you need to know about using it, so we recommend looking at the INSTALL.DOC file for help setting it up.

Application: Visual Resume
Where on CD: \BOOKSTUF\VRESUME
Where Online: Can be found in software libraries on AOL and CompuServe

Description: This is the freeware version of Visual Resume, a program that allows you to add pictures and graphics to your text resume, and send the entire diskette to a prospective employer. You can use your text file resume and add pictures as directed, or simply modify the sample resume that belongs to "Joe Jones."

Application: Building Yourself
Where on CD: \BOOKSTUF\BUILD
Where Online: http://jcsm.com/homepers/index.htm

Description: Building Yourself is a unique, step-by-step shareware guide to giving yourself the tools for personal success. It helps you consider experience versus book learning, thinking for yourself, strategic alliances, and more. This program is easy to use, fun to look at, and even has sound effects. It contains quite a bit of good information, and tests throughout.

Application: The Right Resume
Where on CD: \BOOKSTUF\TRR
Where Online: CompuServe

Description: The Right Resume is a powerful Windows-based job hunting package that provides you with all the necessary tools to help you get the job you want. It allows you to create your choice of a chronological, functional, or targeted resume that can be easily modified or enhanced. It also helps you customize your resume for different people and targets.

Application: LifePlan v1.05
Where on CD: \BOOKSTUF\LIFEGOAL
Where Online: http://lehighvalleynet.com/advocate/soft.htm

Description: LifePlan is a powerful tool that helps you decide exactly what you want to achieve in your life, and then helps you to set the goals and targets that will move you, on a daily basis, toward achieving those dreams. LifePlan asks you a series of questions, ranging from your goals for the next month to your goals for the next 25 years.

Application: Job Hunt
Where on CD: \BOOKSTUF\JOBHUNT
Where Online: http://www.acs.oakland.edu/cgi-bin/vsl-front

Description: Job Hunt provides a large database of employers with full contact information. The program prints mail-merged cover letters and follow-up letters for targeted mass mailings, and even has a built-in phone dialer for making follow-up calls. Also included is a built-in resume creator for resumes in color and with borders, and tips on interviewing and other important topics.

Application: You're Hired!
Where on CD: \BOOKSTUF\YHIRED
Where Online: CompuServe

Description: You're Hired! is an informative and comprehensive job interview simulator that provides realistic training and valuable experience to prepare you for your next job interview. It asks common challenging interview questions in a lifelike simulation and records elapsed times as you verbally respond. If you need help answering a question, you can get online professional advice.

Application: Resume Templates
Where on CD: \BOOKSTUF\TEMPLATE

Description: These files are various resume templates that you can open and use in Word for Windows. Save the file as an HTML document, and you can create an HTML resume. If you don't have the ability to save a document as HTML, use Internet Assistant, which can be downloaded from Microsoft's Web site.

Application: Chapters 4, 10, and a List of Internet Service Providers
Where on CD: \BOOKSTUF\CHAPTERS

Description: This section has Chapter 4, with company information and URLs for employment pages. You can load the chapter into your browser, then click on the URLs for each company and you'll go directly to the site. You can also do this with Chapter 10, which has a variety of job hunting resources. Also included is a list of U.S. and international Internet Service Providers.

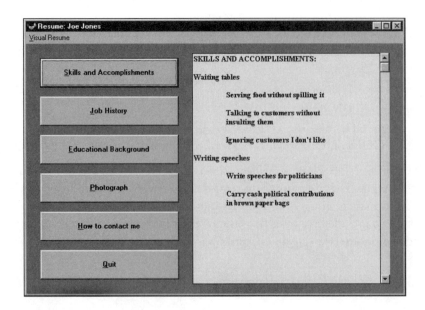

Index